∴ INGMAR

Translated from the Swedish by

FOUR SCREENPLAYS
OF
BERGMAN

LARS MALMSTROM AND DAVID KUSIINER

A TOUCHSTONE BOOK
PUBLISHED BY SIMON AND SCHUSTER

COPYRIGHT © 1960 BY INGMAR BERGMAN
ALL RIGHTS RESERVED
INCLUDING THE RIGHT OF REPRODUCTION
IN WHOLE OR IN PART IN ANY FORM
A TOUCHSTONE BOOK
PUBLISHED BY SIMON AND SCHUSTER
A GULF + WESTERN COMPANY
ROCKEFELLER CENTER, 630 FIFTH AVENUE
NEW YORK, NEW YORK 10020

ISBN 0-671-20353-3
LIBRARY OF CONGRESS CATALOG CARD NUMBER: 60-14283
MANUFACTURED IN THE UNITED STATES OF AMERICA

11   12   13   14   15   16   17   18   19   20

For catalogues or information on other Touchstone titles
available, write to Educational & Library Services, Simon &
Schuster, Inc., 630 Fifth Ave., New York, N.Y. 10020

NOTE: *The screenplays in this book are identical to those used by
Ingmar Bergman when filming, except that:* 1) *the original scripts contain
numbers before each sequence which indicate the estimated number
of shots that will be necessary for that sequence;* 2) *since these
screenplays are prepared before shooting begins, they contain sequences
and dialogue which do not appear in the final film; Bergman has deleted
some material to make the published scripts conform to the movies.*

❁ CONTENTS

The publishers wish to express their gratitude for the help and co-operation received from the staff of Janus Films, Inc., and particularly Cyrus Harvey, Jr.

❀ A PREFACE

by Ingmar Bergman's Producer, Carl Anders Dymling

[CARL ANDERS DYMLING *is the president of Svensk Filmindustri, producers of Ingmar Bergman's films. He has been a major factor in Bergman's film career from its beginning and is largely responsible for the development and establishment of Bergman as a writer-director of world renown. Now in his sixties, Dr. Dymling was previously director-general of the Swedish Broadcasting Corporation and has also been a literary critic and scholar.]*

THE FIRST TIME I saw Ingmar Bergman was during the autumn of 1942, when I had just gone into the motion-picture business as president of Svensk Filmindustri. He was a very young man then, tall, thin, with black hair and burning black eyes. He was still unknown, but trying impatiently to find his way in life and in particular to find an outlet for his erupting creative talents. He began by producing stage plays, on a small scale and with extremely limited resources. I happened to see one of them at the university students' theater in Stockholm. Here, I thought, was a refreshing young talent, a little crazy perhaps, certainly immature, but with a lot of bold and fanciful ideas.

I decided on the spot to find out if he was willing to work in some capacity at the SF (Svensk Filmindustri) studio at Råsunda. He was.

He started by rewriting some scripts, rather poor ones I'm afraid, trying to make them worth while. He wasn't very successful. Then one day about a year later came the first Bergman surprise. A manuscript suddenly appeared on my desk, not a scenario but a short novel intended as a film. (For many years, Bergman preferred to present a film in this way before writing the screenplay.) It was *Hets*, called *Torment* in the United States and *Frenzy* in England. I read it; it was a startling experience. Here was a very angry young man—long before they became the fashion—a writer looking at the world through the eyes of a teen-age rebel harshly criticizing his parents, offending his teachers, making love to a prostitute, fighting everything and everybody in order to preserve his integrity and his right to be unhappy. The dialogue was full of sound and fury, and it is unfortunate that the American audience has so far seen only a disastrously mutilated version of *Torment*. The script promised to be a great success, and we were fortunate in getting Alf Sjöberg to help write the scenario and to direct the picture.

This is how Bergman started his career in motion pictures. It was also the beginning of long years of co-operation and friendship, full of triumphs and frustrations, joys and disappointments, but always exciting. The relationship between a producer and a writer-director is a delicate and complicated thing, and in this particular case the more so because Ingmar Bergman has continued to be a rebel-child. He has always been a problem, not only to others but also to himself, and I think he will remain so. He is a high-strung personality, passionately alive, enormously sensitive, very short-tempered, sometimes quite ruthless in the pursuit of his own goals, suspicious, stubborn, capricious, most unpredictable. His will power is extraordinary. There are bound to be misunderstandings and disagreements; we both know this, and they are soon forgotten. After all, we have a common cause: we want to make good pictures.

This common goal has probably been the most important element in our relationship. When I originally became president of Svensk Filmindustri, I didn't realize how an ambitious producer is inevitably caught up in a conflict between artistic aims and commercial interests. My main problem and aim as a producer has been to balance these interests. It is the problem of everyone working in mass media. And I feel that this search for balance has underlined my relationship with Bergman and enabled him to use the film as a means of self-expression to an extent which few directors in the world today have done.

It has not always been easy. I can remember when Bergman got very bad reviews, when he was considered difficult, bizarre, incomprehensible, pretentious; times when he really needed support and understanding. And also when, among the governing board of SF itself, I sometimes had to fight rather hard for him. From a financial point of view, a Bergman picture seemed a risky business until not long ago; it was only when *Smiles of a Summer Night* was shown at the Cannes Festival in 1956 that he won general recognition in Sweden and other countries, and even with that recognition his films cannot yet be considered great commercial successes.

Ingmar Bergman usually keeps me informed of his plans and ideas long before he has put anything on paper. Sometimes, when he is not too sure of my approval, he is in the habit of dropping supposedly confidential hints to members of the staff which are intended to reach me in due time and prepare me—and him—for the worst. This is how I learned of his intention to make *The Seventh Seal*. His precautions turned out to be unnecessary; I could hardly refuse a screenplay of such quality even if I had wanted to.

As a producer, I was quite aware of the financial risk in a motion picture with so serious a theme. But it promised to be an unusual, an outstanding picture. It *had* to be done. We discussed the script for several days and nights during the Cannes festival in May 1956. We agreed on some changes, on the cast and on the budget. We felt as if we were launching a big ship and we were very happy.

A year or two before, he had told me the story which was to become *Smiles of a Summer Night*. The idea seemed brilliant, and I was pleased with his wish to make a new comedy. For a long time I had encouraged him to write comedies, but he didn't dare. His first attempt was the now famous elevator scene in *Secrets of Women*; then he wrote *A Lesson in Love*. But you never can tell what is going to happen to a Bergman idea. Some disappear mysteriously and are never heard of again. Some are dropped even after a screenplay is written. Others change completely. The story of *Smiles of a Summer Night* turned out to be quite different from the one he had told me about originally, so different, as a matter of fact, that he could use the original story for another comedy without anybody noticing the connection—if Bergman should ever run out of ideas, which seems most unlikely.

As a rule he and I discuss a picture in detail and at length *before* he starts shooting it. Then we go on talking about it *after* he has finished shooting and editing the picture. I refuse to look at the rushes or parts of the picture. Only when the rough cut is ready do we look at it together. It is one of my few rules never to interfere with work in the studio. I want to leave the director alone during the difficult time he must go through. This is not a special privilege given to Bergman but to any director working in our studios.

I have been asked many times by journalists from abroad, particularly from the United States, about the unusual amount of freedom allowed the Swedish film director. This freedom is part of a heritage from the good old days of the Swedish cinema. Svensk Filmindustri is in fact one of the oldest motion-picture companies in the world; we started producing pictures more than fifty years ago. The head of the company at the time was a man of pioneer spirit, Charles Magnusson. He had courage and vision. He wanted to give the public something more than cheap entertainment; he wanted motion pictures to become a cultural force comparable to the theater. In order to raise the standards of production he persuaded two prominent actor-directors of the stage, Victor Sjöström and Mauritz Stiller, to join his company. Magnusson, who was a photographer himself, taught them how to use this new medium. Within a few years they were ready for the great adventure in Swedish film history which began with *Terje Vigen,* (*A Man There Was*), based on Ibsen's poem of the same name, continued with *The Phantom Carriage* and *Sir Arne's Treasure* and came to an end with the Garbo picture, *Gösta Berling's Saga.* Magnusson provided the money but did not interfere; Sjöström and Stiller had an entirely free hand.

Thus the origins of Swedish motion-picture production had an intimate connection with the art and standards of the theater. Ever since that golden age of the Swedish cinema classics, our directors have taken their ideals from the theater. This approach has been an important influence, and it is the reason, I think, that our attitude toward film-making has always been and still is profoundly different from, let us say, that of Hollywood. It is painfully true that motion-picture making has a Janus face: it is both an art and an industry. But the tradition established by Magnusson, Sjöström and Stiller has prevented the surrender of artistic aims to commercial interests.

This difference in attitude explains a good many things. It certainly explains why some of the Bergman pictures have ever been produced. It may also explain why some foreign critics seem anxious to place Ingmar Bergman on a pedestal as a kind of prophet, half hidden in clouds of deep mystery and unintelligible symbolism. We in Sweden don't regard him as a prophet. To us he is a fascinating personality, an outstanding writer-director, an artist of vision but with his feet planted solidly on the ground. Above all, Bergman is a link in the chain which joins the past and the present in Swedish film history.

CARL ANDERS DYMLING

❋ INTRODUCTION:

BERGMAN DISCUSSES FILM-MAKING

DURING THE SHOOTING of *The Virgin Spring*, we were up in the northern province of Dalarna in May and it was early in the morning, about half past seven. The landscape there is rugged, and our company was working by a little lake in the forest. It was very cold, about 30 degrees, and from time to time a few snowflakes fell through the gray, rain-dimmed sky. The company was dressed in a strange variety of clothing—raincoats, oil slickers, Icelandic sweaters, leather jackets, old blankets, coachmen's coats, medieval robes. Our men had laid some ninety feet of rusty, buckling rail over the difficult terrain, to dolly the camera on. We were all helping with the equipment—actors, electricians, make-up men, script girl, sound crew—mainly to keep warm. Suddenly someone shouted and pointed toward the sky. Then we saw a crane floating high above the fir trees, and then another, and then several cranes, floating majestically in a circle above us. We all dropped what we were doing and ran to the top of a nearby hill to see the cranes better. We stood there for a long time, until they turned westward and disappeared over the forest. And suddenly I thought: this is what it means to make a movie in Sweden. This is what can happen, this is how we work together with our old equipment and little money, and this is how we can suddenly drop everything for the love of four cranes floating above the tree tops.

My association with film goes back to the world of childhood.

My grandmother had a very large old apartment in Uppsala. I used to sit under the dining-room table there, "listening" to the sunshine which came in through the gigantic windows. The cathedral bells went ding-dong, and the sunlight moved about and "sounded" in a special way. One day, when winter was giving way to spring and I was five years old, a piano was being played in the next apartment. It played waltzes, nothing but waltzes. On the wall hung a large picture of Venice. As the sunlight moved across the picture the water in the canal began to flow, the pigeons flew up from the square, people talked and gesticulated. Bells sounded, not those of Uppsala Cathedral but from the picture itself. And the piano music also came from that remarkable picture of Venice.

A child who is born and brought up in a vicarage acquires an early familiarity with life and death behind the scenes. Father performed funerals, marriages, baptisms, gave advice and prepared sermons. The devil was an early acquaintance, and in the child's mind there was a need to personify him. This is where my magic lantern came in. It consisted of a small metal box with a carbide lamp—I can still remember the smell of the hot metal—and colored glass slides: Red Riding Hood and the Wolf, and all the others. And the Wolf was the Devil, without horns but with a tail and a gaping red mouth, strangely real yet incomprehensible, a picture of wickedness and temptation on the flowered wall of the nursery.

When I was ten years old I received my first, rattling film projector, with its chimney and lamp. I found it both mystifying and fascinating. The first film I had was nine fect long and brown in color. It showed a girl lying asleep in a meadow, who woke up and stretched out her arms, then disappeared to the right. That was all there was to it. The film was a great success and was projected every night until it broke and could not be mended any more.

This little rickety machine was my first conjuring set. And even today I remind myself with childish excitement that I am really a conjurer, since cinematography is based on deception of the human eye. I have worked it out that if I see a film which has a running time of one hour, I sit through twenty-seven minutes of complete darkness—the blankness between frames. When I show a film I am guilty of deceit. I use an apparatus which is constructed to take advantage of a certain human weakness, an apparatus with which I can sway my audience in a highly emotional manner—make them laugh, scream with fright, smile, believe in fairy stories, become indignant, feel shocked, charmed, deeply moved or perhaps yawn with boredom. Thus I am either an impostor or, when the audience is willing to be taken in, a conjurer. I perform conjuring tricks with apparatus so expensive and so wonderful that any entertainer in history would have given anything to have it.

A film for me begins with something very vague—a chance remark or a bit of conversation, a hazy but agreeable event unrelated to any particular situation. It can be a few bars of music, a shaft of light across the street. Sometimes in my work at the theater I have envisioned actors made up for yet unplayed roles.

These are split-second impressions that disappear as quickly as they come, yet leave behind a mood—like pleasant dreams. It is a mental state, not an actual story, but one abounding in fertile associations and images. Most of all, it is a brightly colored thread sticking out of the dark sack of the unconscious. If I begin to wind up this thread, and do it carefully, a complete film will emerge.

This primitive nucleus strives to achieve definite form, moving in a way that may be lazy and half asleep at first. Its stirring is accompanied by vibrations and rhythms which are very special and unique to each film. The picture sequences then assume a pattern in accordance with these rhythms, obeying laws born out of and conditioned by my original stimulus.

If that embryonic substance seems to have enough strength to be made into a film, I decide to materialize it. Then comes something very complicated and difficult: the transformation of rhythms, moods, atmosphere, tensions, sequences, tones and scents into words and sentences, into an understandable screenplay.

This is an almost impossible task.

The only thing that can be satisfactorily transferred from that original complex of rhythms and moods is the dialogue, and even dialogue is a sensitive substance which may offer resistance. Written dialogue is like a musical score, almost incomprehensible to the average person. Its interpretation demands a technical knack plus a certain kind of imagination and feeling—qualities which are so often lacking, even among actors. One can write dialogue, but how it should be delivered, its rhythm and tempo, what is to take place between lines—all this must be omitted for practical reasons. Such a detailed script would be unreadable. I try to squeeze instructions as to location, characterization and atmosphere into my screenplays in understandable terms, but the success of this depends on my writing ability and the perceptiveness of the reader, which are not always predictable.

Now we come to essentials, by which I mean montage, rhythm and the relation of one picture to another—the vital third dimension without which the film is merely a dead product from a factory. Here I cannot clearly give a key, as in a musical score, nor a specific idea of the tempo which determines the relationship of the elements involved. It is quite impossible for me to indicate the way in which the film "breathes" and pulsates.

I have often wished for a kind of notation which would enable me to put on paper all the shades and tones of my vision, to record distinctly the inner structure of a film. For when I stand in the artistically devastating atmosphere of the studio, my hands and head full of all the trivial and irritating details that go with motion-picture production, it often takes a tremendous effort to remember how I originally saw and thought out this or that sequence, or what was the relation between the scene of four weeks ago and that of today. If I could express myself clearly, in explicit symbols, then this problem would be almost eliminated and I could work with absolute confidence that whenever I liked I could prove the relationship between the part and the whole and put my finger on the rhythm, the continuity of the film.

Thus the script is a very imperfect *technical* basis for a film. And there is another important point in this connection which I should like to mention. Film has nothing to do with literature; the character and substance of the two art forms are usually in conflict. This probably has something to do with the receptive process of the mind. The written word is read and assimilated by a conscious act of the will in alliance with the intellect; little by little it affects the imagination and the emotions. The process is different with a motion picture. When we experience a film, we consciously prime ourselves for illusion. Putting aside will and intellect, we make way for it in our imagination. The sequence of pictures plays directly on our feelings.

Music works in the same fashion; I would say that there is no art form that has so much in common with film as music. Both affect our emotions directly, not via the intellect. And film is mainly rhythm; it is inhalation and exhalation in continuous sequence. Ever since childhood, music has been my great source of recreation and stimulation, and I often experience a film or play musically.

It is mainly because of this difference between film and literature that we should avoid making films out of books. The irrational dimension of a literary work, the germ of its existence, is often untranslatable into visual terms—and it, in turn, destroys the special, irrational dimension of the film. If, despite this, we wish to translate something literary into film terms, we must make an infinite number of complicated adjustments which often bear little or no fruit in proportion to the effort expended.

I myself have never had any ambition to be an author. I do not want to write novels, short stories, essays, biographies, or even plays for the theater. I only want to make films—films about conditions, tensions, pictures, rhythms and characters which are in one way or another important to me. The motion picture, with its complicated process of birth, is my method of saying what I want to my fellow men. I am a film-maker, not an author.

Thus the writing of the script is a difficult period but a useful one, for it compels me to prove logically the validity of my ideas. In doing this, I am caught in a conflict—a conflict between my need to transmit a complicated situation through visual images, and my desire for absolute clarity. I do not intend my work to be solely for the benefit of myself or the few, but for the entertainment of the general public. The wishes of the public are imperative. But sometimes I risk following my own impulse, and it has been shown that the public can respond with surprising sensitivity to the most unconventional line of development.

When shooting begins, the most important thing is that those who work with me feel a definite contact, that all of us somehow cancel out our conflicts through working together. We must pull in one direction for the sake of the work at hand. Sometimes this leads to dispute, but the

more definite and clear the "marching orders," the easier it
is to reach the goal which has been set. This is the basis for
my conduct as director, and perhaps the explanation of
much of the nonsense that has been written about me.

While I cannot let myself be concerned with what people think and say about me personally, I believe that re-
viewers and critics have every right to interpret my films as
they like. I refuse to interpret my work to others, and I cannot tell the critic what to think; each person has the right
to understand a film as he sees it. Either he is attracted or
repelled. A film is made to create reaction. If the audience
does not react one way or another, it is an indifferent work and worthless.

I do not mean by this that I believe in being "different"
at any price. A lot has been said about the value of originality, and I find this foolish. Either you are original or
you are not. It is completely natural for artists to take from
and give to each other, to borrow from and experience one
another. In my own life, my great literary experience was
Strindberg. There are works of his which can still make my
hair stand on end—*The People of Hemsö*, for example.
And it is my dream to produce *Dream Play* some day. Olof
Molander's production of it in 1934 was for me a fundamental dramatic experience.

On a personal level, there are many people who have
meant a great deal to me. My father and mother were certainly of vital importance, not only in themselves but because they created a world for me to revolt against. In my
family there was an atmosphere of hearty wholesomeness
which I, a sensitive young plant, scorned and rebelled
against. But that strict middle-class home gave me a wall to
pound on, something to sharpen myself against. At the same
time they taught me a number of values—efficiency, punc-
tuality, a sense of financial responsibility—which may be
"bourgeois" but are nevertheless important to the artist.
They are part of the process of setting oneself severe stand-

ards. Today as a film-maker I am conscientious, hard-working and extremely careful; my films involve good craftsmanship, and my pride is the pride of a good craftsman.

Among the people who have meant something in my professional development is Torsten Hammaren of Gothenburg. I went there from Hälsingborg, where I had been head of the municipal theater for two years. I had no conception of what theater was; Hammaren taught me during the four years I stayed in Gothenburg. Then, when I made my first attempts at film, Alf Sjöberg—who directed *Torment*—taught me a great deal. And there was Lorens Marmstedt, who really taught me film-making from scratch after my first unsuccessful movie. Among other things I learned from Marmstedt is the one unbreakable rule: you must look at your own work very coldly and clearly; you must be a devil to yourself in the screening room when watching the day's rushes. Then there is Herbert Grevenius, one of the few who believed in me as a writer. I had trouble with script-writing, and was reaching out more and more to the drama, to dialogue, as a means of expression. He gave me great encouragement.

Finally, there is Carl Anders Dymling, my producer. He is crazy enough to place more faith in the sense of responsibility of a creative artist than in calculations of profit and loss. I am thus able to work with an integrity that has become the very air I breathe, and one of the main reasons I do not want to work outside of Sweden. The moment I lose this freedom I will cease to be a film-maker, because I have no skill in the art of compromise. My only significance in the world of film lies in the freedom of my creativity.

Today, the ambitious film-maker is obliged to walk a tightrope without a net. He may be a conjurer, but no one conjures the producer, the bank director or the theater owners when the public refuses to go see a film and lay down the money by which producer, bank director, theater owner and conjurer can live. The conjurer may then be de-

prived of his magic wand; I would like to be able to meas-
ure the amount of talent, initiative and creative ability
which has been destroyed by the film industry in its ruth-
lessly efficient sausage machine. What was play to me once
has now become a struggle. Failure, criticism, public indifference all hurt more today than yesterday. The brutality
of the industry is undisguised—yet that can be an advantage.

So much for people and the film business. I have been
asked, as a clergyman's son, about the role of religion in my
thinking and film-making. To me, religious problems are
continuously alive. I never cease to concern myself with
them; it goes on every hour of every day. Yet this does not
take place on the emotional level, but on an intellectual
one. Religious emotion, religious sentimentality, is something I got rid of long ago—I hope. The religious problem
is an intellectual one to me: the relationship of my mind to
my intuition. The result of this conflict is usually some kind
of tower of Babel.

Philosophically, there is a book which was a tremendous
experience for me: Eiono Kaila's *Psychology of the Personality*. His thesis that man lives strictly according to his
needs—negative and positive—was shattering to me, but
terribly true. And I built on this ground.

People ask what are my intentions with my films—my
aims. It is a difficult and dangerous question, and I usually give an evasive answer: I try to tell the truth about the
human condition, the truth as I see it. This answer seems
to satisfy everyone, but it is not quite correct. I prefer to
describe what I *would like* my aim to be.

There is an old story of how the cathedral of Chartres
was struck by lightning and burned to the ground. Then
thousands of people came from all points of the compass,
like a giant procession of ants, and together they began to
rebuild the cathedral on its old site. They worked until the
building was completed—master builders, artists, laborers,

clowns, noblemen, priests, burghers. But they all remained anonymous, and no one knows to this day who built the cathedral of Chartres.

Regardless of my own beliefs and my own doubts, which are unimportant in this connection, it is my opinion that art lost its basic creative drive the moment it was separated from worship. It severed an umbilical cord and now lives its own sterile life, generating and degenerating itself. In former days the artist remained unknown and his work was to the glory of God. He lived and died without being more or less important than other artisans; "eternal values," "immortality" and "masterpiece" were terms not applicable in his case. The ability to create was a gift. In such a world flourished invulnerable assurance and natural humility.

Today the individual has become the highest form and the greatest bane of artistic creation. The smallest wound or pain of the ego is examined under a microscope as if it were of eternal importance. The artist considers his isolation, his subjectivity, his individualism almost holy. Thus we finally gather in one large pen, where we stand and bleat about our loneliness without listening to each other and without realizing that we are smothering each other to death. The individualists stare into each other's eyes and yet deny the existence of each other. We walk in circles, so limited by our own anxieties that we can no longer distinguish between true and false, between the gangster's whim and the purest ideal.

Thus if I am asked what I would like the general purpose of my films to be, I would reply that I want to be one of the artists in the cathedral on the great plain. I want to make a dragon's head, an angel, a devil—or perhaps a saint —out of stone. It does not matter which; it is the sense of satisfaction that counts. Regardless of whether I believe or not, whether I am a Christian or not, I would play my part in the collective building of the cathedral.

INGMAR BERGMAN

SMILES OF A SUMMER NIGHT

A ROMANTIC COMEDY

SMILES OF A SUMMER NIGHT

THE CAST

Anne Egerman	Ulla Jacobsson
Desirée Armfeldt	Eva Dahlbeck
Charlotte Malcolm	Margit Carlquist
Pctra, the maid	Harriet Andersson
Fredrik Egerman	Gunnar Björnstrand
Count Malcolm	Jarl Kulle
Frid, the groom	Åke Fridell
Henrik Egerman	Björn Bjelvenstam
Mrs. Armfeldt	Naima Wifstrand
The cook	Jullan Kindahl
Malla, Desirée's maid	Gull Natorp

THE CREDITS

Screenplay	Ingmar Bergman
Director	Ingmar Bergman
Director of photography	Gunnar Fischer
Music	Erik Nordgren
Sets	P. A. Lundgren

Costumes	Mago
Make-up	Carl M. Lundh
Sound	P. O. Petterson
Editor	Oscar Rosander
Production supervisor	Allan Ekelund

Running time: 108 *minutes*

Produced by Svensk Filmindustri; distributed in the United States by Janus Films, Inc., and in Great Britain by Intercontinental Films Ltd.

Anne and Fredrik Egerman . . .

Lawyer Egerman and Count Malcolm...

Henrik Egerman
with Petra...

...and the Countess Charlotte

...and with Anne

Madam
Armfeldt
and Desirée

... the meeting

The dinner
Charlotte Malcolm
and Fredrik Egerman

Fredrik and
Count Malcolm

Petra and Frid

IT IS A LATE spring day in 1901.

Fredrik Egerman, attorney, closes his large ledger with a bang so that the dust flies, places it on the shelf behind his desk, takes off his pince-nez, puts it away in its case, looks at his watch, winds it several times, sets his desk in order —pens, inkwell, ruler, writing paper and books—combs his beard quickly with a small comb, rises resolutely and begins to whistle as he walks into the next room, which is occupied by his notary and his secretary, who runs forward to help him with his coat. Egerman smiles amiably to his employees; they bow respectfully.

FREDRIK: Good afternoon, gentlemen.
EMPLOYEES (*chorus*): Good afternoon, Mr. Egerman.
FREDRIK: Close up for the day.
EMPLOYEES: Thank you Mr. Egerman.
FREDRIK: Out in the sun, gentlemen. Summer is here.

He bids them farewell with a salute of his cane, puts his hat on his head and walks out on the street.

NOTARY: What's happened to the boss?
ASSISTANT: Oh, I guess it's that young wife of his, making him act foolish.

NOTARY: Yes, yes. Yes, yes. (*He makes a face and dusts off his roll-top desk*)

Fredrik Egerman whistles contentedly as he walks down the street at a rapid, springy pace, occasionally greeting a passer-by. He is a well-known and highly regarded man in this small town.

Now he walks into Almgren's Photo Studio and is greeted at the door by the shop owner's wife, a fat, sweet-smelling woman in a light summer gown. She curtsies politely and asks him to be seated in the outer office.

WIFE: Adolf! Lawyer Egerman is here for his photographs.

Adolf comes out from the studio. He is an elderly man with an artistic appearance, bushy hair and a beautifully dyed mustache. In his hand he has a number of photographs, which he places on the table in front of Mr. Egerman. A white ribbon of sunlight lies across the dazzlingly clean tablecloth.

ADOLF (*proud*): I must say that these pictures of your young wife are among the finest studies that have ever been made at my studio.

Fredrik lays out the pictures side by side, one after another, and it becomes breathlessly quiet in the small shop. Adolf has clasped his hands together and placed one of his legs forward. His head leans to one side and a proud smile is on his lips. Mrs. Almgren stands with her arms crossed over her large bosom and looks quite touched by the many studies of the beautiful young woman. When the inspection is over, Adolf draws a deep breath and Mr. Egerman quickly gathers the photographs together. Mrs. Almgren rouses from her enchantment with an odd little cluck of her tongue.

FREDRIK: An extraordinary, artistic achievement.
ADOLF: The subject! The subject is always the most important thing.
FREDRIK: Yes, she is beautiful, Anne Egerman.

He cannot conceal a small tremor of pride in his voice. He places the photographs in his wallet while a bill changes ownership.

Mutual bows.

Adolf holds the door open. Fredrik steps out into the sunlight, places his hat jauntily on his head and whistles a completely new melody.

Now he stops outside Hermanson's Tobacco Shop and his gaze falls on a poster announcing that a renowned theater company is in town. The evening's performance will be a French comedy, A Woman of the World, and the title role is to be played by Miss Desirée Armfeldt.

After some hesitation Egerman walks into the tobacco shop, buys two parquet seats and an expensive cigar. He lights it on a small gas flame, pays and trots out again into the sunshine.

Glancing quickly at the poster, he assures himself that it is indeed Miss Armfeldt who is playing the title role.

With slow steps and a thoughtful mien, Fredrik Egerman rounds the corner and arrives home.

It is a long, low eighteenth-century house of two stories, surrounded by a garden with budding fruit trees.

Inside, the redheaded housemaid takes his hat, coat and cane.

FREDRIK: Is my wife in?
PETRA: Of course! Mrs. Egerman is waiting with tea. She asked several times for you, sir.
FREDRIK: I've been slightly delayed.

Fredrik goes to the large wall mirror, straightens his tie

and smoothes his hair with his hands. Petra stands right behind him, watching his actions expectantly.

FREDRIK: Now summer is really here.
PETRA: I like fall best.
FREDRIK: Aha.
PETRA: Not the late fall, but early fall.
FREDRIK: By the way, how old are you, Petra?
PETRA: Eighteen, sir.
FREDRIK: A pleasant age.
PETRA: Do you think so too?
FREDRIK: Hm! Apropos of that, has my son come home?
PETRA: He is in the drawing room reading aloud to your wife.

Fredrik nods smilingly to Petra, who curtsies deeply and returns his smile.

The table near the window is set for tea. The pot bubbles quietly and the smell of bird-cherry blossoms comes from the drawing-room table. In the center of a sunbeam sits Anne, dressed in a yellow gown with a pattern of flowers woven into the skirt and a finely worked silver belt around her slender waist. The big red velvet chair embraces her small body; she is energetically occupied with a piece of embroidery stretched across a large circular frame.

On a stool at her feet sits Fredrik's son, Henrik, a handsome youth of about nineteen. Now he reads in a low voice.

HENRIK: . . . in discussing *temptation*, Martin Luther says: You cannot prevent the birds from flying over your head, but you can prevent them from nesting in your hair.
FREDRIK: Good day, my children.

Both of them look up. Anne, a happy look on her face, throws down her embroidery, runs forward to her husband, puts her arms around him and allows herself to be kissed.

FREDRIK: Hello, Mrs. Egerman. Forgive me for keeping you waiting for tea, but I see that you've had company.

He turns with an ironic expression toward his son. They shake hands and bow slightly.

FREDRIK: Hello, son. How was your examination? What a silly question. Naturally you passed it superbly.
ANNE: Henrik was praised by his professor. He said that it was nice to know a theologian who, for a change, was not an idiot.
FREDRIK: And your decision to become a minister is still firm.
ANNE: Fredrik! Don't be cruel now.
HENRIK: Papa!
FREDRIK: Yes, yes! But I didn't say anything.

Fredrik pulls out the theater tickets and places them in front of his wife.

ANNE: Oh, Fredrik! How nice. Are we going to the theater tonight? What am I going to wear? How did you find time? How wonderful. What shall I wear? Just think, you've found time to go to the theater with your little Anne. Look, Henrik, a theater ticket.

FREDRIK: Perhaps you'd rather go with Henrik. I thought that—
ANNE: When I have a chance to go with you! You never have time. How silly you are. What shall I wear? The blue dress with the feathers or perhaps the yellow one? Is it a comedy we're going to? Yes! I know! The white one! The white one is suitable for both laughter and tears.

She is already in the bedroom and has opened the doors of the large, mirrored wardrobes. Dresses foam out around her.

FREDRIK (*apologetic*): It was thoughtless of me to buy only two tickets, but I assumed that a comedy is too mundane an amusement for a man of the cloth.
HENRIK (*pained*): Naturally.
FREDRIK: To be able to really enjoy the performance, I suggest that we take a nap for a few hours. Will you forgive us, dear Henrik, if we leave you for a while? We'll see each other at dinner.

Fredrik smiles boldly, puts his teacup aside and walks into the bedroom, closing the door behind him. Henrik bites his lip and paces around on the soft carpet. The red-haired Petra appears and begins to pick up the tea service. Henrik stops behind the grand piano and looks shyly at the young woman.

HENRIK: Stop walking like that.
PETRA: What do you mean, Master Henrik?
HENRIK: What I say. Stop walking that way.
PETRA: How?
HENRIK: You're swaying your hips.
PETRA: Am I! How funny. Yes, look.

She looks over her shoulder at herself in the large wall mirror. Henrik pinches her arm and kisses her fiercely with his lips tightly pressed together. He gets a quick slap. The young woman straightens the coil of hair at her ear and lifts the heavy tray in her strong arms. Then she leaves, hips swaying broadly.

Henrik sinks down at the piano and improvises some stormy passages. The door opens carefully and from the twilight of the bedroom Anne emerges, dressed in a languishing, angelic-looking negligee. He stops playing and turns violently toward her, but she puts her fingers over his lips and speaks in a whisper.

ANNE: You must be a little quieter. Your father is already asleep.

Henrik lowers his head and Anne gently pats it. Then she returns to the quiet gloom of the bedroom, where the drawn shutters keep out the sharp afternoon light.

Her husband sleeps solemnly, lying on his back with his fingers entwined across his breast. He looks like a dead king on a sarcophagus—a dead king who is satisfied with his death. Anne lies down at his side and closes her eyes. The silence is complete. A lonely fly strolls in the sunbeam across the night table. A little clock ticks eagerly somewhere in the room. Now Fredrik Egerman turns on his side. He stretches his neck with a contented smile and curls his lips. Ann's eyes open slightly and she looks furtively at her sleeping husband.

Yes, he's smiling quite happily, one would almost say with zest.

FREDRIK: Mmm . . . mum . . . m . . . m . . . uh . . .

His nose dilates, his eyebrows lower, his eyelids quiver slightly. Anne finds a completely new and secret amusement in this. She lies on her back and turns her face toward her husband. It's difficult for her to keep from laughing.

Now Fredrik lifts his right hand and places it quite lightly against his wife's cheek. She is completely immobile now, and when the hand slowly begins to caress her throat and shoulder, she shivers and carefully kisses the palm.

Now the hand imperceptibly touches her breast and the finger tips search farther on across the shoulder's soft curve.

Slowly and carefully Anne moves closer to her husband. Her mouth is very close to his and in his sleep he seems to perceive her nearness. He kisses her with sudden passion, clutches her and pulls her to him. She follows him willingly, secretly tempted by this unknown man.

He repeats his kiss, even stronger, this time almost painfully. His mouth searches its way down the girl's throat while he murmurs more and more passionately.

FREDRIK: Desirée . . . how I have longed for you. Desirée . . . how I have longed . . .

Anne's eyes clear, and she trembles as if she had hurt herself. For a moment she tries to answer his passion, but tears come to her eyes and carefully, with infinite gentleness, she pulls away from his embrace. With a sigh that discloses an undefined state of mind, Fredrik Egerman reassumes his attitude of a dead king on a sarcophagus. The only difference is that he doesn't seem so contented any longer. His wife wipes the tears from her eyes and sits up in bed. She has something to think about.

The town has a very beautiful old theater where the bourgeoisie, the military and the country nobility meet ever so often to look at themselves and each other as well as at some high-class performances by some high-class companies.

Fredrik Egerman and his wife occupy two box seats rather close to the stage.

Anne sits in front at the rail, her face calm and expectant. Her hands rest in her lap; she seems completely absorbed in the play. Fredrik sits immediately behind his wife and a little to the side. He is also dressed in evening clothes and looks more at Anne than at the play.

The stage represents an elegant salon, with an immense Brussels carpet covering the sloping stage floor on which pieces of furniture are scattered according to the conventions of French comedy. Two extremely elegant young ladies are in the midst of a lively and quite artificial conversation.

FIRST LADY: Tell me something about the Countess. As you know, I've never met her, only seen her from a distance.

SECOND LADY: Your request is completely understandable, my dear Madame Vilmorac, and I shall try as best I can to depict the personality of the Countess, although it is too rich in mysterious contradictions to allow itself to be described in a few short moments.

FIRST LADY: It is said that the Countess' power over men is most extraordinary.

SECOND LADY: There is great truth in that, Madame, and her lovers are as many as the pearls in the necklace which she always wears.

FIRST LADY: Your own husband, Madame de Merville, is supposed to be one of the handsomest pearls, isn't he?

SECOND LADY: He fell immediately in love with the Countess. She took him as a lover for three months and after that I had him back.

FIRST LADY: And your marriage was crushed.

SECOND LADY: On the contrary, Madame! My husband had become a tender, devoted, admirable lover, a faithful husband and an exemplary father. I feel eternally grateful to the Countess. I sent her a few small gifts and we became the strongest of friends.

FIRST LADY: I tremble at such a lack of decency.

SECOND LADY: I assure you that the Countess' lack of decency is most moral, and her influence is very ennobling to all men, whatever their class.

Now the door opens in the rear center stage and a servant enters.

SERVANT: The Countess Celimène de Francen de la Tour de Casas.

At that moment, Desirée Armfeldt appears in a huge, dazzling gown. The storm of applause from the darkness of the theater reaches her like waves breaking on the beach. Fredrik applauds and Anne also lets her consent be known by a light tapping of her gloved hands.

ANNE: Who plays the Countess?
FREDRIK: Miss Armfeldt, if I'm not mistaken.
ANNE: Isn't her name Desirée?
FREDRIK: Of course, Desirée Armfeldt.
ANNE: May I borrow the opera glasses?

Anne grasps the binoculars and carefully examines Miss Armfeldt, who has stepped forward to the apron of the stage. Suddenly Anne turns toward her husband.

ANNE: She looked at us. Why did she do that?
FREDRIK: I don't think that she looked especially at us.
ANNE: She looked at us and then she smiled. Why did she do that?
FREDRIK: All actresses smile when they thank the audience.
ANNE (*fiercely*): She is extremely beautiful.
FREDRIK: Dear child, that's only make-up.
ANNE: How can you be so sure? Have you seen her offstage? Look at the necklace she's wearing! All the lovers, of course.
FREDRIK: Yes, yes, yes, yes, yes, yes. (*Sighs*)

Anne gives her husband a dark suspicious glance. Fredrik Egerman smiles uncertainly, sticks out his chin and pretends to return to the play. Anne moves uneasily on her chair. The silk rustles; her bare shoulders are tense. Fredrik sighs once more but this time quietly, to himself.

DESIRÉE: . . . we know that every man has his dignity. We women have a right to commit any crime toward our husbands, our lovers, our sons, as long as we don't hurt their dignity. If we do, we are stupid and have to bear the consequences. We should make men's dignity our best ally, and caress it, cradle it, speak tenderly to it, and handle it as our most beloved toy. Then a man is in our hands, at our feet, or anywhere else we momentarily wish him to be.
FIRST LADY: Do you think that this can be combined with real and sincere love?
DESIRÉE: Don't forget, Madame, that love is a perpetual juggling of three balls. Their names are heart, word and sex. How easily these three balls can be juggled, and how easily one of them can be dropped.

Now Fredrik discovers that his wife is quietly crying, as miserably as a small child. Her round, delicate shoulders shake, and her head is deeply bowed. Tears drop profusely over the white silk dress, and her full lower lip trembles sadly, moistly. Fredrik leans gently over her.

ANNE (whispers): I want to go home!

Fredrik nods reassuringly and leads his wife out of the box after he has placed the wide evening wrap around her shoulders with great care.

Petra looks a little touseled when she opens the gate. She has pulled her skirt over her nightgown. Her arms are bare; her red hair is uncoiled and wells down over her shoulders.

PETRA: Is the play over already?
FREDRIK: My wife became a little ill. Will you help her to bed, Petra.
PETRA: Of course, sir.

She curtsies, and her eyes look curiously from one to the other. She has placed the candle on the table and helps Anne with her wrap. Fredrik Egerman walks into the drawing room and turns up the gaslight. Henrik stares at his father as if he were seeing a ghost. He sits on the sofa near the window and holds a guitar in a spasmodic grip, as if it were a life preserver. His hair and clothes are disheveled, and his cheeks are blushing violently. On the table near the sofa stand two wineglasses and a bottle of champagne in an ice bucket.

His father pretends not to notice the boy's confusion, but walks up to the cupboard, takes out a glass, pours some champagne and nods to his son.

FREDRIK: Skoal, my son.

Henrik does not answer the greeting. He merely rises and looks out the window. His father watches him for a moment, walks away and turns down the gas so that the room rests in twilight once more. Then he sits down on the sofa.

FREDRIK: So you've taken up the guitar. I didn't know that was part of the education of the high church clergy.

Henrik still doesn't answer, but he releases the guitar. Fredrik leans forward and serves himself another glass of champagne.

FREDRIK: An excellent wine. You have good taste. I'm happy that you're celebrating your examination.
HENRIK: I'm so terribly unhappy.

FREDRIK: Yes, of course.

HENRIK: You're being ironic.

FREDRIK: You say that you're unhappy and I can't understand why. You are young, it is spring, there is moonlight, you have passed an exam, you have champagne and a girl who is really very attractive. Yet you say that you're unhappy. Youth is very demanding.

HENRIK: But I don't love her.

FREDRIK: Another reason to be content.

HENRIK: We have sinned and it was a complete failure.

FREDRIK: If you're thrown, mount again before you become frightened. That rule can be applied both to love and horseback riding.

HENRIK: Oh, how sickening.

Fredrik shrugs his shoulders and sips his wine. Henrik sits down on an uncomfortable chair.

FREDRIK: Why do you have to mix up everything, my boy? Sex is the young boy's and old man's toy. Love is . . . is . . . hmm . . .

HENRIK: So young men cannot love.

FREDRIK: Yes, of course. A young man always loves himself, loves his self-love, and his love of love itself.

HENRIK (*ironic*): But at your mature age, of course, one knows what it means to love.

FREDRIK: I think so.

HENRIK (*ironic*): That must be wonderful.

FREDRIK: It's terrible, my son, and one doesn't know how to stand it.

HENRIK: Are you being sincere now, Father?

His father makes a small grimace which is supposed to be a smile. Henrik looks at him almost shyly.

HENRIK: You can't imagine how kind Petra was. "Better luck next time," she said laughingly.

FREDRIK: What did you say? Yes, of course. The premiere is always a miserable farce, my boy, and it's very lucky that women don't take it half as seriously as we do, because then the human race would die out.
HENRIK: You make fun of everything.

Petra stands in the door of the bedroom. She says something into the room and then turns to Fredrik Egerman.

PETRA: Your wife wants to say good night to you, sir.

Fredrik immediately rises but stops at the door and looks with amusement at the youngsters. Henrik blushes deeply and shamefully, but Petra smiles back with happy, mischievous eyes.

FREDRIK: You are a capable girl, Petra! I'll see that you get an increase in salary from the first.

The bedroom is dark except for the soft gleam of a small, flickering night lamp. The large bed shimmers at the rear of the room, but Fredrik can't see his wife's face. He is greeted by a sorrowful little voice which he barely recognizes.

ANNE: Can't you sit down over there in the chair? No, you mustn't come closer because I've cried so much that my face is completely swollen.

Fredrik sits down in the big chair, lights his pipe and draws some deep puffs.

ANNE: It's nice when you smoke a pipe. Then everything becomes calmer.
FREDRIK: How do you feel, little girl?
ANNE: Am I a worthless person?

FREDRIK: You are a great joy to many people.

ANNE: Am I really? But one can't be a success from the very beginning, of course. Do you love me? You mustn't love anyone else.

FREDRIK: My little child.

ANNE: That's what you always say. Have you loved many women? Were they beautiful? Sometimes I become frightened of all your memories.

FREDRIK: Before you and I were married, I was rather lonely. Sometimes I thought that I wasn't even truly real.

ANNE: Do you remember when I was a little girl and you came to my father's and mother's home at night and told fairy tales to me until I fell asleep? Do you remember that?

FREDRIK: Yes, I do.

ANNE: Then you were "Uncle Fredrik" and now you are my husband. (*Giggles*) Isn't it funny? Now I have to laugh, even though I'm crying.

There are a few moments of silence.

ANNE: If you won't look at me, you may come here and hug me.

Fredrik gets up from the chair, walks over to the bed, sits down at the edge and leans over his wife. She puts her arms around him and pulls him down toward her cheek.

ANNE: Would you be jealous?

FREDRIK: Jealous?

ANNE: If Henrik began courting me? Or if I became a little infatuated with him? I say this only as an example.

FREDRIK: What silly ideas you have.

ANNE: *Would* you be jealous? Tell me.

FREDRIK: I can't answer if I'm not allowed to sit up. Yes, I think that I would be jealous, because you are so young

and I am so old (*in a low voice*) and because I love you
both.

ANNE: Yes, you are really terribly old. Why did you marry
me? Can you answer that?

FREDRIK: Is this a cross-examination?

ANNE: Maybe you thought that I was pretty.

FREDRIK: Yes, of course. Very pretty.

ANNE: Different from your other women.

FREDRIK: That too.

ANNE: And I was only sixteen years old then.

FREDRIK: Yes, yes, that too.

ANNE: And I was a good housekeeper and almost always
happy.

FREDRIK: You made me happy.

ANNE: So the wolf thought: I wonder how it would taste
with a really young girl?

FREDRIK: Do you think so?

ANNE: Admit that the wolf thought wicked thoughts.

FREDRIK: Yes, perhaps the wolf thought sometimes—

ANNE: And then the wolf was disappointed.

FREDRIK: Why would he be disappointed?

She doesn't answer, but pulls him closer and holds him
fast.

ANNE: You were so lonely and sad that summer, I felt
terribly sorry for you, and then we were engaged and it was
I who suggested it. You silly goose, have you forgotten?

FREDRIK: One becomes so forgetful when one gets old.

ANNE: Now I'm going to sleep.

She seeks out his mouth and kisses him passionately. He
returns the kiss, but she withdraws immediately and looks
smilingly at him.

ANNE: One day I will become your wife, really, and then
we will have a child.

FREDRIK: Yes, of course.
ANNE: You must be patient with me.

Fredrik nods quietly and pulls away from her. She holds his hand tightly and presses it against her mouth. Then she yawns.

ANNE: Are you going to bed right away?
FREDRIK: I may sit up for a little while.
ANNE: Then good night.

She rolls herself over into a sleeping position and Fredrik quietly sneaks toward the door.

ANNE: That wasn't an amusing play.
FREDRIK: But we didn't see much of it.
ANNE: I wonder how old that Armfeldt woman can be.
FREDRIK: I don't really know.
ANNE: Definitely fifty. What do you think?
FREDRIK: Oh no, I don't think so.
ANNE: Good night.
FREDRIK: Good night.

Fredrik tiptoes out of the bedroom and carefully closes the door. The drawing room is empty. The champagne bottle still stands on the table. He begins to walk along the edge of the carpet; he is bewildered and thoughtful. The door to Henrik's room stands ajar. From the dark corridor Fredrik can see Petra sitting in a rocking chair. She yawns and becomes rather distracted. From inside the room a stubborn murmur is heard. It is Henrik, who is reading aloud about virtue.

HENRIK: Virtue is a continuous thing which must not be interrupted because if Virtue is interrupted, it is no longer Virtue. Nor does newly resolved and recently acquired

Virtue deserve the name of Virtue. Virtue always stands opposed not only to the indecent action but also, and even more, to the shameless thought or imagined act. Virtue places a weapon in the hand of the Virtuous, and although temptation implies an attack, it does not necessarily mean a downfall. About all this Martin Luther says . . . But you aren't listening to what I'm reading.

PETRA: I'm listening carefully, but I don't understand it.

HENRIK: So you sit there and think about something else.

PETRA (*hurt*): No, I'm not thinking of *that* at all. I was thinking about your father.

HENRIK: My father is an old cynic.

PETRA: I think that he's nice. He has such piercing eyes. When your father looks at me, I can feel all my curves tingling.

HENRIK: You are wanton and voluptuous, do you know that?

PETRA (*sighs*): It's such a pity that you're so sweet at one end and so complicated at the other.

HENRIK: What do you mean by that?

PETRA: Nothing really. You are as sweet as a little puppy.

The girl giggles delightedly and rocks in the chair. Henrik looks at her with dark seriousness.

HENRIK: Why does temptation have a beautiful face, and why is the straight and narrow path so rocky? Can you tell me why?

PETRA: I guess that's because you need something nice to look at when you walk there among the stones.

Henrik sighs and shakes his head; so does Fredrik Egerman in the darkness. Petra gets up from the rocking chair and pats the boy on the cheek. Then she yawns and walks out, up to her room. Henrik slams the book to the floor

and is very unhappy. His father steals away quietly and un-
noticed.

When Fredrik enters the backstage of the theater, the
night's performance has just ended and the actors are taking their bows. The man who pulls the curtain works like
a monkey on his ropes and the houselights are turned up.

Finally Desirée stands alone, acclaimed with flowers and
applause. The curtain descends, she walks off, stands re-
laxed with a bowed head right beside Fredrik but oblivious
to him. The applause continues, the curtain goes up. Just
as the actress is about to go on again for the last curtain
call, she discovers him standing there. Her face, which is
small and tired, lights up. She offers him her hand and
grasps his, presses it without a word and then walks on the
stage.

Now the curtain falls for the last time and the audience
becomes quiet. The stage hands take over the theater.
Desirée walks off, hands her flowers to a little lady dressed
in a black smock and an old straw hat.

Desirée takes his hand again. Followed by her wardrobe
mistress, she leads him upstairs and along a long corridor
where some oil lamps burn with sleepy yellow flames.

Desirée's dressing room is large but with a low ceiling.
There are two small windows covered by painted window
shades. In the center of the room is the make-up table and
at the far wall stands a ceiling-high mirror. A high screen,
some comfortable armchairs, a divan and a large bathtub
filled with water complete the interior. On the table are
four bottles of beer and a plate of thick, tempting sandwiches.

As soon as Desirée has pulled Fredrik into the dressing
room and Malla, the wardrobe mistress, has closed the
door, she embraces him with great warmth.

DESIRÉE: Fredrik!

She caresses his cheeks and looks into his eyes. She is almost a little touched.

DESIRÉE: Fredrik. How nice. Do you want a sandwich?
FREDRIK: Yes, thank you.

Malla has served the foamy beer and begins to take off Desirée's dress.

DESIRÉE: I become so terribly hungry.

Both eat sandwiches silently and drink beer. Fredrik is a little uncomfortable at having his mouth full of food.
Desirée takes off her dress, stepping out of it as if she were Venus emerging from her shell. The stays follow it. She draws her breath so that her ribs creak.

DESIRÉE: Oh God! Now I can live again. Sit down! No, not there. There!

She leads him to the divan and stands opposite him with her legs slightly apart, while she continues munching happily on her sandwich. In her other hand she holds a glass of beer.

DESIRÉE: But, Fredrik, you're blushing.
FREDRIK: I guess it's because you smell so good.
DESIRÉE: Same perfume as always.
FREDRIK: Yes, that's why.
DESIRÉE: And you've gotten married.
FREDRIK: Yes, I have remarried. It became a bit lonely to live alone.
DESIRÉE: Get up. Come here. Now give me another hug.

Fredrik rises obediently and walks over to her. She puts her sandwich on the table, puts down both their beer glasses and wipes her mouth with the back of her hand. Then she puts her bare arms around his waist, presses him close to her and looks smilingly into his eyes.

DESIRÉE: You have troubles, don't you?

FREDRIK: Is it that noticeable?

DESIRÉE: You old goat, you brute, you long-nosed camel, how unusually human you look.

FREDRIK: Thanks for the compliments.

DESIRÉE: Have you got a pain in the old pump, or the heart as most people call it?

FREDRIK: That isn't why I came.

DESIRÉE: No indeed. It has always been your most noble feelings which led you to Desirée.

FREDRIK: Yes, it's really funny. Today when I took a nap before dinner with my wife, I began dreaming of you in a—hmm—short dream of you. Suddenly I realized that I had been whispering your name in my sleep over and over again while I caressed my wife. Fortunately, I don't think that Anne noticed anything.

DESIRÉE (laughs): Dear Lord, how touching! "In his dreams she was always alive."

She pushes him away from her with a dissatisfied, hurt expression and returns to her beer and sandwich.

FREDRIK (politely): I didn't know that you had become cruel in your old age.

DESIRÉE: Old, old—what are you saying? For the past three years I've been twenty-nine, and that's no age for a woman of my age.

FREDRIK: My young wife guessed that you must be around fifty. What do you say to that?

DESIRÉE: What a little shrew! (Seriously) Fredrik! I'm sure she knows about it.

FREDRIK: What does she know?

DESIRÉE: Whatever you said in your dreams about me.
FREDRIK: Now that I think about it, she was rather upset.
She cried and asked me the strangest questions. Anne is no
goose.
DESIRÉE: She can't be if she risked marrying you.

Fredrik suddenly becomes serious. He presses his palms
together and stares at his finger tips in embarrassment.

FREDRIK: If you won't laugh, I'll tell you something.
DESIRÉE: Do you want some more beer or another sandwich?

He shakes his head and Desirée lights a small cigar,
which she smokes with satisfaction.

DESIRÉE: Well, what were you going to say?
FREDRIK: Oh, laugh if you want to, but Anne and I have
been married for two years and I have not—in short, she is
still untouched.

Desirée splutters with laughter and gets some smoke
caught in her throat. Fredrik smiles a little sourly.

DESIRÉE: Now the world is really going awry when the
wolf turns into a tender shepherd.
FREDRIK: She's frightened of me and I understand her.·

There are a few moments of silence. Desirée sits at her
make-up table with her back toward Fredrik, but she hasn't
started removing the grease paint. The wardrobe mistress
has departed.

FREDRIK: I want her to mature calmly and quietly. I want
her to come to me one day, without fear, of her own free
will and not as a duty or by force.

DESIRÉE: It sounds as though you love her.
FREDRIK: That's a dirtied word. But if I ever loved anyone, it is that girl.
DESIRÉE: Fredrik Egerman loves! It isn't possible.

Desirée's voice trembles a bit. Fredrik raises his head; he looks tired and old.

FREDRIK: One gets such strange ideas with the passing years. I mean things like consideration and tenderness and caution . . . and . . . and . . . yes, love.
DESIRÉE: What a remarkable girl she is to have enabled you to be hurt by something besides a toothache or an ingrown toenail.
FREDRIK: When I come home in the afternoon, she embraces me and laughs because she is happy that I'm home. She is as obstinate as a spoiled child; she has a violent temper and becomes terribly angry. She is so full of life that my old house has started to settle and the walls have begun to crack. She is tender and affectionate, she likes me to smoke my pipe, she likes me . . . *as if I were her father.*

Fredrik gets up violently and begins to pace the floor. Desirée says nothing and plays with a silver box on the table. A smile passes across her lips every so often, but her eyes are serious.

FREDRIK: Dear Lord, I'm a grown man. The old buck only too often raises his ugly head and brays right in my face and then I become discontented and angry with myself because it wasn't exactly what I intended.
DESIRÉE: And what do you want from me?
FREDRIK: I want you to tell me that it's hopeless with Anne. Or the opposite. Or anything else.
DESIRÉE: How can I do that without knowing her?

FREDRIK: You must help me, Desirée. You must help me for the sake of an old friendship.
DESIRÉE (*laughs*): Well, that's *one* reason, isn't it?

Fredrik stops in front of her, takes her by the shoulders and meets her glance in the mirror.

FREDRIK: Regardless of all our magnificent moments of love, you are my only friend in the world. The only human being to whom I've dared show myself in all my terrible nakedness.
DESIRÉE: Spiritual nakedness, I assume.
FREDRIK: Well, will you help me?
DESIRÉE: And what do I get in return?
FREDRIK: I have a young son; you may take him.
DESIRÉE: Shame on you.
FREDRIK: A riding horse, a fine runner.
DESIRÉE: That's not enough.
FREDRIK: A string of genuine pearls.
DESIRÉE: I have as many as I want.
FREDRIK: You'll get your reward in heaven, then.

Desirée pinches his little finger with her sharpest nails so that it begins to bleed.

DESIRÉE: No, Fredrik Egerman, I want my reward in this world.

There is a knock on the door and the wardrobe mistress enters. She brings some articles of clothing. The silk rustles and from the old woman's gray arms gushes a cascade of white lace.

DESIRÉE: Will you excuse me while I dress?
FREDRIK: Of course. Do you want me to leave?
DESIRÉE: Don't be silly.

She goes behind the screen and with the help of her wardrobe mistress she is freed from one undergarment after another.

FREDRIK: It's still bleeding.
DESIRÉE: Have you some warm water, Malla?
MALLA: What do you think, my little girl? Here's a tub full of water.

They both dive down behind the screen and loud splashing is heard.

DESIRÉE: Fredrik.
FREDRIK: Yes.
DESIRÉE: Come here a moment.

He walks up to the screen.

DESIRÉE: Am I as beautiful as then? Have the years changed me? Answer honestly.
FREDRIK: You are as beautiful and as desirable. The years have given your body the perfection which perfection itself lacks, an excitement which perfection does not have.
DESIRÉE: Did you read that in a book?
FREDRIK: You inspire me so that I surprise myself. I read only lawbooks.
DESIRÉE: This is the end of the demonstration. Go sit down on the sofa.

Fredrik laughs and shakes his head, but walks obediently away from the screen. Now Desirée steps out draped in a full-length bath towel. She raises her hands and arms in a regal movement.

DESIRÉE: "Oh pain that I have never felt before!
      Saved I myself but for a wound more sore?

Each pain I suffered in the heated course
Of past love's glow, with all its cruel remorse
And insult's scorch which so unbearably burns
Only foretold the way my heart now yearns."

For a moment she allows herself to be carried away by her declamation. Her eyes darken, she clenches her hands and then she looks up just as suddenly and smiles almost embarrassedly.

DESIRÉE: That was Madame Fedra, very pathetic but a bit of a gambler.

Malla, who has watched all this with great patience from under her old straw hat, finally takes the floor.

MALLA: Desirée, do you intend to perform that way for the rest of the night or am I going to get a chance to dress you?
DESIRÉE: Oh, now you're becoming sour, Malla.
MALLA: Malla isn't sour, but she is sleepy.
DESIRÉE: If I didn't have Malla to keep after me, I'd be a straw in the wind.

Desirée is suddenly girlish and submissive. She pats the old woman so that it can be heard and allows herself to be dressed without protest.

MALLA: Dammit, she's a straw in the wind anyway.
DESIRÉE: Do you think this gentleman is handsome and someone to be considered seriously?
MALLA: I know Fredrik Egerman well. There's never anything definite with him, we both know that.
DESIRÉE: No, with him there's nothing definite.
MALLA: You are coming of age, Desirée, and before you know it you'll be on the wrong side of springtime and well into the summer.

DESIRÉE: I threw away my youth on the wrong men, Malla says.

MALLA: Recklessness has its time, and so has seriousness. But you mustn't become a spinster with too many scratches showing.

DESIRÉE: Where did you put my red gown?

MALLA: Are you going to a party?

DESIRÉE: I'm going to a party with Fredrik Egerman. We shall awaken old memories.

Fredrik lifts his head and looks at Desirée for a moment. Desirée returns his look, smiling a little provocatively.

DESIRÉE: You are hereby solemnly invited for a glass of wine.

She disappears into her red gown, which is an explosion of gorgeous flowers and foaming silk. At the same moment there is a knock on the door and the stage manager sticks in his thin, ulcerous face.

FERDINAND: Do you intend to stay here all night, or when can a poor, sick man close the theater and go home to pamper his ulcer?

DESIRÉE: Ferdinand, you are sad! Here are two bottles of beer. Take the rest of the sandwiches and this bouquet home to your wife, if you have a wife, and then you may kick me in the bottom.

FERDINAND: Yes, but why? There's no premiere now.

MALLA (sour): No, but perhaps a return premiere.

DESIRÉE: Keep quiet now, Malla. Don't be silly.

Then Ferdinand grasps the situation and his strange, inebriated face is split in half by a big grin. He takes hold of Desirée and kicks her twice in the bottom with bent knee.

FERDINAND: She has something in the behind, that girl.
FREDRIK: And something in front as well.
DESIRÉE: And also at the very top, but no one believes it.
MALLA: Nor do I.

They march out of the theater. Ferdinand, who seems almost intoxicated, waves goodbye and the heavy gate closes behind them. Overhead the moon shines enormously from the clear, colorless sky. Like a little witch out of some fairy tale, Malla patters ahead, bent over her lantern. Fredrik and Desirée follow after her, walking arm in arm in the middle of the narrow street. The trees cast enormous black shadows. From the river the water's continuous murmuring is heard. Now Desirée begins to sing; first she hums, and then the words come forth.

DESIRÉE (sings): "Gone are worries, grief and sadness.
This is a place for love and gladness.
Let us then be happy here,
Take pleasure in love, my dear.
Love is wisdom's law on earth.
Love is life in eternal rebirth."

Malla opens a heavy gate and they enter a dark passage paved with large cobblestones.

DESIRÉE (in the dark): Watch out, Fredrik, there's a big puddle here. Look out that you don't . . .

The small lantern sways helplessly and cannot light up this sudden darkness after the strong moonlight. A shuffling of feet, a sudden splash, a muffled curse and then Desirée's laughter. Malla brings the lantern to light up the sad scene. Fredrik sits in the puddle, wet and dirty up to his ears.

Desirée laughs unrestrainedly. Malla offers a helping hand, but Fredrik is annoyed and gets up by himself.

DESIRÉE: Oh, now we can really pamper our guest. Really, really take care of him so that he doesn't catch a cold or get an ache.

They walk across a yard where a large linden tree whispers in the night wind, up a little stairs and onto a porch.
Malla unlocks the door with its tinted windowpanes and then they are home.

DESIRÉE: You'll have to take off your clothes in the kitchen. I'll look around to see if we have something for you to wear. Malla, will you make a hot toddy?

Light in the kitchen. Desirée brings a robe, a nightshirt and a nightcap, and disappears. Malla is busy at the stove. Fredrik shrugs his shoulders resignedly and loosens his wet clothing; he is rather embarrassed. Malla grins and blows on the tinder.
The small drawing room is beautifully furnished in contemporary style. Desirée kneels in front of the open fireplace and is busy making a lively fire when Fredrik enters dressed in slippers, robe and nightshirt.

DESIRÉE: You must also wear the nightcap.
FREDRIK: Only under protest.
DESIRÉE: You might catch a cold. You should wear a nightcap.

Laughingly she places it on his head and leads him to the mirror. He looks at himself with a serious expression.

FREDRIK: How can a woman ever love a man—can you answer me that?

DESIRÉE: A woman's point of view is seldom aesthetic, and in the worst cases you can always turn off the light.

FREDRIK: And to whom do these clothes belong?

DESIRÉE (*ironically*): A man.

FREDRIK: Yes, but it's for—

DESIRÉE: Would you prefer to sit here in the nude?

FREDRIK: And if he comes?

DESIRÉE: Don't worry. He's on maneuvers.

FREDRIK: So he's in the army.

DESIRÉE: And what's wrong with the military? Under their uniforms they're remarkably like other men.

FREDRIK: Is he a dragoon?

DESIRÉE: A *very* handsome man.

FREDRIK: Are you in love?

DESIRÉE: That's no concern of yours.

FREDRIK: Why do I sound so jealous, by the way? Ha!

DESIRÉE: Yes. Why so jealous?

FREDRIK: Why? (*Lightly*) Many since *that* time?

DESIRÉE: No. One tires of the meaningless rides which always become so lonely.

FREDRIK: So.

DESIRÉE: One suddenly finds oneself thinking of something else.

FREDRIK: With a yawn?

DESIRÉE: I don't know. Besides, one always longs for something one cannot have.

She fans the fire with a pair of large hand bellows. Then something remarkable happens.

The door to another room is slowly opened and both of them turn around. Nothing is seen at first; then a boy about four years old appears, dressed in a long nightshirt. He marches through the room and marches out through another door without taking notice of Fredrik and Desirée.

FREDRIK: What was that?

DESIRÉE: That was Fredrik.

FREDRIK: Fredrik?

DESIRÉE: Yes, Fredrik.

FREDRIK: *Fredrik?*

DESIRÉE: How strange you look.

FREDRIK: Have . . . I . . . I mean have you . . . I mean
. . . it isn't possible, or is it?

DESIRÉE (*laughs*): Look at Fredrik Egerman now. He's
terribly shaken and as pale as a pickled herring. At the same
time he's a little flattered, touched and terribly sentimental.
"Desirée, my love, have you been struggling along by yourself all these years, sacrificing everything for our love's
pawn?"

Now the door opens again and the boy marches right up
to Desirée, who lifts him and carries him toward the bedroom.

FREDRIK: Answer my question.

DESIRÉE: The child is mine and mine alone.

FREDRIK (*his voice rising in a squeak*): But his name is
Fredrik.

DESIRÉE: Named after Fredrik the Great of Prussia.

She goes into the bedroom. Fredrik is still standing there,
as if someone had driven a nail through him. From the
darkness of the adjoining room, Desirée's voice is heard.

DESIRÉE: And I can tell you one thing: if I should have a
child it wouldn't be with you.

She comes out again and closes the door behind her.

FREDRIK: You are not fit to have a child.

He gets a lightninglike slap that sends his nightcap

down over his ears. His cheek flames bright crimson with
the mark of a strong and determined hand. At that moment Malla enters with a steaming hot toddy made of red
wine.

DESIRÉE: You can drink your toddy and then go.
MALLA: May I wish you both good night?
DESIRÉE: You're always the same. Dead serious when you
are involved, but cynical and stupid when it comes to oth-
ers.
FREDRIK: May I say something . . .
DESIRÉE: No, you may not. This is a historic moment. You
have finally been stricken by tremors of feeling above the
navel. This is terribly interesting and touching. (*Angry*)
But *I* also have feelings!
FREDRIK: Calm down now, Desirée.
DESIRÉE: I am completely calm; it's you who's making the
noise. Can I help it if I have a temper?
FREDRIK: *May* I say one thing?
DESIRÉE (*angrier*): I've said *no*. You big baboon, I'd like to
see you so ground down into the dirt that not a trace of
you is left behind.
FREDRIK: I've suffered quite a bit.
DESIRÉE: You've suffered! From *what?* Tight shoes? Law-
yer Fredrik Egerman, whose head is always as orderly as his
desk.
FREDRIK (*in a loud voice*): Now I want to talk.
DESIRÉE: No! I'll do the talking and when I talk, I'll talk
even if I have nothing to say, but I am so furious with you
that I forgot what I was thinking about and that's so typical
of you. Well, what were you going to say?
FREDRIK: I've forgotten.
MALLA: May I go to bed?
DESIRÉE: Good night, Malla.

The old lady departs with a sigh. Fredrik sips his toddy.

DESIRÉE: Do you want sugar?
FREDRIK: No, thanks.

Silence again. The clock on the wall strikes one. Desirée sits down in one of the armchairs near the fire. She rests her head in her hand and looks tired. Fredrik reaches out and touches her arm.

FREDRIK: Forgive my thoughtlessness.
DESIRÉE: I guess you know what loneliness means too. Despite a young wife and a grown son.
FREDRIK (*smiles*): Sometimes it seems to me as if my house is a kindergarten for love.
DESIRÉE: That's very suitable.
FREDRIK: The two of us were adults anyway. We knew what we were doing.
DESIRÉE: So we were adults. We knew what we were doing. Especially when we called it off. Correct?
FREDRIK: It was *you* who ended it. Not me.
DESIRÉE: How bitter that sounded.
FREDRIK: I would like to remind you, Madame, that you can on occasion be rather inconsiderate.
DESIRÉE: I got a chance and took it.
FREDRIK: A paunchy, balding actor.
DESIRÉE: He was kind, talented, and a *very* good lover.
FREDRIK: And then goodbye to me!
DESIRÉE: What could you give me? Security? A future? Were you even in love with me? I was a nice playmate, a pretty thing to boast about to your bachelor friends. Did you ever intend to marry me?
FREDRIK: Well, I . . . my former wife had just died . . .
DESIRÉE: Don't be stupid. *Did you intend to marry me?*
FREDRIK: It's possible that I didn't intend to at that time.
DESIRÉE: There, you see. Besides, you amused yourself rather easily with other women. Do you deny that?
FREDRIK: No, but you were headquarters.

DESIRÉE: When I think of how I let myself be treated, I almost become angry again. You were a real scoundrel, Fredrik Egerman.

FREDRIK: Why do you get so angry? And why do you quarrel, slap me, call me all kinds of ugly names?

DESIRÉE: You've always had a long memory.

FREDRIK: Oh, long memory, long memory. Who was it that started to dig into the past?

DESIRÉE: Why does it matter to me if you love your little child bride and can't master her? Do you think that I give a hoot if your heart is bleeding? Just let it bleed and feel how it hurts.

FREDRIK: I thought that we were friends, but now I see that I'm mistaken and I curse my honesty of a moment ago.

DESIRÉE: Why should I be friends with you, you who have never had any other friend but yourself?

FREDRIK: In that case, I'm exactly like you.

DESIRÉE: I have the *theater*, sir, and the theater is my life and I am a rather talented actress. And I don't need to ask help from anyone on this earth, except to tie my corset.

Fredrik sets his glass down with a thud and gets up. He is rather upset.

FREDRIK: And that's why we will now say good night. In the future, my dreams will be strictly monogamous.

DESIRÉE: I'll be most grateful if I may be spared participation in your shameful fantasies, my dear sir!

FREDRIK: I'll try to forget that you even exist. I don't intend seeing you at the theater either, my dear Miss Armfeldt.

DESIRÉE: I'm extremely happy that I don't have to risk your presence on the other side of the footlights, my dear sir.

FREDRIK: Besides, I didn't think you were particularly good as the Countess. It should definitely have been played by one of the theater's younger members. But you still have a name, Mademoiselle Armfeldt.

DESIRÉE: Watch out, Fredrik Egerman, that one of your family's younger members doesn't take *your* role.

At that moment a heavy pounding is heard on the door. Fredrik turns around and looks at Desirée, who seems a bit frightened for a second.

FREDRIK: Who is that?
DESIRÉE: I'm afraid it's Malcolm.
FREDRIK: You mean the dragoon?
DESIRÉE: I guess I'll have to go and open the door.
FREDRIK: I forbid you to open it.
DESIRÉE: Are you frightened?
FREDRIK: Desirée! A gentleman can't meet his rival without his trousers on.

Now the pounding on the door resumes, this time with emphasis. Malla's anxious little rat-face appears at the door. Fredrik opens his mouth to say something, but sits down again, dumfounded.

DESIRÉE: Go, Malla, you open it.
FREDRIK: Now you're relishing it.
DESIRÉE: I must warn you that Malcolm is very jealous.
FREDRIK: Is he armed?
DESIRÉE: Oh, he could wipe the floor with you without a weapon, if he's in the mood.
FREDRIK: Maybe I can hide somewhere . . .
DESIRÉE: We're not on the stage, dear Fredrik.
FREDRIK: But, dammit, it's still a farce.

Now steps are heard in the hallway. A voice speaks to Malla. The steps become louder and a captain, Count Carl-

Magnus Malcolm, enters. He is a tall, obviously handsome man with fine features and unusually large eyes. He walks straight over to Desirée and kisses her hand.

MALCOLM: Please excuse the dust and grime. Just outside town my faithful horse, Rummel, fell. Here are some simple flowers which I managed to pick from a nearby garden. I didn't want to come empty-handed.

DESIRÉE: How delightful, dear Carl-Magnus, and what beautiful flowers. Are you staying long?

MALCOLM: I have twenty hours' leave. Three hours coming here, nine hours for you, five hours for my wife, and three hours back—that makes twenty hours. Do you mind if I remove my uniform and put on my robe?

DESIRÉE: I'm sorry, but it's taken.

MALCOLM: I can see that, but I thought that it would be available in a few moments.

DESIRÉE: May I present Mr. Egerman—Count Malcolm.

MALCOLM: Charmed.

DESIRÉE: Lawyer Egerman fell in the puddle just outside the door.

MALCOLM: I hope that you didn't hurt yourself.

FREDRIK: Not at all. Not a scratch.

MALCOLM: I'm happy for you. Are you visiting Mademoiselle Armfeldt in a professional capacity at this time of night?

DESIRÉE: We are old friends.

MALCOLM: I also see that my nightshirt is being used. It fits well, I hope. Not too small or too large.

FREDRIK: Thank you, it fits excellently. Neither too small or too large.

DESIRÉE: I'll go into the kitchen and see if your clothes are dry. Don't you think I should, Fredrik?

Desirée departs. She looks as if she were enjoying the situation. The two men eye each other coldly. Malcolm begins paring an apple and whistles a tune. At the same time, Fredrik strikes up a little song quite timidly. Malcolm suddenly becomes silent. Fredrik also shuts up.

MALCOLM: For the past six months Mademoiselle Armfeldt has been my mistress. I am extremely jealous. Other husbands are generally ashamed of this weakness. I am not ashamed. I admit frankly that I don't tolerate lap dogs, cats, or so-called old friends. Have I made myself quite clear?
FREDRIK: There is no possibility of my misunderstanding you.
MALCOLM: Are you fond of duels, sir?
FREDRIK: It's possible. I've never tried.
MALCOLM: I have dueled eighteen times. Pistol, rapier, foil, spear, bow and arrow, poison, hunting rifle. I've been wounded six times, but otherwise fortune has been kind to me, or else I've profited from that "cold rage" which, according to the great Commander August Sommer, creates the victorious soldier.
FREDRIK: I am really very impressed.
MALCOLM: Do you see this fruit knife? I'll throw it across the room and the target will be the photograph of that old lady. Her face, her eye. Watch.

Malcolm throws the knife; with a hard, dead sound it lands and sticks in its target.

FREDRIK: You ought to perform in a circus.

Malcolm doesn't answer, but bites into his apple and observes Fredrik with his big, completely calm eyes.

MALCOLM: You are a lawyer?
FREDRIK: At your service.
MALCOLM: I consider your profession a kind of parasite on society.

FREDRIK: I must express my admiration of your military bluntness. By the way, will there be war?
MALCOLM: Why should there be a war?
FREDRIK: Yes, I wonder too.
MALCOLM: Are you being insolent?
FREDRIK: Of course.

Malcolm changes his position and places one leg across the other. A vein swells on his temple, but he doesn't answer. Desirée enters.

DESIRÉE: Well, have you enjoyed yourselves?
FREDRIK: The Count has been extremely entertaining. Are my clothes dry?
DESIRÉE: Not at all.
MALCOLM: Then you may borrow my nightshirt to go home in.

Desirée hears the tone, sees the thick vein at Carl-Magnus' temple and turns, a little frightened, to Fredrik, but the smile still glitters in her eyes.

DESIRÉE: Perhaps it's just as well that you accept Carl-Magnus' generous offer.
MALCOLM: The robe I will keep—that is, if you have no objections.
FREDRIK: I thank you for your generosity, but in that case I prefer to put on my own clothes even if they are wet.
MALCOLM: Unfortunately you won't have time for that, Mr. Egerman. It's very late and you are in a great hurry.
DESIRÉE (anxiously): Do what he says.
FREDRIK: Good night.
MALCOLM: Good night.
DESIRÉE: Good night.

A few minutes later, Fredrik finds himself in the hallway. After a few more moments he stands in the yard.

It is the beginning of dawn. Birds in the large linden tree have started to sing their morning concert. The air is very fresh and it's cold. Fredrik shivers. When he reaches the street, he hears a step behind him, and turns. It is old Malla, who comes running.

MALLA: Here are your clothes. Desirée sends her best regards and says that you shouldn't take it too hard.
FREDRIK: Thank you. That was kind.
MALLA: She sent her regards and said that she thought the quarrel was very stimulating.
FREDRIK: So that's what she said.
MALLA: She said she was sorry that there were obstacles.
FREDRIK: Obstacles? Which?
MALLA: She said that she had expected a lot from the *reconciliation*, whatever she meant by that.

Fredrik stands there slightly bewildered and looks after the old woman until the door shuts behind her. At that moment, a policeman walks by.

POLICEMAN: Good morning, Mr. Egerman.
FREDRIK: Good morning, Constable.
POLICEMAN: Have you been walking in your sleep?
FREDRIK: No, I've been to a party.

Fredrik smiles. The policeman nods and salutes. The two men part with mutual esteem.

Early, very early in the morning, Desirée orders a hansom cab and starts out for Ryarps Castle to visit her mother, old Mrs. Armfeldt.

She gets out of the hansom cab and walks up the steps to the terrace, into the hallway and through the big, bright dining room. She climbs the stairs, turns down a corridor and knocks at the door of the bedroom.

It is a very large room and old Mrs. Armfeldt is a very small lady. She sits in her bed, which is also enormous, and amuses herself with her morning solitaire. When her daughter enters, she looks up, surprised.

OLD LADY: What has happened now to bring my daughter Desirée here at seven in the morning?

Desirée leans over the old lady, who allows herself to be kissed on the cheek. She sits down on the edge of the bed and butters some bread from the breakfast tray, which stands at the side of the bed.

DESIRÉE: I've broken off with Count Malcolm.
OLD LADY: Someone else?
DESIRÉE: Maybe.
OLD LADY: Do I know him?
DESIRÉE. Maybe.
OLD LADY: Better or worse?
DESIRÉE: It depends on how you look at it. Besides, he doesn't know about his promotion.
OLD LADY: Now the game is completed.
DESIRÉE: If you cheat a little, it always comes out.
OLD LADY: You are wrong there. Solitaire is the only thing in life which demands absolute honesty. What were we talking about?
DESIRÉE: About my intended.
OLD LADY: That's an interesting subject. (*Yawns*) At least for you, my girl. Why did it end between you and the Count, by the way?
DESIRÉE: He threatened me with a poker.
OLD LADY: That was ungracious of the Count. But he probably had his reasons.
DESIRÉE: For once, I was really innocent.
OLD LADY: In that case it must have been rather early in the evening. What did *you* do?

DESIRÉE: I hit the Count on the head with the poker.

OLD LADY: What did the Count say to that?

DESIRÉE: We decided to part without bitterness.

OLD LADY: A very good idea. A cast-off lover on good terms can be most useful. What were you saying, by the way?

DESIRÉE: I suppose we were talking about what we were talking about.

OLD LADY: Things were different in my youth. Once your father threw me out the window.

DESIRÉE: Was it open?

OLD LADY: No, it was closed. I fell right on the head of a lieutenant colonel. Later he became your father.

DESIRÉE: Wasn't it my father who threw you out?

OLD LADY: He became your father *later*. Can't you hear me? God, how I loved him.

DESIRÉE: Which one?

OLD LADY: The one who threw me out the window, of course. The other one was a beast. He could never do anything amusing.

DESIRÉE: Why don't you write your memoirs?

OLD LADY: Dear daughter, I got this mansion for promising not to write my memoirs. What were we talking about?

DESIRÉE: I thought you might arrange a party for me.

OLD LADY: Did I promise that? I can't recall.

DESIRÉE: For once, dear Mother, say yes.

OLD LADY: Bring the invitation cards. Who will come? If they are actors they will have to eat in the stables.

The old lady takes pen and ink and correspondence cards. She sits herself upright in the bed and seems a bit stimulated by the thought of a party.

DESIRÉE: The Count and Countess Malcolm. Lawyer Egerman, his wife and his son, Henrik.

OLD LADY: And your intentions?

DESIRÉE: I intend to do a good deed.

OLD LADY: Watch out for good deeds, my girl. They cost too much and then they smell rather bad.
DESIRÉE: You don't know *how* good this deed will be.

Desirée takes a few paces around the room. She seems uneasy but rather excited. The old lady sucks on the top of the penholder like a reluctant school girl.

OLD LADY: A lawyer is always good to have around.
DESIRÉE: Sometimes I admire your muddled astuteness.
OLD LADY: Do you really love that ass?
DESIRÉE: Which one?
OLD LADY: Which one do *you* mean?
DESIRÉE: That one! Yes, I love him.
OLD LADY: That's what I've always said. "Desirée, you worry me! You have altogether too much character, but then, you are like your father!"
DESIRÉE: Which one? I can take my choice.
OLD LADY: What did you say?
DESIRÉE: You don't listen.
OLD LADY: I've never listened.
DESIRÉE: Is that why you're so healthy, in spite of your years?
OLD LADY: If people only knew how unhealthy it is to listen to what people say they never would and then they would feel so much better. Was it something important we were discussing?
DESIRÉE: Is anything important to you?
OLD LADY: I'm tired of people, but it doesn't stop me from loving them.
DESIRÉE: That was well said.
OLD LADY: Yes, wasn't it! I could have had them stuffed and hung in long rows, as many as I wanted.
DESIRÉE: Are the invitations finished?

OLD LADY: I think that I've done particularly well with the capital letters.

DESIRÉE: Thank you. I'll take them.

The old lady has shrunk. Desirée kisses her cheek. The old lady pats her daughter on the forehead.

OLD LADY: You can never protect a single human being from suffering. That's what makes one so terribly tired.

Desirée turns around at the door and waves to the old lady. She returns the farewell with a tiny hand.

The captain, Count Carl-Magnus Malcolm, shoots fast and skillfully. Each morning he practices with a pistol on his private range in the skittles pavilion. At his side stands his batman, Niklas, loading the weapons. He is a young scoundrel of twenty with a shock of yellow hair and happy eyes.

MALCOLM: Niklas!

NIKLAS: Yes, Captain.

MALCOLM: Semiramis will be saddled at nine. Understood?

NIKLAS: Understood, sir.

MALCOLM: Moreover, you will arrange to have fifty red roses sent to Mademoiselle Desirée Armfeldt with my compliments, and fifty-five yellow roses sent to my wife without my compliments. Is that clear?

NIKLAS: That's clear, sir.

Malcolm fires the last shot, blows the smoke from the breech of the pistol and hands the weapon to Niklas, who stands at attention.

MALCOLM: Get on with it.

Niklas makes a noisy click with his heels and departs. Malcolm walks up to the target, takes it down from the wall and counts the hits. At the same time he takes out a cigarette and looks on the table for matches. Suddenly a flame flashes at the tip of his cigarette. It is his wife, Charlotte, who offers him a light. He says "Oh" and kisses her good morning. Charlotte is really a very beautiful woman, dressed for the morning in an exquisite riding costume. She lays her riding crop on the table and takes one of the pistols.

MALCOLM: Watch out, it's loaded.

Charlotte doesn't answer, but aims at a target to the left —aims long and carefully.

CHARLOTTE: Aren't you on maneuvers?
MALCOLM: A quick visit.
CHARLOTTE: Inspection?
MALCOLM: You can call it that.

Malcolm laughs kindly. Charlotte shoots.

CHARLOTTE: That was a miss.
MALCOLM: You didn't even hit the target, my dear. You aimed too long.

He hands her the second pistol and sits down on the edge of the table.

CHARLOTTE: Well, how was Mademoiselle Desirée Armfeldt?
MALCOLM: She had a visitor. A lawyer. In a nightshirt.
CHARLOTTE: What did you do?
MALCOLM: I kicked him out.
CHARLOTTE: In a nightshirt?

MALCOLM: In a nightshirt.
CHARLOTTE: A lawyer?
MALCOLM: Egerman.

The shot goes off. Charlotte lowers the weapon. Malcolm has loaded the other pistol.

CHARLOTTE: That was better.

Malcolm hands the loaded weapon to his wife.

MALCOLM: Lawyer Egerman himself. People have no morals these days.
CHARLOTTE: Poor little Anne. Are you leaving today?
MALCOLM: At nine o'clock.
CHARLOTTE: That's nice.
MALCOLM: The pleasure is all mine.
CHARLOTTE: And when are you returning?
MALCOLM: We are invited to old Mrs. Armfeldt's at Ryarp for the weekend. The Egermans will also be there.
CHARLOTTE: That will be interesting.

She fires her third shot.

MALCOLM: Look at that—a bulls-eye.

He hands her the newly loaded pistol.

CHARLOTTE: Just think if I shot you instead. What would you say then?
MALCOLM: What do you intend to do today?
CHARLOTTE: It'll be a boring day, as usual.
MALCOLM: Perhaps you can pay a visit to your friend, Anne Egerman.
CHARLOTTE: That's an idea.

Malcolm puts on his tunic and fastens its many buttons; his monocle glistens.

MALCOLM: She's probably totally ignorant of her husband's escapades.
CHARLOTTE: Poor Malcolm, are you so jealous?

Malcolm touches his elegant mustache with his forefinger. Charlotte has lowered the weapon and keeps it cocked in both hands. He takes his cap and walks toward the door. He is suddenly furious, but his large eyes are calm.

MALCOLM: I can tolerate my wife's infidelity, but if anyone touches my mistress, I become a tiger. Good morning!

He kisses her fingers and closes the door behind him. Charlotte raises the pistol and fires at the mirror on the door, splintering it into a thousand pieces.

The same morning, while Anne is still in bed drinking her chocolate, Fredrik enters, but now he is very elegantly dressed in a faultless morning coat and carrying a large book under his arm.

FREDRIK: Good morning, dearest.

The girl's face lights up and she holds out her arms to him. He gets his morning kiss.

ANNE: Just think, I was still sleeping when you got up this morning. Have *you* slept well?
FREDRIK: Well, not altogether.
ANNE: No, now I can see. You're pale and your eyes are tired. Did you work late last night?
FREDRIK: Yes, it was rather wearisome. I'll be in my room if you need me.

He kisses her quickly on the forehead and departs. When he enters the dining room, Henrik is still sitting at the breakfast table.

FREDRIK: Good morning, son. Are you planning to leave today?
HENRIK: I may stay for a little while longer.
FREDRIK: Has a bird built a nest in your hair yet?
HENRIK: No.
FREDRIK: It almost managed to lay an egg in mine.
HENRIK: What did you say, Father?
FREDRIK: Nothing. Enjoy your breakfast.

Fredrik goes into his study and closes the door. Henrik looks after him with a long questioning glance. Petra walks through the room singing and quite rosy. When she passes Henrik, she musses up his hair. He springs up and stares at her as if he had gone insane. She approaches him slowly with a friendly smile. When she has come right up to him, she opens her blouse so that her rounded breast is visible. She takes his hand and wants to place it against her heart, but he breaks loose and runs into his room, slamming the door. The girl looks slightly astonished, buttons up her blouse and begins to sing happily while gathering the breakfast dishes. The old cook comes waddling in on aching legs. She carries a large tray.

COOK: I saw what you did.
PETRA: And what's wrong with it?
COOK: Nothing wrong, exactly, but it wasn't right either.
PETRA: And since when are you a judge?
COOK: You are just a social climber, Petra, but I can tell you that a silly girl will remain a silly girl even if she makes herself silly with His Majesty the King.

Now a little bell rings and the cook gives her a nod.

PETRA: That's the lady ringing. I'll take care of this later.

Petra knocks on the bedroom door and enters nimbly. Anne sits before the mirror combing her hair. Her shoulders are covered with a little cape.

ANNE: Will you please brush my hair with the big brush? It's so pleasant.
PETRA: Yes, Ma'am.

Anne closes her eyes and enjoys Petra's long, strong, rhythmic brush strokes. Both girls are silent for a few moments.

ANNE: Are you a virgin, Petra?
PETRA: God forbid, Ma'am.
ANNE: I am.
PETRA: I know, Ma'am.
ANNE (*frightened*): How can you tell, Petra?
PETRA: It can be seen from your skin and in your eyes, Ma'am.
ANNE (*sad*): Can everyone see it?
PETRA: I don't think so.
ANNE: How old were you, Petra?
PETRA: Sixteen, Ma'am.
ANNE: Was it disgusting?
PETRA: Disgusting! (*Laughs*) Gee, it was so exciting and so much fun, I almost died.
ANNE: Were you in love with the boy?
PETRA: Yes, I suppose so.
ANNE: Have you been in love with many boys since then?
PETRA: I'm always in love, Ma'am.
ANNE: Not with the same one?
PETRA: No, once in a while I get tired, of course, but then it's so exciting with the next boy.

ANNE: Almost everything that's fun isn't virtuous, you know that, don't you, Petra?
PETRA: Then I say, hooray for vice, every inch of it.
ANNE: I think that I'll just wear a ribbon in my hair today.
PETRA: You should wear your hair in an upsweep; it looks more feminine.
ANNE: Today I don't want to have it up.
PETRA: As you like, Ma'am.
ANNE: Which gown shall I wear?
PETRA: The yellow, I think, the one with the lace.
ANNE: I'll wear the blue.

Petra brings the requested gown and is just about to assist Anne when she stops. Anne stands in front of the mirror and turns around, looking at herself both in front and back.

ANNE: Anyway, I don't have a bad figure. It's just as good as yours.

Then she receives the gown with the manner of a princess and Petra buttons up the back.

ANNE: Do you think it would be more fun to be a man?
PETRA: Oh no, God forbid. What a terrible thought.
ANNE: I wouldn't want to be a man either.

Suddenly she giggles, puts her arms around Petra's shoulders and lowers her head. Then she really begins to giggle foolishly. Petra is also caught up in this contagion of laughter and they both act like two silly school girls with a thought which is so indecent that neither of them dares mention it, still less think it. The only thing to do is to giggle about it. When Anne comes to her senses again, she wipes her eyes and gets up from the bed where she has collapsed. She tries to look very dignified.

ANNE (*seriously*): Now I'm going to care for my little flowers and feed the birds. In spite of everything, we have our chores, don't we, Petra?

Anne begins to sing and patters happily into the kitchen, where the cook is supervising the weekly baking.

ANNE: Hello, Beata. I thought that we should have a really good steak for dinner.
COOK: Today it's fish.
ANNE: Yes, but I want steak.
COOK: Of course you can have a steak, Ma'am, but the gentlemen and the rest of us will have fish for dinner.

Anne swallows the defeat, takes the green watering can and fills it from the pail with a wooden dipper.

COOK: Where are you going with the watering can, Ma'am?
ANNE: It's for the flowers.
COOK: They were watered at seven in the morning.
ANNE: But that's my work.
COOK: Yes, but now it's been done anyway.

Anne puts away the watering can and walks wordlessly out of the kitchen. She stops in the center of the drawing room rather thoughtfully and then walks decisively into Henrik's room. Henrik is bent over his books. He smokes a sour pipe, has a pair of very ancient slippers on his feet and a robe of indefinite color over his shoulders.

ANNE: What are you reading?

Henrik gets up and stands politely at attention. His face is shut, almost unfriendly.

HENRIK: A book.

ANNE: Yes, I can see that. But what is it called?
HENRIK: If I told you, you wouldn't understand anyhow.
ANNE: I demand to know the name of your book.

Silently he hands her the book. She reads the incomprehensible Hebrew letters and flings it on the table.

HENRIK: There, you see.
ANNE: That's a disgusting old robe. Give it to me. I want to burn it.

Henrik takes off the robe with a submissive expression and gives it to Anne.

ANNE: Phew, how it smells. It's probably never been cleaned. And what kind of slippers are those? Take them off immediately, you pig. I'll burn them too.

Without a word, Henrik takes off his slippers and hands them to Anne. Her eyes sparkle with suppressed rage and her sensitive mouth trembles. Henrik's submissiveness irritates her even more and she points to his pipe.

ANNE: How *can* you smoke such a nauseating old pipe? It smells so bad that I can barely breathe. Give me the pipe.

Henrik hesitates for a moment and a cloud of anger darkens his face. After some thought he hands her the pipe.

ANNE: And now you'll get a slap because you flirted with Petra. Aren't you ashamed of yourself?

She slaps him. Henrik looks at her steadily and tears come to his eyes. When she notices that he is sad, her own eyes fill with tears. They look at each other mutely. Then she throws the robe, pipe and slippers to the floor. The door bangs violently and Henrik is left alone, looking after the girl as if he had seen an apparition.

Now she stands again in the drawing room, bewildered and sad. The sun shines through the window curtains, the facets on the crystal chandeliers gleam, the canaries sing in their cage.

With fearful caution, she knocks at Fredrik's door. A curt "Come in" is heard from within.

In the big dark room—the shades are drawn—diligence and thick cigar smoke prevail. Fredrik sits in a high-backed chair at a large table cluttered with books and papers. He puffs on a fat cigar and wears a pince-nez, which makes his face somewhat unfamiliar. Anne walks quietly up to her husband, takes the cigar out of his mouth and creeps into his lap. She puts her arms around his neck and presses her cheek against his chin.

Fredrik patiently allows himself to be fondled and caresses the girl on her back and shoulders. Carefully he gropes for his cigar and takes a puff so that it won't go out. Anne looks at him, smiles sadly, struggles to her feet and starts toward the door with a bowed head.

FREDRIK: Did my little girl want anything in particular?
ANNE: No, nothing. Forgive me if I disturbed you.

The only thing she can see is the back of a large chair and a cloud of smoke. She closes the door silently and for the third time finds herself alone in the drawing room.

With a small sigh of sadness and desertion she walks up to the canary cage and stands for some moments looking at the birds hopping from perch to perch.

Then she sits down at her small sewing table and reaches for the embroidery frame.

The quiet around her is complete.

The clock on the rococo bureau strikes ten.

Petra walks through the room humming. She sways her

behind and takes a dance step across the threshold. Anne sees all this and sighs again. Then the doorbell rings. She raises her head and listens. Two voices. Then Petra is standing in the doorway.

PETRA: Countess Malcolm to see you, Ma'am.

At that moment Charlotte enters. Anne becomes happy and greets her with open arms. The embrace is returned; the two young women greet each other most cordially.

ANNE: But, Charlotte, how nice. Petra, please bring some lemonade, some ice and some cookies.
CHARLOTTE: Oh my, how hot it is. Really midsummer heat.
ANNE: What a nice gown you're wearing.
CHARLOTTE: May I return the compliment?
ANNE: But you have such nice coloring too. Oh, if I only looked like you.
CHARLOTTE: And I've always wished that I looked like you. I can tell you one thing—I could never wear my hair loose like a young girl.
ANNE: Yet we are almost the same age, aren't we? How old are you really, Charlotte?
CHARLOTTE: How old are you, dear Anne?
ANNE: Nineteen, but I'll be twenty soon.
CHARLOTTE: Yes, then I'm a few years older, of course. And what else is happening?
ANNE: Henrik is home. He did very well on his last examination.
CHARLOTTE: Apropos of that, how is your husband?
ANNE: He's well, I believe.

Just then Petra enters with the lemonade and the cookies. During the following conversation, Anne serves Charlotte and herself. She does so with complete self-control and without betraying herself by a single expression or gesture.

CHARLOTTE: So the worthy Lawyer Egerman is well. He hasn't got a cold?

ANNE: Why should he have a cold in this warm weather?

CHARLOTTE: Last night it wasn't so warm, of course.

ANNE: Now I don't understand what you mean, dear.

CHARLOTTE: It's really so amusing. Your husband was supposed to have been seen out on the town last night.

ANNE: I guess he had insomnia and took a walk.

CHARLOTTE: In his nightshirt?

ANNE: Why shouldn't he walk around in his nightshirt if he wants to?

CHARLOTTE: He was supposed to have come from Mademoiselle Armfeldt's apartments. You know—the actress.

ANNE: Fredrik has always been interested in the theater.

CHARLOTTE: That actress is supposed to have absolute orgies in her home.

ANNE: Do you want another cookie, Charlotte?

CHARLOTTE: Did your old Beata bake them?

ANNE: Yes, she's a treasure.

CHARLOTTE: As you know, I don't run around with gossip.

ANNE: And if I already knew?

CHARLOTTE: You mean he confessed?

ANNE: Of course.

CHARLOTTE: Don't try to tell me that.

ANNE: It happens to be so, in any case.

CHARLOTTE: I don't believe you.

ANNE: I imagine that he met *your* husband at Miss Armfeldt's.

CHARLOTTE: I don't understand what you mean.

ANNE: But, dear Charlotte, the whole town knows that the Count is having an affair with Mademoiselle Armfeldt.

Anne's nose is a little pale and her eyes have become a

bit dark, but she doesn't allow her thoughts and feelings to be guessed.

CHARLOTTE: Perhaps. It doesn't matter to me what that filthy swine does, and I pay him back in his own coin.
ANNE: Poor Charlotte.

Then Charlotte breaks into such violent tears that the lemonade in her glass pours out over the silver tray, the cookies and the carpet. She cries quite openly and without shame in front of Anne, who sits silent and immobile.

CHARLOTTE: I hate him, I hate him, I hate him, I hate him.

When she thinks of how much she hates him she suddenly stops crying and bites her fingers.

CHARLOTTE: Men are beastly! They are silly and vain and have hair all over their bodies.

She wipes away her tears with the palms of her hands and takes a deep breath. Her mouth trembles, as if she wanted to burst into tears again.

CHARLOTTE: He smiles to me, he kisses me, he comes to me at night, he makes me lose my reason, he caresses me, talks kindly to me, gives me flowers, always yellow roses, talks about his horses, his women, his duels, his soldiers, his hunting—talks, talks, talks.

Her voice is convulsed by a sob. She turns away her face so that Anne won't be able to see her.
CHARLOTTE (*low-voiced*): Love is a disgusting business!

She bites her lip and turns her face toward Anne in a sudden, violent movement.

CHARLOTTE: In spite of everything, I love him. I would do anything for him. Do you understand that? Anything. Just so that he'll pat me and say: That's a good little dog.

There are a few moments of silence. Anne looks at her friend with a mixture of fright and reluctant admiration.

ANNE: Poor Charlotte.
CHARLOTTE: That Desirée, with her strength and her independence. No one can get the best of her, not even Carl-Magnus. That's why he's so obsessed with her.
ANNE: I don't know her.
CHARLOTTE: All men are drawn to her and I don't know why.

Charlotte sits quietly for a moment, searching for an answer. Then she shrugs her shoulders and suddenly becomes her old self again.

CHARLOTTE: It was good that you knew everything. Then I haven't caused any trouble.
ANNE: No.
CHARLOTTE: She has probably never been in love.
ANNE: Excuse me, what did you say? Who?
CHARLOTTE: Desirée. She has probably never been in love. She probably only loves herself.

Then the door opens and Fredrik enters. He still has a cigar in his mouth and the pince-nez on his nose. He carries a small letter in his hand.

FREDRIK: Good day, Countess! It was nice of you to visit my wife. I hope you're enjoying yourselves.
ANNE: We're enjoying ourselves very much, my friend.
FREDRIK: By the way, dear Anne, I've just received an invitation to old Mrs. Armfeldt's estate at Ryarp.

CHARLOTTE: Oh! Isn't that Desirée Armfeldt's mother?
FREDRIK: I believe so.
CHARLOTTE: Then perhaps we'll meet the great actress
That would be lovely.
FREDRIK: Are you also invited, Countess?
CHARLOTTE: I and my husband. Just think, how amusing.
ANNE: You can go alone. I don't want to.
FREDRIK: I'll say no, then, for both of us.

He nods briefly, bows toward Charlotte and goes to the
door. Anne calls out to him.

ANNE: No, wait! I've changed my mind.
FREDRIK: So we're going?
ANNE: Yes, thanks! It should be very amusing.

Fredrik walks toward the door again.

ANNE: How are you, Fredrik?
FREDRIK: I? Excellent. I may have the beginning of a cold,
but it's only a trifle.

He clears his throat and looks from one woman to the
other, but their faces are impenetrable.

When he has returned to his study, he sits down at the
table, smokes for a few minutes while he looks thoughtfully out of the window. Then he takes out his wallet and
extracts Anne's photographs. He places them on a row on
the table before him, leans forward, touches them one after
another with his forefinger. His eyeglasses cloud up. He
has to take them off and wipe them with his handkerchief.
He holds them up to the light. His face is tense and the
membranes of his eyes feel brittle with suppressed sorrow.

FREDRIK (*mumbles*): I don't understand . . .

The small castle lies under the early-summer foliage, slumbering in the mild sunshine of a Saturday afternoon. Down on the lawn, Mrs. Armfeldt is just receiving the Egerman family. The old lady, whose legs are paralyzed, sits in a large chair. Her grandson, Fredrik, plays nearby. Old Malla sits watchfully at his side on a folding stool. Mrs. Armfeldt carries on a lively conversation with Mr. Egerman. Anne, who is dressed in a light-hued summer dress, plays with a puppy. Henrik hovers near her, reaching out his long arm to pat the little dog on the head once in a while.

Frid, the coachman, is a big, ruddy man of about forty with a large mustache and a pair of icy-blue eyes looking out from the heavy folds of his face. Now he is helping Petra with the baggage.

FRID: So your name is Petra.

PETRA: And yours is Frid.

FRID: You're a nice piece of baggage. I guess no one has said that to you before?

PETRA: All right, calm down now and bring over the large suitcase.

They walk silently through the hallway and enter the dining room.

FRID: Do you have a sweetheart?

PETRA: No, but I have plans for the future.

FRID: Then Frid is the right man for you, because Frid is a man of the future.

PETRA: Have the other guests arrived yet?

FRID: They will arrive soon.

In a niche, lit by the afternoon sun through a narrow window, stands the statue of a magnificently shaped woman.

PETRA: Who is that statue supposed to be?
FRID: It's the old lady when she was young.
PETRA: Oh, my God. (*She is shaken*) Is this the old lady?
My God, what life does to us.
FRID: Take advantage of every moment.

Frid looks at the girl with happy, lustful eyes. She pretends not to notice but feels very flattered. They walk
down a long corridor. Gloomy ancestors gaze down from
the walls. Frid pushes open a door.

FRID: Here is where your master and mistress will stay.
PETRA: And where does their son Henrik sleep?
FRID: So you're interested in that.

Frid puts down the big trunk and walks along the corridor and into the adjoining room, which has only one bed.
Petra follows him.

FRID: Yes, here's where the boy will stay. It's pretty nice
for that little runt. Do you know why? I'm going to tell
you. This is a *royal* guest room.
PETRA: So, has royalty lived here?
FRID: You see, the King had a minister and that minister
had an unusually beautiful wife and the King took a fancy
to the young woman. Then the King and the minister were
going to meet here at Ryarp and the minister and his wife
were placed in the room where the Egermans are going to
stay and the King slept here.
PETRA: And then the wife went to the King?
FRID: No! There you're wrong, little maid. When the minister had fallen asleep, the King pressed this button. Do it
and you'll see what happens.
PETRA: Oh, you're just teasing me.
FRID: Do what I say.

Petra presses the knob and at first nothing happens. Just as Petra turns to reproach Frid for his joke, a little music-box melody is suddenly heard. Soundlessly, as if by magic, a bed glides through the wall and pulls in quietly and faithfully alongside the other bed.

FRID (*proudly*): That's how the beautiful lady came through the wall, bed and all, to enjoy herself with His Majesty.

He walks up to the button and presses it again. The bed glides back, this time without music.

PETRA: How clever. I wish I had such a nice bed.
FRID: There's a little bit of the devil in you, did you know that, Petra?
PETRA: Ouch, don't pinch. Look, who's that beautiful lady coming out now and greeting Mr. Egerman? Is it Desirée, the actress? Just think if I looked like that.

Desirée is really very beautiful, dressed in a sweetly feminine summer dress and a wide-brimmed hat. She offers her hand to Egerman and he brings it to his lips.

DESIRÉE: How nice that you could come. And this is your young wife.

A small explosion is heard and then a persistent rattling sound. Up the tree-lined driveway leading to the castle a strange equipage approaches. It is the Count and Countess Malcolm and the batman Niklas in a shiny new automobile. With an elegant turn and an echoing report, the fire wagon stops in a cloud of dust in front of the house. Malcolm jumps out wearing a long leather coat and enormous gauntlets. He walks around the car and helps his wife to get down. Niklas hops out and begins unloading the baggage. Petra has rushed out on the steps to observe the miracle together with Frid, who regards it with reserve and a certain scorn.

Malcolm leads his wife by the arm over to the old Mrs. Armfeldt. Polite greetings are exchanged. Malcolm and Desirée, very formal. Malcolm and Fredrik, very severe. Anne and Charlotte, very hypocritical. Malcolm and Anne, very curious. Charlotte and Desirée, very armed.

DESIRÉE: I'm very happy to see you here.
CHARLOTTE: Oh, both of us have heard so much about you and looked forward to meeting you.
DESIRÉE: Do you want to see your room, Countess?
CHARLOTTE: Yes, it would be pleasant to wash off the dirt from the journey.

The two ladies depart, conversing amiably. There are a few moments of meaningful silence and the remainder of the party look after them. Then all eyes turn toward Captain Malcolm. He is aware of his responsibility and draws a deep breath.

MALCOLM: Yes, speaking of automobiles. When the road was smooth we attained a speed of nearly thirty kilometers an hour.

Desirée and Charlotte are already in the large sunny guest room with its white curtains, light furniture and broad plank flooring.

DESIRÉE: I'll call someone to arrange a bath for you.
CHARLOTTE: Miss Armfeldt.
DESIRÉE: Countess?
CHARLOTTE: Why did you invite us?
DESIRÉE: I have a plan.

CHARLOTTE: Does it concern me?

DESIRÉE: Very much so.

CHARLOTTE: Are you prepared to speak frankly?

DESIRÉE: Why shouldn't I be frank? We're enemies, aren't we?

CHARLOTTE: Do you want a cigarette?

DESIRÉE: No, thanks. I only smoke cigars. Now, it is possible that enemies can have mutual interests. Should they continue to remain enemies and ignore their common interest?

CHARLOTTE: Not two women.

DESIRÉE: Then let us make peace, at least for the moment.

CHARLOTTE: Unfortunately my husband doesn't have a ring in his nose so that he can be tethered in one place.

DESIRÉE: That's true. He has his free will, whatever that means. And then there's his perpetually functioning masculinity, which bothers him quite a lot.

CHARLOTTE: He's a corpse.

DESIRÉE: I rather pity him.

CHARLOTTE: Pity *him!*

DESIRÉE: Yes. Look, now they're playing croquet down there. Who is the undisputed master? Who is the rover? Who makes an innocent game into an offensive battle for prestige?

They play croquet. The sun shines over the green lawn. Anne is like a big flower. Henrik's eyes never leave her for a moment. Cracked ice clinks in the lemonade glasses; bees are humming in the rose bushes; a mild breeze chases light shadows across the lawn. The old lady has taken little Fredrik on her lap and is reading to him from a large book. Fredrik and Malcolm stand close together, each smoking a cigar, swinging their croquet mallets.

MALCOLM: It's your turn, Mr. Egerman.

FREDRIK: I'm afraid it is.

MALCOLM: As you know, I'm a rover and have the right to put you out of position.

Malcolm puts his ball next to Fredrik's and puts his foot on top of it. Then he hits it with a hard blow and Fredrik's ball rolls out of bounds. Malcolm laughs jauntily.

CHARLOTTE: When he laughs that way, he's angry.
DESIRÉE: Angry and jealous.
CHARLOTTE: Of you?
DESIRÉE: Of you.
CHARLOTTE: Why in heaven's name should he be jealous of me?
DESIRÉE: He is furious about the way you looked at Mr. Egerman when you said hello to each other a moment ago.
CHARLOTTE: How ridiculous! How utterly ridiculous!
DESIRÉE (*seriously*): Yes, that's how ridiculous it is.
CHARLOTTE: So you have a plan. And how does it work?
DESIRÉE: Very simple. You get back your husband, and I . . .
CHARLOTTE: And you . . .
DESIRÉE: Can I really depend on you?
CHARLOTTE: And you get back your lawyer Egerman. Right?
DESIRÉE (*nods*): Men can never see what's good for them. We have to help them find their way. Isn't it so?
CHARLOTTE: And the plan?
DESIRÉE: First let's arrange the seating for dinner.

The warm candlelight from the long table clashes with the pale light from the summer evening outside the lofty windows. The old lady acts as hostess, with Frid behind her chair dressed in livery and wearing white gloves. Petra and the maids from the house serve the meal. The seating has been planned with subtle strategy. Lawyer Egerman is paired off with Charlotte, Count Malcolm

with Desirée, and Henrik Egerman with his young step-
mother. The gentlemen are dressed in evening clothes and
the ladies wear grand evening gowns. Now Desirée leans
forward and tries to catch Charlotte's glance. Charlotte
nods imperceptibly.

Malcolm has just told a joke and everyone laughs except
Henrik.

CHARLOTTE: So you think, my dear Carl-Magnus, that all
woman can be seduced?
MALCOLM: Absolutely. Age, class, condition and looks
play no part at all.
DESIRÉE: Those that are married too?
MALCOLM: Married women above all.
OLD LADY: Then your best ally is not your own charm but
the wife's matrimonial gloom.
FREDRIK: Bravo.
CHARLOTTE: What's your opinion, Mr. Egerman? Can't
the woman ever be the seducer?
FREDRIK: I think that we men are always seduced.
MALCOLM: Idiotic. I have never been seduced in my whole
life. A man is always on the offensive.
CHARLOTTE: Apparently not Mr. Egerman.
MALCOLM: Oh, he just wants to make himself more inter-
esting.
CHARLOTTE: I assure you that I can seduce Mr. Egerman
in less than a quarter of an hour.
MALCOLM: No, my love. We men don't swallow such large
hooks.
CHARLOTTE: Yes, you do.
MALCOLM: By no means.
DESIRÉE: Charlotte is right.
CHARLOTTE: Shall we make a bet?
MALCOLM: Very funny. (*laughs*)
DESIRÉE: Don't you have the courage to make a bet with
your wife?

MALCOLM: You're on!

Everyone laughs but Henrik and Anne. They are quiet and embarrassed in the presence of this gaiety without happiness.

MALCOLM: Here comes the man, marches up, shoots his broadside. Bang. The enemy retreats, takes new positions. New offensive. The positions are ripped up. Bang. Bang. Then the chase goes over stock and stone until the game— I mean the enemy—lays down his arms in front of superior forces, but I give no quarter. I raise my weapon and there she lies bleeding with love and devotion—I mean the enemy. Then I secure my position and make a wonderful meal, the feast of truce; passions rage, intoxication mounts, and the morning sun finds the soldier in the arms of the enemy, slumbering sweetly. After a little while he gets up, girds his loins and starts out to do new deeds of bravery . . . New games—I mean enemies . . . (*He is at a loss for words*)

OLD LADY: My dear Count, before you begin your offensive, as you call it, the ground has been long since mined and the enemy is wise in the ways of both you and your strategy.

HENRIK (*angry*): Strategy, enemy, offensive, mines. Is this love or a field battle that you're talking about?

DESIRÉE: My dear young man, mature human beings treat love as if it were either a battle or a calisthenic exhibition.

HENRIK: *But we are put into this world to love each other.*

There is silence. Then they smile a little embarrassedly, as wise people smile at such banalities.

OLD LADY: My children . . . my friends . . .

She raises her glass. Out of the twilight, out of nowhere, a melody is heard. It seems to have been born out of the night, out of the bouquet of the wine, out of the secret life of the walls and the objects around them.

OLD LADY: A story is told that this wine is pressed from grapes whose juice wells forth like drops of blood on the white skin of the peel. It is also said that to every cask filled with this wine a drop of milk from the swelling breasts of a woman who has just given birth to her first child and a drop of seed from a young stallion are added. This gives the wine a mysterious, stimulating power, and whoever drinks of it does so at his own risk.

Desirée's smile deepens and her hand closes tightly around the finely shaped goblet. She drinks deeply and holds the cut glass up to the candelabra's flickering light. A flame falls across her cheek and forehead.

Malcolm finishes his glass in one draught and then allows the tip of his tongue to play over his lips, smacking them discreetly but pleasurably.

ANNE (*quietly*): I drink to my love . . .

She lifts the glass to her lips and sniffs its bouquet. Then she lets the mild juice flow in a fine stream over her tongue. Her shoulders quiver with a small tremor of pleasure.

CHARLOTTE: My success.

She grasps the glass in her cupped hands and raises it to her mouth like a sorceress. She drinks with closed eyes and in small, greedy swallows. When she has finished, she draws her breath deeply.

FREDRIK (*quietly*): Anne.

He drinks, and a mist comes over his eyes. He tries to brush it away, but it remains.

Henrik's glass stands full and untouched in front of him. He stares at it as if he were hypnotized by it. Then he grips it, brings it to his mouth, but changes his mind and puts it down again.

The old lady dips a small, bony finger into her glass and allows it to be colored by the wine. She licks her finger like a cat.

Then Henrik drinks, emptying the whole glass and putting it down so violently that he cracks its fragile stem. Fredrik is startled, wakes up from his feeling of unreality. His forehead wrinkles with irritation.

FREDRIK: Watch what you're doing.
HENRIK: Watch what *you're* doing yourself.

Henrik flares up; his eyes flash and his mouth trembles. He has turned absolutely white. Petra runs forward and tries to wipe up the red stain which grows and swells across the white tablecloth.

FREDRIK: What kind of language is that?
HENRIK: Do you think that I can tolerate everything from you? Are you some kind of emperor who decides what everyone in your house can think and do?
FREDRIK: Calm down now, Henrik. You don't know what you're saying.
HENRIK: But you do, don't you? You with your lack of normal decency. When I come with my sorrow, you answer with your sarcasm. I'm ashamed that you're my father.
FREDRIK: Now shut up or leave the table.
HENRIK: For once I don't feel like keeping quiet. Now I want to throw this glass on the floor.
DESIRÉE (*smiling*): Here is another glass. You can throw as many as you like.

HENRIK: You who are such a great artist, don't you suffer from the lies, the compromises? Doesn't your own life torment you?
DESIRÉE: Why don't you try to laugh at us?
HENRIK: It hurts too much to be funny.
ANNE: *Henrik, calm down now!*

Her voice is like a little silver bell and it rings in the air above their heads, above the candelabra and the mild twilight of the room. The dinner guests listen, astonished and thoughtful. Yes, that is how it is. Anne has laid her small hand on top of his, but she doesn't look at Henrik; she has closed her eyes and withdrawn into herself.

Once again the silver bell sounds.

ANNE (*low voice*): Calm down now, Henrik.

Fredrik is suddenly stricken; his chest constricts so that he can barely breathe. He opens his mouth like a fish on land and raises his hand toward his face as if to ward off a blow.

OLD LADY (*quietly*): Why is youth so terribly unmerciful? And who has given it permission to be that way?

No one answers. The old lady drinks another mouthful of the strange wine and shakes her head.

OLD LADY: Who has given it permission?
DESIRÉE: The young live on the sheer chance that they will never need to become as old as we.
HENRIK: Then one might as well be dead.

Desirée lets her glance glide toward Fredrik. He is no longer present. He sits with a cramped, dead smile and stares at his wineglass. Once in a while he blinks as if incapable of stopping the flow which is almost ready to burst from his eyes. Now he draws his breath deeply, but that also hurts. It is better not to breathe, not to move.

MALCOLM: Good Lord! The boy is going to become a minister. He'll get paid to produce some small tremors in the reluctant soul.

Then Henrik gets up. He is deathly pale and looks as if he is going to faint. Swaying like a drunk, he walks up to Malcolm, who is calmly wiping his mouth with his napkin.

MALCOLM: Are you going to hit me? Very well, if you want to, but it will be all the worse for you.
HENRIK (*whispers*): Forgive me! Forgive me, all of you!

He staggers from the room, pulls open the door leading to the large stone-paved hallway and disappears like a shadow into the summer night. Anne rises from the table.

ANNE (*shouts*): Henrik, don't hurt yourself!

But he doesn't hear her, or care to hear her, and she sits down on her chair with a bowed head, like a punished school girl.

OLD LADY: Yes, let's leave the table. Coffee and liqueurs await us in the yellow pavilion.
ANNE: May I retire?

Fredrik hardly sees her, but nods.
Anne stretches out her right hand and grasps Petra's firm little fist. Fredrik pats Anne on the cheek. The surface of the wound in his heart has clotted; it doesn't bleed any more, but each movement is terribly painful. Anne pulls

Petra to her and the two girls disappear with their arms around each other's waists.

Desirée lights a cigar from one of the candelabra. She leans forward to speak to Charlotte.

CHARLOTTE: And we thought that the first step would be the most difficult one.

DESIRÉE: Maybe the most difficult but not the most delicate, because that comes next.

Both ladies turn their eyes toward Fredrik Egerman, who has walked over to the window. Their quiet thoughtfulness is interrupted when Malcolm steps up.

MALCOLM: What are you gossiping about?

DESIRÉE: Come now, Count, let us go to the yellow pavilion and have coffee.

MALCOLM: What is my wife going to do?

DESIRÉE: You can see quite well. She's taking care of Fredrik Egerman.

MALCOLM (*laughs*): Yes, he's had enough to make him quiet, poor wretch.

Charlotte has come up to the window and stands behind Fredrik.

CHARLOTTE: Are you crying?

FREDRIK: I! No.

CHARLOTTE: Shall we go or stay, or laugh or cry? Or make funny faces?

The others have gone out into the light summer night. The moon's enormous globe rolls over the horizon, the bulrushes murmur, and once in a while you can hear the voice of the nightjar bird. Malcolm and Desirée walk arm in arm

down the path. Frid walks in front, carrying the old lady
like an ikon.

CHARLOTTE: May I put some salve on the wound?

She stands on her toes and kisses Fredrik.

FREDRIK: Why did you do that?
CHARLOTTE: Was it unpleasant?
FREDRIK: You want to make your husband jealous.
CHARLOTTE: But he can't see us.
FREDRIK: You are not much older than Anne.
CHARLOTTE: I'm a much greater risk.
FREDRIK: For yourself, perhaps.
CHARLOTTE: For myself and others, but I generally give
warning first. I am an honest little rattlesnake. Now I'm
giving warning.

She raises her forefinger, holds it high in front of his face
and then rattles her bracelets.

FREDRIK: The rattlesnake may well bite to kill something
left over.

The moon has risen higher; it drenches the countryside
with a mysterious shimmer. The water in the small bay
gleams like melted lead; the trees stand quiet and waiting;
the tower clock strikes its soft chimes; the yellow pavilion
is lit like a jewel. Now Desirée sings a song in German:
*"Freut Euch des Lebens, weil noch das Lämpchen glüht!
Flücket die Rose eh' sie verblüht . . .*
Henrik looks at all this from the terrace, shakes his head
and doesn't want to know, feel or live.

HENRIK: No, no, not know, not feel, not live . . .

His head sinks down on his breast and he clenches his fist against all this beauty.

HENRIK: Oh, how I suffer. And how ashamed I am.

He staggers through the large door, through the flagstone-paved hallway, into the dining room, which lies empty and quiet, with moonlight floating in through the tall windows. He sinks down at the grand piano and plays some stormy bars from Chopin's Fantasy-Impromptu. Then he stops and bends over, covering his face with his hands and mumbling to himself.

HENRIK: Why am I so ugly, so evil, so stupid? The only right thing to do is to commit suicide. I'm going to die. I know I am. Pass away with quiet dignity.

The thought consoles him; he rises from the piano stool and walks with dignified if rather shaky steps through the patterns of moonlight. When he reaches the stairs, the moon suddenly disappears and it becomes dark—immensely, completely dark.

HENRIK (*mumbles*): I walk in darkness, a blood-red sorrow lights my way. Oh, horror, you who erode my mind so that I may never see the light . . .

But suddenly the moon's strange light has returned, and there, lit by the tall, narrow staircase window, a woman's body shimmers nakedly. The boy stares transfixedly at this beautiful creature, whose mysterious, arrogant smile seems to come alive in the mild light.

HENRIK: Oh God, God . . .

He raises his hand and touches the marble. He starts,

as if he had been burned. Then he turns his face away in fear and disgust, climbs upstairs and staggers down the corridor to his big, lonely room.

A breeze flows through the garden; the white curtains balloon inward and the branches of the trees form a moving pattern on the ceiling and the walls.

Now a flute is heard down among the shrubbery. It is Niklas, drunk and blissful, sitting among the flowers under the trees, playing his instrument.

Now a girl laughs loud and provocatively. A little pantomime is being performed on the moonlit terrace. Petra is chased by Frid, who makes small leaps in the air like a gay, giant Pan. She is amused, tempted, but constantly escaping until they both disappear in the shadow of the house. The end of the chase can be surmised, a cascade of white petticoats and a single blurred shape that disappears under the trees, staggering and bent.

Henrik stands at the window of his room and sees all this. The sweetness of the night, the flute's sad arabesques, overwhelm his heart, which is already filled to the brim with a strange madness.

HENRIK: O Lord, if your world is sinful, then I want to sin. Let the birds build nests in my hair; take my miserable virtue away from me, because I can't bear it any longer.

He hiccups from sorrow and drunkenness, searches for the belt of his robe, ties a strong noose around his neck, pulls a chair out on the floor, climbs up on it and fastens the belt to the flue of the porcelain furnace. Thus prepared, he throws a last look on all the wonders of the earth and takes his leap toward eternity.

He lands on the floor and staggers against the wall. When he retrieves his balance he loses his sense of comprehension for the last time.

The night wind has returned and the moonlight seems stronger than before.

From out of nowhere, a small music box plays a fragile tune. A bed comes gliding through the wall, dreamlike, soundless, unreal, as if materialized by the moonlight. And in the bed Anne lies sleeping. At first he stands there motionless.

HENRIK: I think I must be dead after all.

He rouses himself, takes a towel, dips it deeply into the water pitcher and lets the cold water splash over his head and shoulders. With surprise he discovers that he is still alive, awake and real.

Then he ventures over to the bed. He falls on his knees and feels the warmth of the girl; the fragrance from her body makes him dizzy and he closes his eyes. Now the music box falls silent, and so do the wind and the flute. It is as if everything had stopped breathing. He leans over the girl's face with closed eyes and kisses her lightly.

She awakens slowly from her deep slumber and looks for a long time at the boy, at his wet, pale face, and she smiles.

ANNE: Henrik.
HENRIK: Anne.
ANNE: I love you.
HENRIK: I love you.
ANNE: I've loved you all the time.
HENRIK: I've loved you all the time.

Frid empties a mug of foaming beer. He sits comfortably, leaning back against the cushions of the open carriage, while Petra rests against his hairy chest. They have a wide view through the open door of the shed, out over meadows and plowed fields and verdant farms. Frid points with his mug toward the horizon, which is beginning to lighten with dawn.

FRID: Look, little one, the summer night is smiling.
PETRA: Just think, you're a poet too.
FRID: Oh yes! The summer night has three smiles, and this is the first—between midnight and daybreak—when young lovers open their hearts and bodies. Can you see it back there at the horizon, a smile so soft that one has to be very quiet and watchful to see it at all?
PETRA: The young lovers . . .

Tears come to Petra's eyes and she sighs.

FRID: Did you have a pang of the heart, my little pudding?
PETRA: Why have I never been a young lover? Can you tell me that?
FRID: Oh, my dear, don't feel sorry! There are only a very few young lovers on this earth. Yes, one can almost count them. Love has smitten them both as a gift and as a punishment.
PETRA: And we others?
FRID: We others . . . Ha!

He makes a violent gesture with his beer mug and smiles to himself, so that his icy-blue eyes sparkle. He lays a large hand on Petra's round, girlish head.

PETRA: Yes, what becomes of us?
FRID: We invoke love, call out for it, beg for it, cry for it, try to imitate it, think that we have it, lie about it.
PETRA: But we don't have it.
FRID: No, my sugar plum. The love of lovers is denied to us. We don't have the gift.
PETRA: Nor the punishment.

A dark shadow suddenly appears at the edge of the carriage. Petra shrieks with fright. A hand is raised, a face approaches, a pale face with burning eyes. Henrik's face. He whispers to her; her eyes open with astonishment. Then another figure, a smaller one, frees itself from the shadows behind the shed.

Petra nods in complete agreement. Henrik climbs down from the carriage and Petra says something to Frid, whispering in a low voice so that no one will hear.

Anne takes a few steps over the broad, dusty floorboards. She stretches out her arms in front of her like a blind woman. She cries and laughs with excitement and she takes the boy in her arms.

Fredrik Egerman sees all this. He is standing by the large trees, lit up by the reflection of the white roadway. He simply stands there, with no thought or desire to conceal himself. His arms lie still along his sides and his chin protrudes tautly.

Now boots and hoofbeats pound on the floor of the stable. The horse is led out into the yard and harnessed to a light carriage.

Petra embraces her mistress and they whisper bewildered and tender words into each other's hair. Henrik helps Frid with the baggage and then the two young ones climb in.

At that point, Fredrik takes a step forward and his lips form a cry, but it becomes a soundless cry, a toneless whisper.

The whip flicks across the back of the horse, and the carriage turns toward the white ribbon of road. A cloud of dust rises around the hoofs of the horse.

Fredrik finds the strength to move. He withdraws quickly into the darkness of the big tree. The big horse falls into a trot; the carriage rattles and tosses over the road and disappears in a cloud, as if in a dream.

Now they are gone.

Now it is quiet. Now they are finally gone.

Fredrik hears Frid laugh and Petra telling him to be quiet. Their steps die away. Fredrik Egerman is alone; he has only his heavy breathing for company, and his pounding heart, his pain, his fear.

The clock in the old tower strikes one. First there are four quarter-hour beats, then the mighty hour beat. Now the trumpeters step out through their portals in the clock as the carillon sounds over the sleeping estate. There is the priest, the knight, the peasant with his staff, the dwarf with his poodle. There is the merchant, the warrior with his lance, the jester, death with his scythe, and the maiden with her mirror.

The moon sinks behind the islands of the bay; the stars turn pale and the sky whitens in the east.

Desirée opens her window. She has changed her dress and wears a loose gray gown with soft lines and large pockets on the skirt. The light flickers in the draft; on the table lies the handwritten script of her next role.

DESIRÉE (*mumbling*): "Do you know, my friend, how loneliness feels? How the mere thought of it frightens me? I am too faint to . . ."

She looks at the script, holding it up to the flickering light.

DESIRÉE: . . . "I am too faint to give answer to your kind proposal. But if you ask for me as wife, I may decide to tie the bond of life."

But she has difficulty concentrating on the role. A secret anxiety drives her around the room, over to the large bed where her son sleeps burrowed in the soft pillows, back to the window to look out on the grounds, down to the pavilion.

The pavilion is silhouetted against the pale, white water.

The windows are dark and gleam lifelessly in the night light. She sharpens her glance. Is she seeing wrong, or is there a small flame flickering inside, a tiny flame which disappears almost as fast as it has been lit?

DESIRÉE (*mumbles*): Charlotte! Charlotte! I can't depend on you after all.

Now someone moves in the shadows under the trees, the light flickers brightly in the doorway at the top of the pavilion stairs, and someone hurries silently out of the darkness, silhouetted against the water's reflection, and into the shelter of the pavilion. There is a flash of white skirt, the blurred oval of a face, and the door is closed as silently as it had been opened. The night is warm and quiet.

Charlotte's eyes gleam in the twilight of the pavilion. She looks to either side several times. Now another shadow can be seen.

CHARLOTTE: It's so dark in here. I can barely see you. Where are you?

He comes quite close to her and puts his hand on her bare shoulder.

FREDRIK: My wife, Anne, has eloped with my son, Henrik.

Charlotte tries to hold back a laugh.

FREDRIK: I saw them in the stable yard. They stood embracing in the moonlight. They stood embracing, embracing so that everyone could see them.
CHARLOTTE: Poor Fredrik. (*Laughs*)
FREDRIK (*in a low voice*): I could have stopped them.
CHARLOTTE: Poor, poor Fredrik.

FREDRIK: If you continue to laugh that way I'll do—

CHARLOTTE: Do what! (*Giggles*) Poor, poor, poor, poor Fredrik.

FREDRIK: I look ridiculous.

CHARLOTTE: Do you know that your face has shrunk? Your eyes are sitting on your cheekbones and your nose has become very long.

FREDRIK: I loved them.

CHARLOTTE: And that was the great love.

FREDRIK: I loved them. Henrik and Anne, they were my most precious possessions. Oh, I knew they were infatuated with each other—I wasn't blind. But I was never jealous. I liked it. Their movements, their fragrance, their voices and laughter gladdened my heart, and I found pleasure in their games.

CHARLOTTE: And now you hate them.

FREDRIK: No, Charlotte, it's hopeless. But I would like to beat them with my fists, beat them for what they have stolen from me.

Charlotte puts her wrap over Fredrik's head. A pale, embittered face looks at her between the wrap's loose weave. She raises her hand and presses her thumb against his eye.

CHARLOTTE: Prisoner, imprisoned one, locked in, raging, hurt, wounded without reason or sense. There he sits, the wise lawyer amidst his little catastrophe, like a child in a puddle.

She pulls the wrap off him and kisses his lips. He makes a strong move toward her, but she withdraws. Fredrik's mouth bleeds.

FREDRIK: You have sharp teeth.

CHARLOTTE: Sharp tongue, sharp teeth, sharp nails.

FREDRIK: Sore heart, gashed hands, blood in your eyes.

CHARLOTTE: Yes, now you know how it feels.

FREDRIK: Are you really real, by the way?

CHARLOTTE: Haven't you noticed that I am a character in a play, a ridiculous farce?

FREDRIK: Yes, that's true.

CHARLOTTE: We deceived, we betrayed, we deserted. We who are *really* ridiculous.

Now she is serious, calm, almost mild. Her face, half averted, rests in the shadow and is sad, dignified.

FREDRIK: Now you are dangerous, Charlotte.

CHARLOTTE: You have no reason to reproach yourself.

Desirée's anxiety grows as she stands there in the window looking down on the dark pavilion.

DESIRÉE: How stupid I've been.

She raises her hands to her mouth as she mumbles to herself. The light flickers and she blows it out in irritation. Now the door opens quite carefully and Malcolm appears. He seems tangled and sour, stretches himself, yawns, is quite out of humor.

DESIRÉE: So now you come.

Malcolm stares and stiffens in the middle of a yawn.

MALCOLM: What have I done? Why do you say that?

DESIRÉE: I mean . . . I'll be brief. It's nice to see you. But I think you're terribly late.

MALCOLM: Are you brewing some kind of mischief! Have you cooked up something?

DESIRÉE: By the way, where is your wife?

MALCOLM: She's asleep.

DESIRÉE: Are you sure that she's sleeping?

MALCOLM: Absolutely.

DESIRÉE: Have you never imagined that Charlotte could deceive you?

MALCOLM: An unusually ridiculous idea. Why should she? She has nothing to complain about.

DESIRÉE: No, of course not.

MALCOLM: Now you have a tone in your voice which irritates me.

DESIRÉE: I only said "Of course not."

MALCOLM: Do you know anything?

DESIRÉE: Your wife is not sleeping, *that* I know.

MALCOLM: Where is she?

DESIRÉE: In the pavilion.

MALCOLM: With whom?

DESIRÉE: Fredrik Egerman.

MALCOLM: Fredrik Eger . . . Devil take it!

DESIRÉE: They have already been there for a quarter of an hour.

MALCOLM: Now I'm really going to fix that damned shyster.

DESIRÉE: Are you so jealous, poor Malcolm?

MALCOLM: I can tolerate someone dallying with my mistress, but if anyone touches my wife, then I become a tiger.

He looks around wildly and strides off with long steps.

After a few moments, Desirée sees him hurrying across the terrace of the castle and down to the pavilion. Now she smiles, relieved.

Malcolm lights a couple of candles and puts them on the table in the pavilion.

MALCOLM: Leave the room, Charlotte! Mr. Egerman and I want to be alone.

Charlotte hesitates and looks from one to the other.

MALCOLM: I seriously recommend that you leave. The lawyer and I want to play roulette.
FREDRIK: Roulette?

Charlotte has a worried, hesitant expression on her face, but she departs and closes the door silently. For a moment she can be seen outside the window.
Malcolm turns again towards Fredrik.

MALCOLM: Of course, *Russian* roulette.

He pulls out a revolver and places it on the table between them.

FREDRIK: I don't understand.
MALCOLM: A kind of duel. If we met with weapons in our hands, there would be no hope for you. I therefore suggest a duel which gives both of us exactly the same chance.
FREDRIK: I still don't understand.
MALCOLM: The revolver is loaded with only *one* bullet. You close your eyes, roll the cylinder, and then point the weapon at your temple and press the trigger. Each one of us repeats this procedure twice. That means the odds are twelve to two.

When Charlotte comes around the corner, she meets Desirée on the path leading to the beach.

DESIRÉE: Are they still in the pavilion?
CHARLOTTE: I think that the gentlemen wish to be left alone.
DESIRÉE: And why, may I ask?
CHARLOTTE: It's some kind of roulette.
DESIRÉE (*astonished*): Roulette?

Malcolm pours cognac first into Fredrik's glass and then

into his own. They sit in armchairs opposite each other. Between them stands the table. On the table lies the small revolver. Malcolm leans forward.

MALCOLM: Now I'll spin the weapon. Whoever the muzzle points at goes first.

Fredrik nods and wets his lips. Malcolm reaches out with his hand and spins the weapon. It turns several times and then the muzzle points at him. He raises his glass. Fredrik returns the toast.

MALCOLM: To all faithful wives.

They empty their glasses. Malcolm raises the weapon and closes his eyes. He rolls the cylinder and aims the muzzle at his temple. He opens his eyes and looks smilingly at Fredrik. Then he presses the trigger. A sharp click is heard.

A cold sweat breaks out on Fredrik's forehead. Malcolm lays down the revolver, pushes it across the table toward Fredrik with a friendly smile. Then he pours another round of cognac for himself and his opponent. Now it is Fredrik's turn to raise his glass. He hesitates for a moment.

FREDRIK: To you, Count Malcolm!

The Count bows and forces a smile. The two gentlemen empty their glasses.

FREDRIK: An exquisite cognac.
MALCOLM: It was supposedly imported in the 1850s by a very dear friend of old Mrs. Armfeldt. He was later killed in a duel.

Fredrik grips the weapon, closes his eyes, rolls the cylinder and points the muzzle toward his temple. He hesitates for a moment. Malcolm looks at him with a smile. He pulls the trigger.

A sharp click is heard.

Fredrik opens his eyes and blinks, somewhat surprised; he looks at the weapon.

FREDRIK: The bullet was in the next slot.

He puts down the revolver and now it's his turn to serve cognac.

MALCOLM: Allow me to say that you impress me, Lawyer Egerman.
FREDRIK: This is not courage, sir.

Malcolm lifts his glass.

MALCOLM (*cordially*): To you.

Fredrik bows and drinks. Malcolm puts down his glass, takes the weapon and closes his eyes. He rolls the cylinder and places the muzzle of the revolver against his temple.

He pulls the trigger.

A sharp click.

FREDRIK: I hope there is nothing wrong with the mechanism.

Malcolm shakes his head and serves the cognac. The two gentlemen raise their glasses.

MALCOLM: I have been told that your wife eloped tonight with your son.
FREDRIK: It's true.
MALCOLM: To youth, Mr. Egerman.

The gentlemen empty their glasses. Fredrik lifts the

weapon, closes his eyes, rolls the cylinder, points the revolver toward his temple and looks calmly in front of him.

When the sound of the shot dies down, Desirée and
Charlotte are on their way toward the house. They turn
around.

The door of the pavilion opens and Malcolm steps out
onto the stairs, weapon in hand. When he sees both
women, their frightened faces, Desirée's unabashed fear,
he bursts into laughter. He laughs so hard that he has to
sit down. He slaps his knees and almost loses his breath.

MALCOLM: Devil take it, I used a blank filled with soot.
CHARLOTTE: With soot!
MALCOLM: Do you think that a nobleman risks his life
with a shyster?
DESIRÉE: You are disgusting.

Desirée enters the pavilion and closes the door. Malcolm
rises. He has finished laughing. Husband and wife look at
each other silently.

MALCOLM: You are equally ridiculous, you and Desirée
and all the others. Bitchy and unfaithful.
CHARLOTTE: Carl-Magnus Malcolm!
MALCOLM: At your service.
CHARLOTTE: Turn around and look at me.
MALCOLM: Well?
CHARLOTTE: You have forgotten our bet.
MALCOLM: Bet? What bet?
CHARLOTTE: At dinner.
MALCOLM: At dinner. My God, the bet at dinner.
CHARLOTTE: I did it in eight minutes. Then I had all kinds
of trouble fighting him off.
MALCOLM: But you enjoyed it.
CHARLOTTE: Carl-Magnus Malcolm, look at me again.
MALCOLM: I can never be at ease, you know that.

CHARLOTTE: Look at me.
MALCOLM: I look at you all the time.
CHARLOTTE: And what do you see?
MALCOLM: You.
CHARLOTTE: That you've never done. Not even now.
MALCOLM: Has everyone gone crazy? Isn't it you I see? What the devil do I see if I don't see you?
CHARLOTTE: Close your eyes.
MALCOLM: I refuse.
CHARLOTTE: Shut them.
MALCOLM: And why should I?
CHARLOTTE: Now you must say: "You have won your bet. What does the winner want?"
MALCOLM: Ridiculous.
CHARLOTTE: Don't you keep your word?
MALCOLM: By all means. What does the winner want?
CHARLOTTE: Shut your eyes.
MALCOLM: What does the winner want? (*He closes his eyes*)
CHARLOTTE: You.
MALCOLM: That's impossible.
CHARLOTTE: Your word!
MALCOLM: I give in.

He falls on his knees, laughing. She falls on her knees opposite him. She is still serious.

CHARLOTTE: Swear to be faithful to me for at least—
MALCOLM: I'll be faithful to you for at least seven eternities of pleasure, eighteen false smiles and fifty-seven loving whispers without meaning. I'll be faithful to you until the last gasp separates us. In short, I'll be faithful to you in my way.

Now it is just before dawn. A light mist lies over the

water like a puff of smoke. The morning breeze stirs the birches. The birds tune up their morning song.

Frid rises from the hay stack where he has lain with Petra. He takes a deep breath and raises his arm in an expansive gesture.

FRID: Now the summer night smiles its second smile: for the clowns, the fools, the unredeemable.
PETRA: Then she smiles for us.
FRID: Are you thirsty? Do you want a beer?
PETRA: I said that she smiles for us.
FRID: I agree. (*Drinks*) Now she smiles for us.
PETRA: Will you marry me?
FRID: Ha-ha-ha-ha-ha!
PETRA: An hour ago you said that you wanted to—
FRID: Ha-ha-ha-ha-ha! That was then.

Petra looks up. Then she gives him a strong slap across his face, but he continues to laugh.

PETRA: You shall marry me.
FRID: Ha-ha-ha-ha-ha! You're a strong little sugar plum.

Petra becomes furious and continues to pound him with her fists, shaking him like a pillowcase.

PETRA (*furious*): You shall marry me. You shall marry me. You shall! You shall! You shall!
FRID: This is what I call love. Ha-ha-ha-ha!

They tumble around in the hay in a wild and affectionate fight.

The trumpeters appear from behind the shutters and now the tower clock announces that the time is three.

The sun rolls up out of the forest and everything takes on its true color in the warm sunlight.

The cocks begin crowing as if possessed.

The mild light reaches through the windows of the pavilion and falls on Fredrik, who sits in his chair with a blackened face. Desirée kneels on the floor and removes the worst of the soot with a sponge. Egerman rouses from his stupor and looks in bewilderment at Desirée. The sunlight strikes him directly in the face and he is forced to shut his eyes again.

He sighs contentedly, but when Desirée touches the scratch on his forehead he awakens and says "Ouch."

FREDRIK: This can't be heaven.
DESIRÉE: Is that because I'm here, perhaps?
FREDRIK: Desirée. You were a fine help.
DESIRÉE: You're right. I was a fine help.
FREDRIK: Why am I not dead?
DESIRÉE: The bullet was a blank.
FREDRIK: Oh.
DESIRÉE: Does it hurt?
FREDRIK: Yes it hurts, hurts, hurts.
DESIRÉE: Lie down here and go to sleep.

He gets up and collapses on the divan. Desirée pulls a blanket over him. He turns his face away.

On the table are the pictures of his young wife. Adolf's artistic studies, the pride of the Almgren Photo Shop.

Desirée quietly gathers the pictures and lets them disappear in her large skirt pocket. Then she closes the door of the pavilion gently and sits down on the steps in the strong sunlight.

She pulls a cigar case out of her pocket and chooses one from it. She lights the cigar with pleasure and draws on it with careful puffs. Out of the other pocket she takes her script.

Then she closes her eyes. Malla comes toddling across

the lawn. Back on the terrace, little Fredrik plays with the
puppy.

MALLA: Good morning, Desirée.
DESIRÉE: Good morning, Malla.
MALLA: Are you studying your new role?
DESIRÉE: Yes, you might say that.

The old woman grins insinuatingly. She is wearing her
straw hat and carries a large basket in one hand.

MALLA: I'm going to pick strawberries. But Fredrik doesn't
want to go along.
DESIRÉE: Let him stay here. I'll look after him.
MALLA (*grins*): There's nowhere that you can sleep as well
as in the country.

Petra has straddled Frid and holds him by the ears. He
laughs and snorts. Both of them are out of breath and excited. The dust from the hay rises up like a cloud around
them in the strong sunlight.

PETRA: Do you promise to marry me?
FRID: Ouch! I'll promise if you let go of my ears.
PETRA: No. First promise.
FRID: I promise. Ouch.
PETRA: Swear by everything you hold sacred.
FRID: By my manhood, I swear.

She lets go of him and gives him a hard slap on the
cheek, then gets up, straightens her clothes and stretches.

PETRA: Then we can consider ourselves engaged?
FRID (*laughs*): The fun is over. Now I'm on my way to
hell.
PETRA: Rise and shine, fatso. The horses have to be curried.

He gets up and turns his face toward the sun, stretches out his arms and breathes deeply.

FRID: There isn't a better life than this.
PETRA: And then the summer night smiled for the third time.
FRID: For the sad, the depressed, the sleepless, the confused, the frightened, the lonely.
PETRA: But the clowns will have a cup of coffee in the kitchen.

She has pulled off her shoes and stockings and walks barefoot through the dewy grass, holding her skirt high above her knees. Frid walks behind her, and the sight of her rounded thighs is so damn beautiful that he begins to sing.

Stockholm
May 27, 1955

A profound intellectual motive

A portrayal of the possibilities to human existence.

Natural evil - the plague
+ death

moral evil - corrupted church
+ persons

THE

SEVENTH

SEAL

What is to be man's response to such a situation? The following possibilities:

(1) Antonius Block
    —an idealistic, rationalistic approach to life. Identified with traditional christianity.

    10 yr. crusade to Holy Land in order to find a sense of meaning. Frustrated he returns home & met by the plague and Death. Chess—betting a sense of meaning against his life.

    In response to every experience the knight asks "How can I know that God exists?" Answer however is never forthcoming

(2) Squire-Jons - portrays a practical perhaps existentialist approach to life. He is an activist (helps others) and seeks no metaphysical and religious questions because he believes they are unanswerable.

Accompanied knight on the crusade. Blames failure not on knight but on the idealistic ideology behind the crusade.

(3) Jof and Mia — traveling actors - son mikael

Portray a personal, simple, somewhat mystical approach to life. Innocent manner and eventual escape.

Faces the difficulties and threats of life with a normal amount of fear. Basis of calmness seems to result from their love for one another and their lack of concern for kind of questions that knight insists on asking.

THE SEVENTH SEAL

THE CAST

The squire	Gunnar Björnstrand
Death	Bengt Ekerot
Jof	Nils Poppe
The knight	Max von Sydow
Mia	Bibi Andersson
Lisa	Inga Gill
The witch	Maud Hansson
The knight's wife	Inga Landgré
The girl	Gunnel Lindblom
Raval	Bertil Anderberg
The monk	Anders Ek
The smith	Åke Fridell
The church painter	Gunnar Olsson
Skat	Erik Strandmark
The merchant	Benkt-Åke Benktsson
Woman at the inn	Gudrun Brost
Leader of the soldiers	Ulf Johansson
The young monk	Lars Lind

THE CREDITS

Screenplay	Ingmar Bergman
Director	Ingmar Bergman

Assistant director	Lennart Ohlsson
Director of photography	Gunnar Fischer
Assistant cameraman	Åke Nilsson
Music	Erik Nordgren
Music directed by	Sixten Ehrling
Choreography	Else Fisher
Sets	P. A. Lundgren
Costumes	Manne Lindholm
Make-up	Nils Nittel and Carl M. Lundh, Inc.
Sound	Aaby Wedin and Lennart Wallin
Special sound effects	Evald Andersson
Editor	Lennart Wallén

Running time: 96 *minutes*

Produced by Svensk Filmindustri; distributed in the United States by Janus Films, Inc., and in Great Britain by Contemporary Films Ltd.

The knight must ask them, The squire will not ask them, and The couple is unable to ask them.

Bergman sees the limitations of idealism, the virtues of a simple mysticism and the value of realistic activism.

Suggests that even though there are values + limitations in each of the 3 approaches, obtained meaning must be achieved through personal struggle and active concern for the welfare of others.

The knight,
Antonius Block

Death

Chess game holds the play together. Symbolizes the importance of personal struggle in the quest for meaning; and even though the outcome is inevitable, the interim can be used for significant acts for the good of others (transcending the physical defeat).

The squire, Jöns, and the church painter ▶

Jof and Mia; below, with Skat

The procession of flagellants; below, the monk

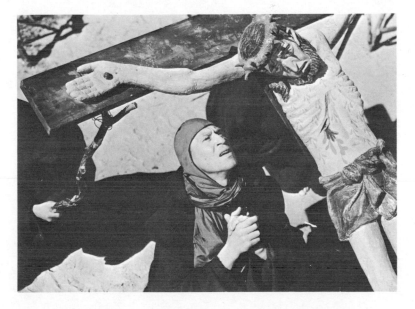

Plog, the smith, and Jöns

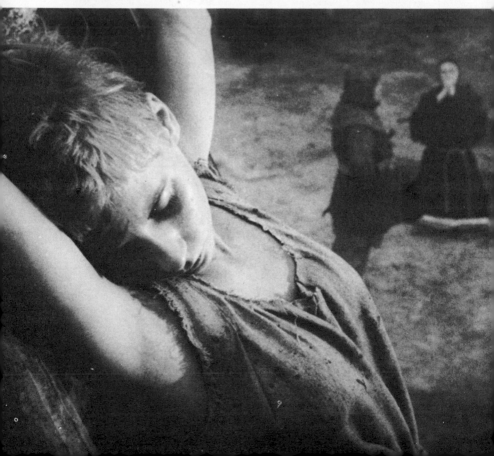

Lisa, Plog, the knight's wife, the knight, the girl, and Jöns

Tyan, the witch

. . . They dance away from the dawn,
and it's a solemn dance toward the dark lands. . . .

THE NIGHT HAD BROUGHT little relief from the heat, and at dawn a hot gust of wind blows across the colorless sea.

The knight, Antonius Block, lies prostrate on some spruce branches spread over the fine sand. His eyes are wide-open and bloodshot from lack of sleep.

Nearby his squire Jöns is snoring loudly. He has fallen asleep where he collapsed, at the edge of the forest among the wind-gnarled fir trees. His open mouth gapes toward the dawn, and unearthly sounds come from his throat.

At the sudden gust of wind the horses stir, stretching their parched muzzles toward the sea. They are as thin and worn as their masters.

The knight has risen and waded into the shallow water, where he rinses his sunburned face and blistered lips.

Jöns rolls over to face the forest and the darkness. He moans in his sleep and vigorously scratches the stubbled hair on his head. A scar stretches diagonally across his scalp, as white as lightning against the grime.

The knight returns to the beach and falls on his knees. With his eyes closed and brow furrowed, he says his morning prayers. His hands are clenched together and his lips

137

form the words silently. His face is sad and bitter. He opens his eyes and stares directly into the morning sun which wallows up from the misty sea like some bloated, dying fish. The sky is gray and immobile, a dome of lead. A cloud hangs mute and dark over the western horizon. High up, barely visible, a sea gull floats on motionless wings. Its cry is weird and restless.

The knight's large gray horse lifts its head and whinnies. Antonius Block turns around.

Behind him stands a man in black. His face is very pale and he keeps his hands hidden in the wide folds of his cloak.

KNIGHT: Who are you?
DEATH: I am Death.
KNIGHT: Have you come for me?
DEATH: I have been walking by your side for a long time.
KNIGHT: That I know.
DEATH: Are you prepared?
KNIGHT: My body is frightened, but I am not.
DEATH: Well, there is no shame in that.

The knight has risen to his feet. He shivers. Death opens his cloak to place it around the knight's shoulders.

KNIGHT: Wait a moment.
DEATH: That's what they all say. I grant no reprieves.
KNIGHT: You play chess, don't you?

A gleam of interest kindles in Death's eyes.

DEATH: How did you know that?
KNIGHT: I have seen it in paintings and heard it sung in ballads.
DEATH: Yes, in fact I'm quite a good chess player.
KNIGHT: But you can't be better than I am.

The knight rummages in the big black bag which he keeps beside him and takes out a small chessboard. He placcs it carcfully on thc ground and begins setting up the pieces.

DEATH: Why do you want to play chess with me?
KNIGHT: I have my reasons.
DEATH: That is your privilege.
KNIGHT: The condition is that I may live as long as I hold out against you. If I win, you will release me. Is it agreed?

The knight holds out his two fists to Death, who smiles at him suddenly. Death points to one of the knight's hands; it contains a black pawn.

KNIGHT: You drew black!
DEATH: Very appropriate. Don't you think so?

The knight and Death bend over the chessboard. After a moment of hesitation, Antonius Block opens with his king's pawn. Death moves, also using his king's pawn.

The morning breeze has died down. The restless movement of the sea has ceased, the water is silent. The sun rises from the haze and its glow whitens. The sea gull floats under the dark cloud, frozen in space. The day is already scorchingly hot.

The squire Jöns is awakened by a kick in the rear. Opening his eyes, he grunts like a pig and yawns broadly. He scrambles to his feet, saddles his horse and picks up the heavy pack.

The knight slowly rides away from the sea, into the forest near the beach and up toward the road. He pretends not to hear the morning prayers of his squire. Jöns soon overtakes him.

Jöns (*sings*): Between a strumpet's legs to lie
Is the life for which I sigh.

He stops and looks at his master, but the knight hasn't heard Jöns' song, or he pretends that he hasn't. To give further vent to his irritation, the squire sings even louder.

Jöns (*sings*): Up above is God Almighty
So very far away,
But your brother the Devil
You will meet on every level.

Jöns finally gets the knight's attention. He stops singing. The knight, his horse, Jöns' own horse and Jöns himself know all the songs by heart. The long, dusty journey from the Holy Land hasn't made them any cleaner.

They ride across a mossy heath which stretches toward the horizon. Beyond it, the sea lies shimmering in the white glitter of the sun.

Jöns: In Färjestad everyone was talking about evil omens and other horrible things. Two horses had eaten each other in the night, and, in the churchyard, graves had been opened and the remains of corpses scattered all over the place. Yesterday afternoon there were as many as four suns in the heavens.

The knight doesn't answer. Close by a scrawny dog is whining, crawling toward its master, who is sleeping in a sitting position in the blazing hot sun. A black cloud of flies clusters around his head and shoulders. The miserable-looking dog whines incessantly as it lies flat on its stomach, wagging its tail.

Jöns dismounts and approaches the sleeping man. Jöns addresses him politely. When he doesn't receive an answer, he walks up to the man in order to shake him awake. He

THE SEVENTH SEAL   141

bends over the sleeping man's shoulder, but quickly pulls
back his hand. The man falls backward on the heath, his
face turned toward Jöns. It is a corpse, staring at Jöns with
empty eye sockets and white teeth.

The squire remounts and overtakes his master. He takes
a drink from his waterskin and hands the bag to the knight.

KNIGHT: Well, did he show you the way?
JÖNS: Not exactly.
KNIGHT: What did he say?
JÖNS: Nothing.
KNIGHT: Was he a mute?
JÖNS: No, sir, I wouldn't say that. As a matter of fact, he
was quite eloquent.
KNIGHT: Oh?
JÖNS: He was eloquent, all right. The trouble is that what
he had to say was most depressing. (*Sings*)

> One moment you're bright and lively,
> The next you're crawling with worms.
> Fate is a terrible villain
> And you, my friend, its poor victim.

KNIGHT: Must you sing?
JÖNS: No.

The knight hands his squire a piece of bread, which
keeps him quiet for a while. The sun burns down on them
cruelly, and beads of perspiration trickle down their faces.
There is a cloud of dust around the horses' hoofs.

They ride past an inlet and along verdant groves. In the
shade of some large trees stands a bulging wagon covered
with a mottled canvas. A horse whinnies nearby and is
answered by the knight's horse. The two travelers do not
stop to rest under the shade of the trees but continue riding until they disappear at the bend of the road.

In his sleep, Jof the juggler hears the neighing of his

horse and the answer from a distance. He tries to go on sleeping, but it is stifling inside the wagon. The rays of the sun filtering through the canvas cast streaks of light across the face of Jof's wife, Mia, and their one-year-old son, Mikael, who are sleeping deeply and peacefully. Near them, Jonas Skat, an older man, snores loudly.

Jof crawls out of the wagon. There is still a spot of shade under the big trees. He takes a drink of water, gargles, stretches and talks to his scrawny old horse.

JOF: Good morning. Have you had breakfast? I can't eat grass, worse luck. Can't you teach me how? We're a little hard up. People aren't very interested in juggling in this part of the country.

He has picked up the juggling balls and slowly begins to toss them. Then he stands on his head and cackles like a hen. Suddenly he stops and sits down with a look of utter astonishment on his face. The wind causes the trees to sway slightly. The leaves stir and there is a soft murmur. The flowers and the grass bend gracefully, and somewhere a bird raises its voice in a long warble.

Jof's face breaks into a smile and his eyes fill with tears. With a dazed expression he sits flat on his behind while the grass rustles softly, and bees and butterflies hum around his head. The unseen bird continues to sing.

Suddenly the breeze stops blowing, the bird stops singing, Jof's smile fades, the flowers and grass wilt in the heat. The old horse is still walking around grazing and swishing its tail to ward off the flies.

Jof comes to life. He rushes into the wagon and shakes Mia awake.

JOF: Mia, wake up. Wake up! Mia, I've just seen something. I've got to tell you about it!
MIA (*sits up, terrified*): What is it? What's happened?

Jof: Listen, I've had a vision. No, it wasn't a vision. It was real, absolutely real.
Mia: Oh, so you've had a vision again!

Mia's voice is filled with gentle irony. Jof shakes his head and grabs her by the shoulders.

Jof: But I did see her!
Mia: Whom did you see?
Jof: The Virgin Mary.

Mia can't help being impressed by her husband's fervor. She lowers her voice.

Mia: Did you really see her?
Jof: She was so close to me that I could have touched her. She had a golden crown on her head and wore a blue gown with flowers of gold. She was barefoot and had small brown hands with which she was holding the Child and teaching Him to walk. And then she saw me watching her and she smiled at me. My eyes filled with tears and when I wiped them away, she had disappeared. And everything became so still in the sky and on the earth. Can you understand . . .
Mia: What an imagination you have.
Jof: You don't believe me! But it was real, I tell you, not the kind of reality you see everyday, but a different kind.
Mia: Perhaps it was the kind of reality you told us about when you saw the Devil paint our wagon wheels red, using his tail as a brush.
Jof (*embarrassed*): Why must you keep bringing that up?
Mia: And then you discovered that you had red paint under your nails.
Jof: Well, perhaps that time I made it up. (*Eagerly*) I did it just so that you would believe in my other visions. The real ones. The ones that I didn't make up.

MIA (*severely*): You have to keep your visions under control. Otherwise people will think that you're a half-wit, which you're not. At least not yet—as far as I know. But, come to think of it, I'm not so sure about that.

JOF (*angry*): I didn't ask to have visions. I can't help it if voices speak to me, if the Holy Virgin appears before me and angels and devils like my company.

SKAT (*sits up*): Haven't I told you once and for all that I need my morning's sleep! I have asked you politely, pleaded with you, but nothing works. So now I'm telling you to *shut up!*

His eyes are popping with rage. He turns over and continues snoring where he left off. Mia and Jof decide that it would be wisest to leave the wagon. They sit down on a crate. Mia has Mikael on her knees. He is naked and squirms vigorously. Jof sits close to his wife. Slumped over, he still looks dazed and astonished. A dry, hot wind blows from the sea.

MIA: If we would only get some rain. Everything is burned to cinders. We won't have anything to eat this winter.

JOF (*yawning*): We'll get by.

He says this smilingly, with a casual air. He stretches and laughs contentedly.

MIA: I want Mikael to have a better life than ours.

JOF: Mikael will grow up to be a great acrobat—or a juggler who can do the one impossible trick.

MIA: What's that?

JOF: To make one of the balls stand absolutely still in the air.

MIA: But that's impossible.

JOF: Impossible for us—but not for him.

MIA: You're dreaming again.

She yawns. The sun has made her a bit drowsy and she lies down on the grass. Jof does likewise and puts one arm around his wife's shoulders.

JOF: I've composed a song. I made it up during the night when I couldn't sleep. Do you want to hear it?
MIA: Sing it. I'm very curious.
JOF: I have to sit up first.

He sits with his legs crossed, makes a dramatic gesture with his arms and sings in a loud voice.

JOF: On a lily branch a dove is perched
          Against the summer sky,
          She sings a wondrous song of Christ
          And there's great joy on high.

He interrupts his singing in order to be complimented by his wife.

JOF: Mia! Are you asleep?
MIA: It's a lovely song.
JOF: I haven't finished yet.
MIA: I heard it, but I think I'll sleep a little longer. You can sing the rest to me afterward.
JOF: All you do is sleep.

Jof is a bit offended and glances over at his son, Mikael, but he is also sleeping soundly in the high grass. Jonas Skat comes out from the wagon. He yawns; he is very tired and in a bad humor. In his hands he holds a crudely made death mask.

SKAT: Is this supposed to be a mask for an actor? If the priests didn't pay us so well, I'd say no thank you.
JOF: Are you going to play Death?

SKAT: Just think, scaring decent folk out of their wits with this kind of nonsense.
JOF: When are we supposed to do this play?
SKAT: At the saints' feast in Elsinore. We're going to perform right on the church steps, believe it or not.
JOF: Wouldn't it be better to play something bawdy? People like it better, and, besides, it's more fun.
SKAT: Idiot. There's a rumor going around that there's a terrible pestilence in the land, and now the priests are prophesying sudden death and all sorts of spiritual agonies.

Mia is awake now and lies contentedly on her back, sucking on a blade of grass and looking smilingly at her husband.

JOF: And what part am I to play?
SKAT: You're such a damn fool, so you're going to be the Soul of Man.
JOF: That's a bad part, of course.
SKAT: Who makes the decisions around here? Who is the director of this company anyhow?

Skat, grinning, holds the mask in front of his face and recites dramatically.

SKAT: Bear this in mind, you fool. Your life hangs by a thread. Your time is short. (*In his usual voice*) Are the women going to like me in this getup? Will I make a hit? No! I feel as if I were dead already.

He stumbles into the wagon muttering furiously. Jof sits, leaning forward. Mia lies beside him on the grass.

MIA: Jof!
JOF: What is it?
MIA: Sit still. Don't move.
JOF: What do you mean?

MIA: Don't say anything.
JOF: I'm as silent as a grave.
MIA: Shh! I love you.

Waves of heat envelop the gray stone church in a strange white mist. The knight dismounts and enters. After tying up the horses, Jöns slowly follows him in. When he comes onto the church porch he stops in surprise. To the right of the entrance there is a large fresco on the wall, not quite finished. Perched on a crude scaffolding is a painter wearing a red cap and paint-stained clothes. He has one brush in his mouth, while with another in his hand he outlines a small, terrified human face amidst a sea of other faces.

JÖNS: What is this supposed to represent?
PAINTER: The Dance of Death.
JÖNS: And that one is Death?
PAINTER: Yes, he dances off with all of them.
JÖNS: Why do you paint such nonsense?
PAINTER: I thought it would serve to remind people that they must die.
JÖNS: Well, it's not going to make them feel any happier.
PAINTER: Why should one always make people happy? It might not be a bad idea to scare them a little once in a while.
JÖNS: Then they'll close their eyes and refuse to look at your painting.
PAINTER: Oh, they'll look. A skull is almost more interesting than a naked woman.
JÖNS: If you do scare them . . .
PAINTER: They'll think.
JÖNS: And if they think . . .
PAINTER: They'll become still more scared.
JÖNS: And then they'll run right into the arms of the priests.
PAINTER: That's not my business.

JÖNS: You're only painting your Dance of Death.
PAINTER: I'm only painting things as they are. Everyone else can do as he likes.
JÖNS: Just think how some people will curse you.
PAINTER: Maybe. But then I'll paint something amusing for them to look at. I have to make a living—at least until the plague takes me.
JÖNS: The plague. That sounds horrible.
PAINTER: You should see the boils on a diseased man's throat. You should see how his body shrivels up so that his legs look like knotted strings—like the man I've painted over there.

The painter points with his brush. Jöns sees a small human form writhing in the grass, its eyes turned upward in a frenzied look of horror and pain.

JÖNS: That looks terrible.
PAINTER: It certainly does. He tries to rip out the boil, he bites his hands, tears his veins open with his fingernails and his screams can be heard everywhere. Does that scare you?
JÖNS: Scare? Me? You don't know me. What are the horrors you've painted over there?
PAINTER: The remarkable thing is that the poor creatures think the pestilence is the Lord's punishment. Mobs of people who call themselves Slaves of Sin are swarming over the country, flagellating themselves and others, all for the glory of God.
JÖNS: Do they really whip themselves?
PAINTER: Yes, it's a terrible sight. I crawl into a ditch and hide when they pass by.
JÖNS: Do you have any brandy? I've been drinking water all day and it's made me as thirsty as a camel in the desert.
PAINTER: I think I frightened you after all.

Jöns sits down with the painter, who produces a jug of brandy.

The knight is kneeling before a small altar. It is dark and quiet around him. The air is cool and musty. Pictures of saints look down on him with stony eyes. Christ's face is turned upward, His mouth open as if in a cry of anguish. On the ceiling beam there is a representation of a hideous devil spying on a miserable human being. The knight hears a sound from the confession booth and approaches it. The face of Death appears behind the grill for an instant, but the knight doesn't see him.

KNIGHT: I want to talk to you as openly as I can, but my heart is empty.

Death doesn't answer.

KNIGHT: The emptiness is a mirror turned toward my own face. I see myself in it, and I am filled with fear and disgust.

Death doesn't answer.

KNIGHT: Through my indifference to my fellow men, I have isolated myself from their company. Now I live in a world of phantoms. I am imprisoned in my dreams and fantasies.
DEATH: And yet you don't want to die.
KNIGHT: Yes, I do.
DEATH: What are you waiting for?
KNIGHT: I want knowledge.
DEATH: You want guarantees?
KNIGHT: Call it whatever you like. Is it so cruelly inconceivable to grasp God with the senses? Why should he hide himself in a mist of half-spoken promises and unseen miracles?

Death doesn't answer.

KNIGHT: How can we have faith in those who believe when we can't have faith in ourselves? What is going to happen to those of us who want to believe but aren't able to? And what is to become of those who neither want to nor are capable of believing?

The knight stops and waits for a reply, but no one speaks or answers him. There is complete silence.

KNIGHT: Why can't I kill God within me? Why does he live on in this painful and humiliating way even though I curse Him and want to tear Him out of my heart? Why, in spite of everything, is He a baffling reality that I can't shake off? Do you hear me?
DEATH: Yes, I hear you.
KNIGHT: I want knowledge, not faith, not suppositions, but knowledge. I want God to stretch out his hand toward me, reveal Himself and speak to me.
DEATH: But he remains silent.
KNIGHT: I call out to him in the dark but no one seems to be there.
DEATH: Perhaps no one is there.
KNIGHT: Then life is an outrageous horror. No one can live in the face of death, knowing that all is nothingness.
DEATH: Most people never reflect about either death or the futility of life.
KNIGHT: But one day they will have to stand at that last moment of life and look toward the darkness.
DEATH: When *that* day comes . . .
KNIGHT: In our fear, we make an image, and that image we call God.
DEATH: You are worrying . . .
KNIGHT: Death visited me this morning. We are playing

chess together. This reprieve gives me the chance to arrange an urgent matter.

DEATH: What matter is that?

KNIGHT: My life has been a futile pursuit, a wandering, a great deal of talk without meaning. I feel no bitterness or self-reproach because the lives of most people are very much like this. But I will use my reprieve for one meaningful deed.

DEATH: Is that why you are playing chess with Death?

KNIGHT: He is a clever opponent, but up to now I haven't lost a single man.

DEATH: How will you outwit Death in your game?

KNIGHT: I use a combination of the bishop and the knight which he hasn't yet discovered. In the next move I'll shatter one of his flanks.

DEATH: I'll remember that.

Death shows his face at the grill of the confession booth for a moment but disappears instantly.

KNIGHT: You've tricked and cheated me! But we'll meet again, and I'll find a way.

DEATH (*invisible*): We'll meet at the inn, and there we'll continue playing.

The knight raises his hand and looks at it in the sunlight which comes through the tiny window.

KNIGHT: This is my hand. I can move it, feel the blood pulsing through it. The sun is still high in the sky and I, Antonius Block, am playing chess with Death.

He makes a fist of his hand and lifts it to his temple.

Meanwhile, Jöns and the painter have gotten drunk and are talking animatedly together.

Jöns: Me and my master have been abroad and have just come home. Do you understand, you little pictor?
Painter: The Crusade.
Jöns (*drunk*): Precisely. For ten years we sat in the Holy Land and let snakes bite us, flies sting us, wild animals eat us, heathens butcher us, the wine poison us, the women give us lice, the lice devour us, the fevers rot us, all for the Glory of God. Our crusade was such madness that only a real idealist could have thought it up. But what you said about the plague was horrible.
Painter: It's worse than that.
Jöns: Ah me. No matter which way you turn, you have your rump behind you. That's the truth.
Painter: The rump behind you, the rump behind you— there's a profound truth.

Jöns paints a small figure which is supposed to represent himself.

Jöns: This is squire Jöns. He grins at Death, mocks the Lord, laughs at himself and leers at the girls. His world is a Jöns-world, believable only to himself, ridiculous to all including himself, meaningless to Heaven and of no interest to Hell.

The knight walks by, calls to his squire and goes out into the bright sunshine. Jöns manages to get himself down from the scaffolding.

Outside the church, four soldiers and a monk are in the process of putting a woman in the stocks. Her face is pale and child-like, her head has been shaved, and her knuckles are bloody and broken. Her eyes are wide open, yet she doesn't appear to be fully conscious.

Jöns and the knight stop and watch in silence. The soldiers are working quickly and skillfully, but they seem frightened and dejected. The monk mumbles from a small book. One of the soldiers picks up a wooden bucket and with his hand begins to smear a bloody paste on the wall of the church and around the woman. Jöns holds his nose.

JÖNS: That soup of yours has a hell of a stink. What is it good for?
SOLDIER: She has had carnal intercourse with the Evil One.

He whispers this with a horrified face and continues to splash the sticky mess on the wall.

JÖNS: And now she's in the stocks.
SOLDIER: She will be burned tomorrow morning at the parish boundary. But we have to keep the Devil away from the rest of us.
JÖNS (*holding his nose*): And you do that with this stinking mess?
SOLDIER: It's the best remedy: blood mixed with the bile of a big black dog. The Devil can't stand the smell.
JÖNS: Neither can I.

Jöns walks over toward the horses. The knight stands for a few moments looking at the young girl. She is almost a child. Slowly she turns her eyes toward him.

KNIGHT: Have you seen the Devil?

The monk stops reading and raises his head.

MONK: You must not talk to her.
KNIGHT: Can that be so dangerous?
MONK: I don't know, but she is believed to have caused the pestilence with which we are afflicted.
KNIGHT: I understand.

He nods resignedly and walks away. The young woman

starts to moan as though she were having a horrible nightmare. The sound of her cries follows the two riders for a considerable distance down the road.

The sun stands high in the sky, like a red ball of fire. The waterskin is empty and Jöns looks for a well where he can fill it.

They approach a group of peasant cottages at the edge of the forest. Jöns ties up the horses, slings the skin over his shoulder and walks along the path toward the nearest cottage. As always, his movements are light and almost soundless. The door to the cottage is open. He stops outside, but when no one appears he enters. It is very dark inside and his foot touches a soft object. He looks down. Beside the whitewashed fireplace, a woman is lying with her face to the ground.

At the sound of approaching steps, Jöns quickly hides behind the door. A man comes down a ladder from the loft. He is broad and thick-set. His eyes are black and his face is pale and puffy. His clothes are well cut but dirty and in rags. He carries a cloth sack. Looking around, he goes into the inner room, bends over the bed, tucks something into the bag, slinks along the walls, looking on the shelves, finds something else which he tucks in his bag.

Slowly he re-enters the outer room, bends over the dead woman and carefully slips a ring from her finger. At that moment a young woman comes through the door. She stops and stares at the stranger.

RAVAL: Why do you look so surprised? I steal from the dead. These days it's quite a lucrative enterprise.

The girl makes a movement as if to run away.

RAVEL: You're thinking of running to the village and telling. That wouldn't serve any purpose. Each of us has to save his own skin. It's as simple as that.

GIRL: Don't touch me.
RAVAL: Don't try to scream. There's no one around to hear you, neither God nor man.

Slowly he closes the door behind the girl. The stuffy room is now in almost total darkness. But Jöns becomes clearly visible.

JÖNS: I recognize you, although it's a long time since we met. Your name is Raval, from the theological college at Roskilde. You are Dr. Mirabilis, Coelestis et Diabilis.

Raval smiles uneasily and looks around.

JÖNS: Am I not right?

The girl stands immobile.

JÖNS: You were the one who, ten years ago, convinced my master of the necessity to join a better-class crusade to the Holy Land.

Raval looks around.

JÖNS: You look uncomfortable. Do you have a stomach-ache?

Raval smiles anxiously.

JÖNS: When I see you, I suddenly understand the meaning of these ten years, which previously seemed to me such a waste. Our life was too good and we were too satisfied with ourselves. The Lord wanted to punish us for our complacency. That is why He sent you to spew out your holy venom and poison the knight.
RAVAL: I acted in good faith.

JÖNS: But now you know better, don't you? Because now you have turned into a thief. A more fitting and rewarding occupation for scoundrels. Isn't that so?

With a quick movement he knocks the knife out of Raval's hand, gives him a kick so that he falls on the floor and is about to finish him off. Suddenly the girl screams. Jöns stops and makes a gesture of generosity with his hand.

JÖNS: By all means. I'm not bloodthirsty. (*He bends over Raval*)
RAVAL: Don't beat me.
JÖNS: I don't have the heart to touch you, Doctor. But remember this: The next time we meet, I'll brand your face the way one does with thieves. (*He rises*) What I really came for is to get my waterskin filled.
GIRL: We have a deep well with cool, fresh water. Come, I'll show you.

They walk out of the house. Raval lies still for a few moments, then he rises slowly and looks around. When no one is in sight, he takes his bag and steals away.

Jöns quenches his thirst and fills his bag with water. The girl helps him.

JÖNS: Jöns is my name. I am a pleasant and talkative young man who has never had anything but kind thoughts and has only done beautiful and noble deeds. I'm kindest of all to young women. With them, there is no limit to my kindness.

He embraces her and tries to kiss her, but she holds herself back. Almost immediately he loses interest, hoists the waterbag on his shoulder and pats the girl on the cheek.

JÖNS: Goodbye, my girl. I could very well have raped you,

but between you and me, I'm tired of that kind of love. It runs a little dry in the end.

He laughs kindly and walks away from her. When he has walked a short distance he turns; the girl is still there.

Jöns: Now that I think of it, I will need a housekeeper. Can you prepare good food? (*The girl nods*) As far as I know, I'm still a married man, but I have high hopes that my wife is dead by now. That's why I need a housekeeper. (*The girl doesn't answer but gets up*) The devil with it! Come along and don't stand there staring. I've saved your life, so you owe me a great deal.

She begins walking toward him, her head bent. He doesn't wait for her but walks toward the knight, who patiently awaits his squire.

The Embarrassment Inn lies in the eastern section of the province. The plague has not yet reached this area on its way along the coast.

The actors have placed their wagon under a tree in the yard of the inn. Dressed in colorful costumes, they perform a farce.

The spectators watch the performance, commenting on it noisily. There are merchants with fat, beer-sweaty faces, apprentices and journeymen, farmhands and milkmaids. A whole flock of children perch in the trees around the wagon.

The knight and his squire have sat down in the shadow of a wall. They drink beer and doze in the midday heat. The girl from the deserted village sleeps at Jöns' side.

Skat beats the drums, Jof blows the flute, Mia performs a gay and lively dance. They perspire under the hot white sun. When they have finished Skat comes forward and bows.

SKAT: Noble ladies and gentlemen, I thank you for your interest. Please remain standing a little longer, or sit on the ground, because we are now going to perform a tragedia about an unfaithful wife, her jealous husband, and the handsome lover—that's me.

Mia and Jof have quickly changed costumes and again step out on the stage. They bow to the public.

SKAT: Here is the husband. Here is the wife. If you'll shut up over there, you'll see something splendid. As I said, I play the lover and I haven't entered yet. That's why I'm going to hide behind the curtain for the time being. (*He wipes the sweat from his forehead*) It's damned hot. I think we'll have a thunderstorm.

He places his leg in front of Jof as if to trip him, raises Mia's skirt, makes a face as if he could see all the wonders of the world underneath it, and disappears behind the gaudily patched curtains.

Skat is very handsome, now that he can see himself in the reflection of a tin washbowl. His hair is tightly curled, his eyebrows are beautifully bushy, glittering earrings vie for equal attention with his teeth, and his cheeks are flushed rose red.

He sits out in back on the tailboard of the wagon, dangling his legs and whistling to himself.

In the meantime Jof and Mia play their tragedy; it is not, however, received with great acclaim.

Skat suddenly discovers that someone is watching him as he gazes contentedly into the tin bowl. A woman stands there, stately in both height and volume.

Skat frowns, toys with his small dagger and occasionally throws a roguish but fiery glance at the beautiful visitor.

She suddenly discovers that one of her shoes doesn't quite fit. She leans down to fix it and in doing so allows her generous bosom to burst out of its prison—no more than honor and chastity allow, but still enough so that the actor with his experienced eye immediately sees that there are ample rewards to be had here.

Now she comes a little closer, kneels down and opens a bundle containing several dainty morsels and a skin filled with red wine. Jonas Skat manages not to fall off the wagon in his excitement. Standing on the steps of the wagon, he supports himself against a nearby tree, crosses his legs and bows.

The woman quietly bites into a chicken leg dripping with fat. At this moment the actor is stricken by a radiant glance full of lustful appetites.

When he sees this look, Skat makes an instantaneous decision, jumps down from the wagon and kneels in front of the blushing damsel.

She becomes weak and faint from his nearness, looks at him with a glassy glance and breathes heavily. Skat doesn't neglect to press kisses on her small, chubby hands. The sun shines brightly and small birds make noises in the bushes.

Now she is forced to sit back; her legs seem unwilling to support her any longer. Bewildered, she singles out another chicken leg from the large sack of food and holds it up in front of Skat with an appealing and triumphant expression, as if it were her maidenhood being offered as a prize.

Skat hesitates momentarily, but he is still the strategist. He lets the chicken leg fall to the grass, and murmurs in the woman's rosy ear.

His words seem to please her. She puts her arms around the actor's neck and pulls him to her with such fierceness that both of them lose their balance and tumble down on the soft grass. The small birds take to their wings with frightened shrieks.

Jof stands in the hot sun with a flickering lantern in his

hand. Mia pretends to be asleep on a bench which has been pulled forward on the stage.

JOF: Night and moonlight now prevail
            Here sleeps my wife so frail . . .
VOICE FROM THE PUBLIC: Does she snore?
JOF: May I point out that this is a tragedy, and in trage-dies one doesn't snore.
VOICE FROM THE PUBLIC: I think she should snore any-how.

This opinion causes mirth in the audience. Jof becomes slightly confused and goes out of character, but Mia keeps her head and begins snoring.

JOF: Night and moonlight now prevail.
        There snores—I mean sleeps—my wife so frail.
        Jealous I am, as never before,
        I hide myself behind this door.
        Faithful is she
        To her lover—not me.
        He soon comes a-stealing
        To awaken her lusty feeling.
        I shall now kill him dead
        For cuckolding me in my bed.
        There he comes in the moonlight,
        His white legs shining bright.
        Quiet as a mouse, here I'll lie,
        Tell him not that he's about to die.

Jof hides himself. Mia immediately ends her snoring and sits up, looking to the left.

MIA: Look, there he comes in the night
            My lover, my heart's delight.

She becomes silent and looks wide-eyed in front of her.

The mood in the yard in front of the inn has, up to now, been rather lighthearted despite the heat.

Now a rapid change occurs. People who had been laughing and chattering fall silent. Their faces seem to pale under their sunbrowned skins, the children stop their games and stand with gaping mouths and frightened eyes. Jof steps out in front of the curtain. His painted face bears an expression of horror. Mia has risen with Mikael in her arms. Some of the women in the yard have fallen on their knees, others hide their faces, many begin to mutter half-forgotten prayers.

All have turned their faces toward the white road. Now a shrill song is heard. It is frenzied, almost a scream.

A crucified Christ sways above the hilltop.

The cross-bearers soon come into sight. They are Dominican monks, their hoods pulled down over their faces. More and more of them follow, carrying litters with heavy coffins or clutching holy relics, their hands stretched out spasmodically. The dust wells up around their black hoods; the censers sway and emit a thick, ashen smoke which smells of rancid herbs.

After the line of monks comes another procession. It is a column of men, boys, old men, women, girls, children. All of them have steel-edged scourges in their hands with which they whip themselves and each other, howling ecstatically. They twist in pain; their eyes bulge wildly; their lips are gnawed to shreds and dripping with foam. They have been seized by madness. They bite their own hands and arms, whip each other in violent, almost rhythmic outbursts. Throughout it all the shrill song howls from their bursting throats. Many sway and fall, lift themselves up again, support each other and help each other to intensify the scourging.

Now the procession pauses at the crossroads in front of the inn. The monks fall on their knees, hiding their faces with clenched hands, arms pressed tightly together. Their song never stops. The Christ figure on its timbered cross is raised above the heads of the crowd. It is not Christ triumphant, but the suffering Jesus with the sores, the blood, the hammered nails and the face in convulsive pain. The Son of God, nailed on the wood of the cross, suffering scorn and shame.

The penitents have now sunk down in the dirt of the road. They collapse where they stood like slaughtered cattle. Their screams rise with the song of the monks, through misty clouds of incense, toward the white fire of the sun.

A large square monk rises from his knees and reveals his face, which is red-brown from the sun. His eyes glitter; his voice is thick with impotent scorn.

MONK: God has sentenced us to punishment. We shall all perish in the black death. You, standing there like gaping cattle, you who sit there in your glutted complacency, do you know that this may be your last hour? Death stands right behind you. I can see how his crown gleams in the sun. His scythe flashes as he raises it above your heads. Which one of you shall he strike first? You there, who stands staring like a goat, will your mouth be twisted into the last unfinished gasp before nightfall? And you, woman, who bloom with life and self-satisfaction, will you pale and become extinguished before the morning dawns? You back there, with your swollen nose and stupid grin, do you have another year left to dirty the earth with your refuse? Do you know, you insensible fools, that you shall die today or tomorrow, or the next day, because all of you have been sentenced? Do you hear what I say? Do you hear the word? You have been sentenced, sentenced!

The monk falls silent, looking around with a bitter face and a cold, scornful glance. Now he clenches his hands, straddles the ground and turns his face upward.

MONK: Lord have mercy on us in our humiliation! Don't turn your face from us in loathing and contempt, but be merciful to us for the sake of your son, Jesus Christ.

He makes the sign of the cross over the crowd and then begins a new song in a strong voice. The monks rise and join in the song. As if driven by some superhuman force, the penitents begin to whip themselves again, still wailing and moaning.

The procession continues. New members have joined the rear of the column; others who were unable to go on lie weeping in the dust of the road.

Jöns the squire drinks his beer.

JÖNS: This damned ranting about doom. Is that food for the minds of modern people? Do they really expect us to take them seriously?

The knight grins tiredly.

JÖNS: Yes, now you grin at me, my lord. But allow me to point out that I've either read, heard or experienced most of the tales which we people tell each other.

KNIGHT (*yawns*): Yes, yes.

JÖNS: Even the ghost stories about God the Father, the angels, Jesus Christ and the Holy Ghost—all these I've accepted without too much emotion.

He leans down over the girl as she crouches at his feet and pats her on the head. The knight drinks his beer silently.

JÖNS (*contentedly*): My little stomach is my world, my head is my eternity, and my hands, two wonderful suns. My legs are time's damned pendulums, and my dirty feet are two splendid starting points for my philosophy. Everything is worth precisely as much as a belch, the only difference being that a belch is more satisfying.

The beer mug is empty. Sighing, Jöns gets to his feet. The girl follows him like a shadow.

In the yard he meets a large man with a sooty face and a dark expression. He stops Jöns with a roar.

Jöns: What are you screaming about?
Plog: I am Plog, the smith, and you are the squire Jöns.
Jöns: That's possible.
Plog: Have you seen my wife?
Jöns: No, I haven't. But if I had seen her and she looked like you, I'd quickly forget that I'd seen her.
Plog: Well, in that case you haven't seen her.
Jöns: Maybe she's run off.
Plog: Do you know anything?
Jöns: I know quite a lot, but not about your wife. Go to the inn. Maybe they can help you.

The smith sighs sadly and goes inside.

The inn is very small and full of people eating and drinking to forget their newly aroused fear of eternity. In the open fireplace a roasting pig turns on an iron spit. The sun shines outside the casement window, its sharp rays piercing the darkness of the room, which is thick with fumes and perspiration.

Merchant: Yes, it's true! The plague is spreading along the west coast. People are dying like flies. Usually business would be good at this time of year, but, damn it, I've still got my whole stock unsold.
Woman: They speak of the judgment day. And all these omens are terrible. Worms, chopped-off hands and other monstrosities began pouring out of an old woman, and

down in the village another woman gave birth to a calf's head.

OLD MAN: The day of judgment. Imagine.

FARMER: It hasn't rained here for a month. We'll surely lose our crops.

MERCHANT: And people are acting crazy, I'd say. They flee the country and carry the plague with them wherever they go.

OLD MAN: The day of judgment. Just think, just think!

FARMER: If it's as they say, I suppose a person should look after his house and try to enjoy life as long as he can.

WOMAN: But there have been other things too, such things that can't even be spoken of. (*Whispers*) Things that mustn't be named—but the priests say that the woman carries it between her legs and that's why she must cleanse herself.

OLD MAN: Judgment day. And the Riders of the Apocalypse stand at the bend in the village road. I imagine they'll come on judgment night, at sundown.

WOMAN: There are many who have purged themselves with fire and died from it, but the priests say that it's better to die pure than to live for hell.

MERCHANT: This is the end, yes, it is. No one says it out loud, but all of us know that it's the end. And people are going mad from fear.

FARMER: So you're afraid too.

MERCHANT: Of course I'm afraid.

OLD MAN: The judgment day becomes night, and the angels descend and the graves open. It will be terrible to see.

They whisper in low tones and sit close to each other. Plog, the smith, shoves his way into a place next to Jof, who is still dressed in his costume. Opposite him sits Raval, leaning slightly forward, his face perspiring heavily. Raval rolls an armlet out on the table.

RAVAL: Do you want this armlet? You can have it cheap.

JOF: I can't afford it.

RAVAL: It's real silver.

JOF: It's nice. But it's surely too expensive for me.

PLOG: Excuse me, but has anyone here seen my wife?

JOF: Has she disappeared?

PLOG: They say she's run away.

JOF: Has she deserted you?

PLOG: With an actor.

JOF: An actor! If she's got such bad taste, then I think you should let her go.

PLOG: You're right. My first thought, of course, was to kill her.

JOF: Oh. But to murder her, that's a terrible thing to do.

PLOG: I'm also going to kill the actor.

JOF: The actor?

PLOG: Of course, the one she eloped with.

JOF: What has he done to deserve that?

PLOG: Are you stupid?

JOF: The actor! Now I understand. There are too many of them, so even if he hasn't done anything in particular you ought to kill him merely because he's an actor.

PLOG: You see, my wife has always been interested in the tricks of the theater.

JOF: And that turned out to be her misfortune.

PLOG: Her misfortune, but not mine, because a person who's born unfortunate can hardly suffer from any further misfortune. Isn't that true?

Now Raval enters the discussion. He is slightly drunk and his voice is shrill and evil.

RAVAL: Listen, you! You sit there and lie to the smith.

JOF: I! A liar!

RAVAL: You're an actor too and it's probably your partner who's run off with Plog's old lady.

PLOG: Are you an actor too?

JOF: An actor! Me! I wouldn't quite call myself that!

RAVAL: We ought to kill you; it's only logical.

JOF (*laughs*): You're really funny.

RAVAL: How strange—you've turned pale. Have you anything on your conscience?

JOF: You're funny. Don't you think he's funny? (*To Plog*) Oh, you don't.

RAVAL: Maybe we should mark you up a little with a knife, like they do petty scoundrels of your kind.

Plog bangs his hands down on the table so that the dishes jump. He gets up.

PLOG (*shouting*): What have you done with my wife?

The room becomes silent. Jof looks around, but there is no exit, no way to escape. He puts his hands on the table. Suddenly a knife flashes through the air and sinks into the table top between his fingers.

Jof snatches away his hands and raises his head. He looks half surprised, as if the truth had just become apparent to him.

JOF: Do you want to hurt me? Why? Have I provoked someone, or got in the way? I'll leave right now and never come back.

Jof looks from one face to another, but no one seems ready to help him or come to his defense.

RAVAL: Get up so everyone can hear you. Talk louder.

Trembling, Jof rises. He opens his mouth as if to say something, but not a word comes out.

RAVAL: Stand on your head so that we can see how good an actor you are.

Jof gets up on the table and stands on his head. A hand pushes him forward so that he collapses on the floor. Plog rises, pulls him to his feet with one hand.

PLOG (*shouts*): What have you done with my wife?

The smith beats him so furiously that Jof flies across the table. Raval leans over him.

RAVAL: Don't lie there moaning. Get up and dance.
JOF: I don't want to. I can't.
RAVAL: Show us how you imitate a bear.
JOF: I can't play a bear.
RAVAL: Let's see if you can't after all.

Raval prods Jof lightly with the knife point. Jof gets up with cold sweat on his cheeks and forehead, frightened half to death. He begins to jump and hop on top of the tables, swinging his arms and legs and making grotesque faces. Some laugh, but most of the people sit silently. Jof gasps as if his lungs were about to burst. He sinks to his knees, and someone pours beer over him.

RAVAL: Up again! Be a good bear.
JOF: I haven't done any harm. I haven't got the strength to play a bear any more.

At that moment the door opens and Jöns enters. Jof sees his chance and steals out. Raval intends to follow him, but suddenly stops. Jöns and Raval look at each other.

JÖNS: Do you remember what I was going to do to you if we met again?

Raval steps back without speaking.

JÖNS: I'm a man who keeps his word.

Jöns raises his knife and cuts Raval from forehead to cheek. Raval staggers toward the wall.

The hot day has become night. Singing and howling can be heard from the inn. In a hollow near the forest, the light still lingers. Hidden in the grass and the shrubbery, nightingales sing and their voices echo through the stillness.

The players' wagon stands in a small ravine, and not far away the horse grazes on the dry grass. Mia has sat down in front of the wagon with her son in her arms. They play together and laugh happily.

Now a soft gleam of light strokes the hilltops, a last reflection from the red clouds over the sea.

Not far from the wagon, the knight sits crouched over his chess game. He lifts his head.

The evening light moves across the heavy wagon wheels, across the woman and the child.

The knight gets up.

Mia sees him and smiles. She holds up her struggling son, as if to amuse the knight.

KNIGHT: What's his name?
MIA: Mikael.
KNIGHT: How old is he?
MIA: Oh, he'll soon be two.
KNIGHT: He's big for his age.
MIA: Do you think so? Yes, I guess he's rather big.

She puts the child down on the ground and half rises to shake out her red skirt. When she sits down again, the knight steps closer.

KNIGHT: You played some kind of show this afternoon.

MIA: Did you think it was bad?

KNIGHT: You are more beautiful now without your face painted, and this gown is more becoming.

MIA: You see, Jonas Skat has run off and left us, so we're in real trouble now.

KNIGHT: Is that your husband?

MIA (*laughs*): Jonas! The other man is my husband. His name is Jof.

KNIGHT: Oh, that one.

MIA: And now there's only him and me. We'll have to start doing tricks again and that's more trouble than it's worth.

KNIGHT: Do you do tricks also?

MIA: We certainly do. And Jof is a very skillful juggler.

KNIGHT: Is Mikael going to be an acrobat?

MIA: Jof wants him to be.

KNIGHT: But you don't.

MIA: I don't know. (*Smiling*) Perhaps he'll become a knight.

KNIGHT: Let me assure you, that's no pleasure either.

MIA: No, you don't look so happy.

KNIGHT: No.

MIA: Are you tired?

KNIGHT: Yes.

MIA: Why?

KNIGHT: I have dull company.

MIA: Do you mean your squire?

KNIGHT: No, not him.

MIA: Who do you mean, then?

KNIGHT: Myself.

MIA: I understand.

KNIGHT: Do you, really?

MIA: Yes, I understand rather well. I have often wondered why people torture themselves as often as they can. Isn't that so?

She nods energetically and the knight smiles seriously. Now the shrieks and the noise from the inn become louder. Black figures flicker across the grass mound. Someone collapses, gets up and runs. It is Jof. Mia stretches out her arms and receives him. He holds his hands in front of his face, moaning like a child, and his body sways. He kneels. Mia holds him close to her and sprinkles him with small, anxious questions: What have you done? How are you? What is it? Does it hurt? What can I do? Have they been cruel to you? She runs for a rag, which she dips in water, and carefully bathes her husband's dirty, bloody face.

Eventually a rather sorrowful visage emerges. Blood runs from a bruise on his forehead and his nose, and a tooth has been loosened, but otherwise Jof seems unhurt.

JOF: Ouch, it hurts.
MIA: Why did you have to go there? And of course you drank.

Mia's anxiety has been replaced by a mild anger. She pats him a little harder than necessary.

JOF: Ouch! I didn't drink anything.
MIA: Then I suppose you were boasting about the angels and devils you consort with. People don't like someone who has too many ideas and fantasies.
JOF: I swear to you that I didn't say a word about angels.
MIA: You were, of course, busy singing and dancing. You can never stop being an actor. People also become angry at that, and you know it.

Jof doesn't answer but searches for the armlet. He holds it up in front of Mia with an injured expression.

JOF: Look what I bought for you.

MIA: You couldn't afford it.
JOF (*angry*): But I got it anyhow.

The armlet glitters faintly in the twilight. Mia now pulls it across her wrist. They look at it in silence, and their faces soften. They look at each other, touch each other's hands. Jof puts his head against Mia's shoulder and sighs.

JOF: Oh, how they beat me.
MIA: Why didn't you beat them back?
JOF: I only become frightened and angry. I never get a chance to hit back. I can get angry, you know that. I roared like a lion.
MIA: Were they frightened?
JOF: No, they just laughed.

Their son Mikael crawls over to them. Jof lies down on the ground and pulls his son on top of him. Mia gets down on her hands and knees and playfully sniffs at Mikael.

MIA: Do you notice how good he smells?
JOF: And he is so compact to hold. You're a sturdy one. A real acrobat's body.

He lifts Mikael up and holds him by the legs. Mia looks up suddenly, remembering the knight's presence.

MIA: Yes, this is my husband, Jof.
JOF: Good evening.
KNIGHT: Good evening.

Jof becomes a little embarrassed and rises. All three of them look at one another silently.

KNIGHT: I have just told your wife that you have a splendid son. He'll bring great joy to you.

Jof: Yes, he's fine.

They become silent again.

Jof: Have we nothing to offer the knight, Mia?
Knight: Thank you, I don't want anything.
Mia (*housewifely*): I picked a basket of wild strawberries this afternoon. And we have a drop of milk fresh from a cow . . .
Jof: . . . that we were *allowed* to milk. So, if you would like to partake of this humble fare, it would be a great honor.
Mia: Please be seated and I'll bring the food.

They sit down. Mia disappears with Mikael.

Knight: Where are you going next?
Jof: Up to the saints' feast at Elsinore.
Knight: I wouldn't advise you to go there.
Jof: Why not, if I may ask?
Knight: The plague has spread in that direction, following the coast line south. It's said that people are dying by the tens of thousands.
Jof: Really! Well, sometimes life is a little hard.
Knight: May I suggest . . . (*Jof looks at him, surprised*) . . . that you follow me through the forest tonight and stay at my home if you like. Or go along the east coast. You'll probably be safer there.

Mia has returned with a bowl of wild strawberries and the milk, places it between them and gives each of them a spoon.

Jof: I wish you good appetite.
Knight: I humbly thank you.
Mia: These are wild strawberries from the forest. I have

never seen such large ones. They grow up there on the hill-
side. Notice how they smell!

She points with a spoon and smiles. The knight nods,
as if he were pondering some profound thought. Jof eats
heartily.

JOF: Your suggestion is good, but I must think it over.
MIA: It might be wise to have company going through the
forest. It's said to be full of trolls and ghosts and bandits.
That's what I've heard.
JOF (*staunchly*): Yes, I'd say that it's not a bad idea, but
I have to think about it. Now that Skat has left, I am re-
sponsible for the troupe. After all, I have become direc-
tor of the whole company.
MIA (*mimics*): After all, I have become director of the
whole company.

Jöns comes walking slowly down the hill, closely followed
by the girl. Mia points with her spoon.

MIA: Do you want some strawberries?
JOF: This man saved my life. Sit down, my friend, and let
us be together.
MIA (*stretches herself*): Oh, how nice this is.
KNIGHT: For a short while.
MIA: Nearly always. One day is like another. There is
nothing strange about that. The summer, of course, is better than the winter, because in summer you don't have to
be cold. But spring is best of all.
JOF: I have written a poem about the spring. Perhaps you'd
like to hear it. I'll run and get my lyre. (*He sprints toward
the wagon*)
MIA: Not now, Jof. Our guests may not be amused by
your songs.
JÖNS (*politely*): By all means. I write little songs myself.

For example, I know a very funny song about a wanton fish which I doubt that you've heard yet.

The knight looks at him.

Jöns: You'll not get to hear it either. There are persons here who don't appreciate my art and I don't want to upset anyone. I'm a sensitive soul.

Jof has come out with his lyre, sits on a small, gaudy box and plucks at the instrument, humming quietly, searching for his melody. Jöns yawns and lies down.

Knight: People are troubled by so much.
Mia: It's always better when one is two. Have you no one of your own?
Knight: Yes, I think I had someone.
Mia: And what is she doing now?
Knight: I don't know.
Mia: You look so solemn. Was she your beloved?
Knight: We were newly married and we played together. We laughed a great deal. I wrote songs to her eyes, to her nose, to her beautiful little ears. We went hunting together and at night we danced. The house was full of life . . .
Mia: Do you want some more strawberries?
Knight (shakes his head): Faith is a torment, did you know that? It is like loving someone who is out there in the darkness but never appears, no matter how loudly you call.
Mia: I don't understand what you mean.
Knight: Everything I've said seems meaningless and unreal while I sit here with you and your husband. How unimportant it all becomes suddenly.

He takes the bowl of milk in his hand and drinks deeply

from it several times. Then he carefully puts it down and looks up, smiling.

MIA: Now you don't look so solemn.
KNIGHT: I shall remember this moment. The silence, the twilight, the bowls of strawberries and milk, your faces in the evening light. Mikael sleeping, Jof with his lyre. I'll try to remember what we have talked about. I'll carry this memory between my hands as carefully as if it were a bowl filled to the brim with fresh milk. (*He turns his face away and looks out toward the sea and the colorless gray sky*) And it will be an adequate sign—it will be enough for me.

He rises, nods to the others and walks down toward the forest. Jof continues to play on his lyre. Mia stretches out on the grass.

The knight picks up his chess game and carries it toward the beach. It is quiet and deserted; the sea is still.

DEATH: I have been waiting for you.
KNIGHT: Pardon me. I was detained for a few moments. Because I revealed my tactics to you, I'm in retreat. It's your move.
DEATH: Why do you look so satisfied?
KNIGHT: That's my secret.
DEATH: Of course. Now I take your knight.
KNIGHT: You did the right thing.
DEATH: Have you tricked me?
KNIGHT: Of course. You fell right in the trap. Check!
DEATH: What are you laughing at?
KNIGHT: Don't worry about my laughter; save your king instead.
DEATH: You're rather arrogant.
KNIGHT: Our game amuses me.

DEATH: It's your move. Hurry up. I'm a little pressed for time.
KNIGHT: I understand that you've a lot to do, but you can't get out of our game. It takes time.

Death is about to answer him but stops and leans over the board. The knight smiles.

DEATH: Are you going to escort the juggler and his wife through the forest? Those whose names are Jof and Mia and who have a small son.
KNIGHT: Why do you ask?
DEATH: Oh, no reason at all.

The knight suddenly stops smiling. Death looks at him scornfully.

Immediately after sundown, the little company gathers in the yard of the inn. There is the knight, Jöns and the girl, Jof and Mia in their wagon. Their son, Mikael, is already asleep. Jonas Skat is still missing.

Jöns goes into the inn to get provisions for the night journey and to have a last mug of beer. The inn is now empty and quiet except for a few farmhands and maidens who are eating their evening meal in a corner.

At one of the small windows sits a lonely, hunched-over fellow, with a jug of brandy in his hands. His expression is very sad. Once in a while he is shaken by a gigantic sob. It is Plog, the smith, who sits there and whimpers.

JÖNS: God in heaven, isn't this Plog, the smith?
PLOG: Good evening.
JÖNS: Are you sitting here sniveling in loneliness?
PLOG: Yes, yes, look at the smith. He moans like a rabbit.
JÖNS: If I were in your boots, I'd be happy to get rid of a wife in such an easy way.

Jöns pats the smith on the back, quenches his thirst with beer, and sits down by his side.

PLOG: Are *you* married?
JÖNS: *I!* A hundred times and more. I can't keep count of all my wives any longer. But it's often that way when you're a traveling man.
PLOG: I can assure you that *one* wife is worse than a hundred, or else I've had worse luck than any poor wretch in this miserable world, which isn't impossible.
JÖNS: Yes, it's hell *with* women and hell *without* them. So, however you look at it, it's still best to kill them off while it's most amusing.
PLOG: Women's nagging, the shrieking of children and wet diapers, sharp nails and sharp words, blows and pokes, and the devil's aunt for a mother-in-law. And then, when one wants to sleep after a long day, there's a new song—tears, whining and moans loud enough to wake the dead.

Jöns nods delightedly. He has drunk deeply and talks with an old woman's voice.

JÖNS: Why don't you kiss me good night?
PLOG (*in the same way*): Why don't you sing a song for me?
JÖNS: Why don't you love me the way you did when we first met?
PLOG: Why don't you look at my new shift?
JÖNS: You only turn your back and snore.
PLOG: Oh hell!
JÖNS: Oh hell. And now she's gone. Rejoice!
PLOG (*furious*): I'll snip their noses with pliers, I'll bash in their chests with a small hammer, I'll tap their heads ever so lightly with a sledge.

Plog begins to cry loudly and his whole body sways in an

enormous attack of sorrow. Jöns looks at him with interest.

Jöns: Look how he howls again.
Plog: Maybe I love her.
Jöns: So, maybe you love her! Then, you poor misguided ham shank, I'll tell you that love is another word for lust, plus lust, plus lust and a damn lot of cheating, falseness, lies and all kinds of other fooling around.
Plog: Yes, but it hurts anyway.
Jöns: Of course. Love is the blackest of all plagues, and if one could die of it, there would be some pleasure in love. But you almost always get over it.
Plog: No, no, not me.
Jöns: Yes, you too. There are only a couple of poor wretches who die of love once in a while. Love is as contagious as a cold in the nose. It eats away at your strength, your independence, your morale, if you have any. If everything is imperfect in this imperfect world, love is most perfect in its perfect imperfection.
Plog: You're happy, you with your oily words, and, besides, you believe your own drivel.
Jöns: Believe! Who said that I believed it? But I love to give good advice. If you ask me for advice you'll get two pieces for the price of one, because after all I really am an educated man.

Jöns gets up from the table and strokes his face with his hands. The smith becomes very unhappy and grabs his belt.

Plog: Listen, Jöns. May I go with you through the forest? I'm so lonely and don't want to go home because everyone will laugh at me.
Jöns: Only if you don't whimper all the time, because in that case we'll all have to avoid you.

The smith gets up and embraces Jöns. Slightly drunk, the two new friends walk toward the door.

When they come out in the yard, Jof immediately catches sight of them, becomes angry and yells a warning to Jöns.

JOF: Jöns! Watch out. That one wants to fight all the time. He's not quite sane.

JÖNS: Yes, but now he's just sniveling.

The smith steps up to Jof, who blanches with fear. Plog offers his hand.

PLOG: I'm really sorry if I hurt you. But I have such a hell of a temper, you know. Shake hands.

Jof gingerly proffers a frightened hand and gets it thoroughly shaken and squeezed. While Jof tries to straighten out his fingers, Plog is seized by great good will and opens his arms.

PLOG: Come in my arms, little brother.

JOF: Thank you, thank you, perhaps later. But now we're really in a hurry.

Jof climbs up on the wagon seat quickly and clucks at the horse.

The small company is on its way toward the forest and the night.

It is dark in the forest.

First comes the knight on his large horse. Then Jof and Mia follow, sitting close to each other in the juggler's wagon. Mia holds her son in her arms. Jöns follows them with his heavily laden horse. He has the smith in tow. The girl sits on top of the load on the horse's back, hunched over as if asleep.

The footsteps, the horses' heavy tramp on the soft path, the human breathing—yet it is quiet.

Then the moon sails out of the clouds. The forest suddenly becomes alive with the night's unreality. The dazzling light pours through the thick foliage of the beech trees, a moving, quivering world of light and shadow.

The wanderers stop. Their eyes are dark with anxiety and foreboding. Their faces are pale and unreal in the floating light. It is very quiet.

PLOG: Now the moon has come out of the clouds.
JÖNS: That's good. Now we can see the road better.
MIA: I don't like the moon tonight.
JOF: The trees stand so still.
JÖNS: That's because there's no wind.
PLOG: I guess he means that they stand *very* still.
JOF: It's completely quiet.
JÖNS: If one could hear a fox at least.
JOF: Or an owl.
JÖNS: Or a human voice besides one's own.
GIRL: They say it's dangerous to remain standing in moonlight.

Suddenly, out of the silence and the dim light falling across the forest road, a ghostlike cart emerges.

It is the witch being taken to the place where she will be burned. Next to her eight soldiers shuffle along tiredly, carrying their lances on their backs. The girl sits in the cart, bound with iron chains around her throat and arms. She stares fixedly into the moonlight.

A black figure sits next to her, a monk with his hood pulled down over his head.

JÖNS: Where are you going?
SOLDIER: To the place of execution.

Jöns: Yes, now I can see. It's the girl who has done it with the Black One. The witch?

The soldier nods sourly. Hesitantly, the travelers follow. The knight guides his horse over to the side of the cart. The witch seems to be half conscious, but her eyes are wide open.

Knight: I see that they have hurt your hands.

The witch's pale, childish face turns toward the knight and she shakes her head.

Knight: I have a potion that will stop your pain.

She shakes her head again.

Jöns: Why do you burn her at this time of night? People have so few diversions these days.
Soldier: Saints preserve us, be quiet! It's said that she brings the Devil with her wherever she goes.
Jöns: You are eight brave men, then.
Soldier: Well, we've been paid. And this is a volunteer job.

The soldier speaks in whispers while glancing anxiously at the witch.

Knight (to witch): What's your name?
Tyan: My name is Tyan, my lord.
Knight: How old are you?
Tyan: Fourteen, my lord.
Knight: And is it true that you have been in league with the Devil?

Tyan nods quietly and looks away. Now they arrive at

the parish border. At the foot of the nearby hills lies a
crossroads. The pyre has already been stacked in the center of the forest clearing. The travelers remain there, hesitant and curious.

The soldiers have tied up the cart horse and bring out
two long wooden beams. They nail rungs across the beams
so that it looks like a ladder. Tyan will be bound to this
like an eelskin stretched out to dry.

The sound of the hammering echoes through the forest.
The knight has dismounted and walks closer to the cart.
Again he tries to catch Tyan's eyes, touches her very
lightly as if to waken her.

Slowly she turns her face toward him.

KNIGHT: They say that you have been in league with the
Devil.
TYAN: Why do you ask?
KNIGHT: Not out of curiosity, but for very personal rea-
sons. I too want to meet him.
TYAN: Why?
KNIGHT: I want to ask him about God. He, if anyone,
must know.
TYAN: You can see him anytime.
KNIGHT: How?
TYAN: You must do as I tell you.

The knight grips the wooden rail of the cart so tightly
that his knuckles whiten. Tyan leans forward and joins
her gaze with his.

TYAN: Look into my eyes.

The knight meets her gaze. They stare at each other for
a long time.

TYAN: What do you see? Do you see *him?*

KNIGHT: I see fear in your eyes, an empty, numb fear. But nothing else.

He falls silent. The soldiers work at the stakes; their hammering echoes in the forest.

TYAN: No one, nothing, no one?
KNIGHT (*shakes his head*): No.
TYAN: Can't you see him behind your back?
KNIGHT (*looks around*): No, there is no one there.
TYAN: But he is with me everywhere. I only have to stretch out my hand and I can feel his hand. He is with me now too. The fire won't hurt me. He will protect me from everything evil.
KNIGHT: Has he told you this?
TYAN: I know it.
KNIGHT: Has he said it?
TYAN: I know it, I know it. You must see him somewhere, you must. The priests had no difficulty seeing him, nor did the soldiers. They are so afraid of him that they don't even dare touch me.

The sound of the hammers stops. The soldiers stand like black shadows rooted in the moss. They fumble with the chains and pull at the neck iron. Tyan moans weakly, as if she were far away.

KNIGHT: Why have you crushed her hands?
SOLDIER (*surly*): We didn't do it.
KNIGHT: Who did?
SOLDIER: Ask the monk.

The soldiers pull the iron and the chains. Tyan's shaven head sways, gleaming in the moonlight. Her blackened mouth opens as if to scream, but no sound emerges.

They take her down from the cart and lead her toward

the ladder and the stake. The knight turns to the monk, who remains seated in the cart.

KNIGHT: What have you done with the child?

Death turns around and looks at him.

DEATH: Don't you ever stop asking questions?
KNIGHT: No, I'll never stop.

The soldiers chain Tyan to the rungs of the ladder. She submits resignedly, moans weakly like an animal and tries to ease her body into position.

When they have fastened her, they walk over to light the pyre. The knight steps up and leans over her.

JÖNS: For a moment I thought of killing the soldiers, but it would do no good. She's nearly dead already.

One of the soldiers approaches. Thick smoke wells down from the pyre and sweeps over the quiet shadows near the crossroads and the hill.

SOLDIER: I've told you to be careful. Don't go too close to her.

The knight doesn't heed this warning. He cups his hand, fills it with water from the skin and gives it to Tyan. Then he gives her a potion.

KNIGHT: Take this and it will stop the pain.

Smoke billows down over them and they begin to cough. The soldiers step forward and raise the ladder against a nearby fir tree. Tyan hangs there motionlessly, her eyes wide open.

The knight straightens up and stands immobile. Jöns is behind him, his voice nearly choked with rage.

JÖNS: What does she see? Can you tell me?
KNIGHT (*shakes his head*): She feels no more pain.
JÖNS: You don't answer my question. Who watches over that child? Is it the angels, or God, or the Devil, or only the emptiness? Emptiness, my lord!
KNIGHT: This cannot be.
JÖNS: Look at her eyes, my lord. Her poor brain has just made a discovery. Emptiness under the moon.
KNIGHT: No.
JÖNS: We stand powerless, our arms hanging at our sides, because we see what she sees, and our terror and hers are the same. (*An outburst*) That poor little child. I can't stand it, I can't stand it . . .

His voice sticks in his throat and he suddenly walks away. The knight mounts his horse. The travelers depart from the crossroads. Tyan finally closes her eyes.

The forest is now very dark. The road winds between the trees. The wagon squeaks and rattles over stones and roots. A bird suddenly shrieks.

Jof lifts his head and wakes up. He has been asleep with his arms around Mia's shoulders. The knight is sharply silhouetted against the tree trunks.

His silence makes him seem almost unreal.

Jöns and the smith are slightly drunk and support each other. Suddenly Plog has to sit down. He puts his hands over his face and howls piteously.

PLOG: Oh, now it came over me again!
JÖNS: Don't scream. What came over you?
PLOG: My wife, damn it. She is so beautiful. She is so

beautiful that she can't be described without the accompaniment of a lyre.

JÖNS: Now it starts again.

PLOG: Her smile is like brandy. Her eyes like blackberries . . .

Plog searches for beautiful words. He gestures gropingly with his large hands.

JÖNS (*sighs*): Get up, you tear-drenched pig. We'll lose the others.

PLOG: Yes, of course, of course. Her nose is like a little pink potato; her behind is like a juicy pear—yes, the whole woman is like a strawberry patch. I can see her in front of me, with arms like wonderful cucumbers.

JÖNS: Saints almighty, stop! You're a very bad poet, despite the fact that you're drunk. And your vegetable garden bores me.

They walk across an open meadow. Here it is a little brighter and the moon shimmers behind a thin sky. Suddenly the smith points a large finger toward the edge of the forest.

PLOG: Look there.

JÖNS: Do you see something?

PLOG: There, over there!

JÖNS: I don't see anything.

PLOG: Hang on to something, my friends. The hour is near! Who is that at the edge of the forest if not my own dearly beloved, with actor attached?

The two lovers discover the smith and it's too late. They cannot retreat. Skat immediately takes to his heels. Plog chases him, swinging his sledge and bellowing like a wild boar.

For a few confusing moments the two rivals stumble among the stones and bushes in the gray gloom of the forest. The duel begins to look senseless, because both of them are equally frightened.

The travelers silently observe this confused performance. Lisa screams once in a while, more out of duty than out of impulse.

SKAT (*panting*): You miserable stubbleheaded bastard of seven scurvy bitches, if I were in your lousy rags I would be stricken with such eternal shame about my breath, my voice, my arms and legs—in short, about my whole body— that I would immediately rid nature of my own embarrassing self.

PLOG (*angry*): Watch out, you perfumed slob, that I don't fart on you and immediately blow you down to the actor's own red-hot hell, where you can sit and recite monologues to each other until the dust comes out of the Devil's ears.

Then Lisa throws herself around her husband's neck.

LISA: Forgive me, dear little husband. I'll never do it again. I am so sorry and you can't imagine how terribly that man over there betrayed me.

PLOG: I'll kill him anyway.

LISA: Yes, do that, just kill him. He isn't even a human being.

JÖNS: Hell, he's an actor.

LISA: He is only a false beard, false teeth, false smiles, rehearsed lines, and he's as empty as a jug. Just kill him.

Lisa sobs with excitement and sorrow. The smith looks around, a little confused. The actor uses this opportunity. He pulls out a dagger and places the point against his breast.

SKAT: She's right. Just kill me. If you thought that I was going to apologize for being what I am, you are mistaken.

LISA: Look how sickening he is. How he makes a fool of himself, how he puts on an act. Dear Plog, kill him!

SKAT: My friends, you have only to push, and my unreality will soon be transformed into a new, solid reality. An absolutely tangible corpse.

LISA: Do something then. Kill him.

PLOG (*embarrassed*): He has to fight me, otherwise I can't kill him.

SKAT: Your life's thread now hangs by a very ragged shred. Idiot, your day is short.

PLOG: You'll have to irritate me a little more to get me as angry as before.

Skat looks at the travelers with a pained expression and then lifts his eyes toward the night sky.

SKAT: I forgive all of you. Pray for me sometimes.

Skat sinks the dagger into his breast and slowly falls to the ground. The travelers stand confused. The smith rushes forward and begins to pull at the actor's hands.

PLOG: Oh dear, dear, I didn't mean it that way! Look, there's no life left in him. I was beginning to like him, and in my opinion Lisa was much too spiteful.

Jof leans over his colleague.

JOF: He's dead, totally, enormously dead. In fact, I've never seen such a dead actor.

LISA: Come on, let's go. This is nothing to mourn over. He has only himself to blame.

PLOG: And I have to be married to *her*.

JÖNS: We must go on.

Skat lies in the grass and keeps the dagger pressed tightly to his breast. The travelers depart and soon they have disappeared into the dark forest on the other side of the meadow. When Skat is sure that no one can see him, he sits up and lifts the dagger from his breast. It is a stage dagger with a blade that pushes into the handle. Skat laughs to himself.

SKAT: Now that was a good scene. I'm really a good actor. After all, why shouldn't I be a little pleased with myself? But where shall I go? I'll wait until it becomes light and then I'll find the easiest way out of the forest. I'll climb up a tree for the time being so that no bears, wolves or ghosts can get at me.

He soon finds a likely tree and climbs up into its thick foliage. He sits down as comfortably as possible and reaches for his food pouch.

SKAT (*yawns*): Tomorrow I'll find Jof and Mia and then we'll go to the saints' feast in Elsinore. We'll make lots of money there. (*Yawns*) Now, I'll sing a little song to myself:

> I am a little bird
> Who sings whate'er he will,
> And when I am in danger
> I fling out a pissing trill
> As in the carnal thrill.

(*Speaks*) It's boring to be alone in the forest tonight. (*Sings*) The terrible night doesn't frighten me . . .

He interrupts himself and listens. The sound of industrious sawing is heard through the silence.

SKAT: Workmen in the forest. Oh, well! (*Sings*) The terrible night doesn't frighten me . . . Hey, what the devil . . . it's *my* tree they're cutting down.

He peers through the foliage. Below him stands a dark figure diligently sawing away at the base of the tree. Skat becomes frightened and angry.

SKAT: Hey, you! Do you hear me, you tricky bastard? What are you doing with my tree?

The sawing continues without a pause. Skat becomes more frightened.

SKAT: Can't you at least answer me? Politeness costs so little. Who are you?

Death straightens his back and squints up at him. Skat cries out in terror.

DEATH: I'm sawing down your tree because your time is up.
SKAT: It won't do. I haven't got time.
DEATH: So you haven't got time.
SKAT: No, I have my performance.
DEATH: Then it's been canceled because of death.
SKAT: My contract.
DEATH: Your contract is terminated.
SKAT: My children, my family.
DEATH: Shame on you, Skat!
SKAT: Yes, I'm ashamed.

Death begins to saw again. The tree creaks.

SKAT: Isn't there any way to get off? Aren't there any special rules for actors?
DEATH: No, not in this case.
SKAT: No loopholes, no exceptions?

Death saws.

SKAT: Perhaps you'll take a bribe.

Death saws.

SKAT: Help!

Death saws.

SKAT: Help! Help!

The tree falls. The forest becomes silent again.

Night and then dawn.

The travelers have come to a sort of clearing and have collapsed on the moss. They lie quietly and listen to their own breathing, their heartbeats, and the wind in the tree tops. Here the forest is wild and impenetrable. Huge boulders stick up out of the ground like the heads of black giants. A fallen tree lies like a mighty barrier between light and shadow.

Mia, Jof and their child have sat down apart from the others. They look at the light of the moon, which is no longer full and dead but mysterious and unstable.

The knight sits bent over his chess game. Lisa cries quietly behind the smith's back. Jöns lies on the ground and looks up at the heavens.

JÖNS: Soon dawn will come, but the heat continues to hang over us like a smothering blanket.
LISA: I'm so frightened.
PLOG: We feel that something is going to happen to us, but we don't know what.
JÖNS: Maybe it's the day of judgment.
PLOG: The day of judgment . . .

Now something moves behind the fallen tree. There is a

rustling sound and a moaning cry that seems to come from a wounded animal. Everyone listens intently, all faces turned toward the sound.

A voice comes out of the darkness.

RAVAL: Do you have some water?

Raval's perspiring face soon becomes visible. He disappears in the darkness, but his voice is heard again.

RAVAL: Can't you give me a little water? (*Pause*) I have the plague.
JÖNS: Don't come here. If you do I'll slit your throat. Keep to the other side of the tree.
RAVAL: I'm afraid of death.

No one answers. There is complete silence. Raval gasps heavily for air. The dry leaves rustle with his movements.

RAVAL: I don't want to die! I don't want to!

No one answers. Raval's face appears suddenly at the base of the tree. His eyes bulge wildly and his mouth is ringed with foam.

RAVAL: Can't you have pity on me? Help me! At least talk to me.

No one answers. The trees sigh. Raval begins to cry.

RAVAL: I am going to die. I. I. *I!* What will happen to me! Can no one console me? Haven't you any compassion? Can't you see that I . . .

His words are choked off by a gurgling sound. He disappears in the darkness behind the fallen tree. It becomes quiet for a few moments.

RAVAL (*Whispers*): Can't anyone . . . only a little water.

Suddenly the girl gets up with a quick movement, snatches Jöns' water bag and runs a few steps. Jöns grabs her and holds her fast.

JÖNS: It's no use. It's no use. I know that it's no use. It's meaningless. It's totally meaningless. I tell you that it's meaningless. Can't you hear that I'm consoling you?

RAVAL: Help me, help me!

No one answers, no one moves. Raval's sobs are dry and convulsive, like a frightened child's. His sudden scream is cut off in the middle.
Then it becomes quiet.
The girl sinks down and hides her face in her hands. Jöns places his hand on her shoulder.

The knight is no longer alone. Death has come to him and he raises his hand.

DEATH: Shall we play our game to the end?
KNIGHT: Your move!

Death raises his hand and strikes the knight's queen. Antonius Block looks at Death.

DEATH: Now I take your queen.
KNIGHT: I didn't notice that.

The knight leans over the game. The moonlight moves over the chess pieces, which seem to have a life of their own.
Jof has dozed off for a few moments, but suddenly he wakens. Then he sees the knight and Death together.

He becomes very frightened and awakens Mia.

JOF: Mia!

MIA: Yes, what is it?

JOF: I see something terrible. Something I almost can't talk about.

MIA: What do you see?

JOF: The knight is sitting over there playing chess.

MIA: Yes, I can see that too and I don't think it's so terrible.

JOF: But do you see who he's playing with?

MIA: He is alone. You *mustn't* frighten me this way.

JOF: No, no, he isn't alone.

MIA: Who is it, then?

JOF: Death. He is sitting there playing chess with Death himself.

MIA: You mustn't say that.

JOF: We must try to escape.

MIA: One can't do that.

JOF: We must try. They are so occupied with their game that if we move very quietly, they won't notice us.

Jof gets up carefully and disappears into the darkness behind the trees. Mia remains standing, as if paralyzed by fear. She stares fixedly at the knight and the chess game. She holds her son in her arms.

Now Jof returns.

JOF: I have harnessed the horse. The wagon is standing near the big tree. You go first and I'll follow you with the packs. See that Mikael doesn't wake up.

Mia does what Jof has told her. At the same moment, the knight looks up from his game.

DEATH: It is your move, Antonius Block.

The knight remains silent. He sees Mia go through the moonlight toward the wagon. Jof bends down to pick up the pack and follows at a distance.

DEATH: Have you lost interest in our game?

The knight's eyes become alarmed. Death looks at him intently.

KNIGHT: Lost interest? On the contrary.
DEATH: You seem anxious. Are you hiding anything?
KNIGHT: Nothing escapes you—or does it?
DEATH: Nothing escapes me. No one escapes from me.
KNIGHT: It's true that I'm worried.

He pretends to be clumsy and knocks the chess pieces over with the hem of his coat. He looks up at Death.

KNIGHT: I've forgotten how the pieces stood.
DEATH (*laughs contentedly*): But I have not forgotten. You can't get away that easily.

Death leans over the board and rearranges the pieces. The knight looks past him toward the road. Mia has just climbed up on the wagon. Jof takes the horse by the bridle and leads it down to the road. Death notices nothing; he is completely occupied with reconstructing the game.

DEATH: Now I see something interesting.
KNIGHT: What do you see?
DEATH: You are mated on the next move, Antonius Block.
KNIGHT: That's true.
DEATH: Did you enjoy your reprieve?
KNIGHT: Yes, I did.
DEATH: I'm happy to hear that. Now I'll be leaving you. When we meet again, you and your companions' time will be up.

KNIGHT: And you will divulge your secrets.
DEATH: I have no secrets.
KNIGHT: So you know nothing.
DEATH: I have nothing to tell.

The knight wants to answer, but Death is already gone.
A murmur is heard in the tree tops. Dawn comes, a
flickering light without life, making the forest seem threatening and evil. Jof drives over the twisting road. Mia sits
beside him.

MIA: What a strange light.
JOF: I guess it's the thunderstorm which comes with
dawn.
MIA: No, it's something else. Something terrible. Do you
hear the roar in the forest?
JOF: It's probably rain.
MIA: No, it isn't rain. He has seen us and he's following
us. He has overtaken us; he's coming toward us.
JOF: Not yet, Mia. In any case, not yet.
MIA: I'm so afraid. I'm so afraid.

The wagon rattles over roots and stones; it sways and
creaks. Now the horse stops with his ears flat against his
head. The forest sighs and stirs ponderously.

JOF: Get into the wagon, Mia. Crawl in quickly. We'll lie
down, Mia, with Mikael between us.

They crawl into the wagon and crouch around the sleeping child.

JOF: It is the Angel of Death that's passing over us, Mia.
It's the Angel of Death. *The Angel of Death, and he's very
big.*
MIA: Do you feel how cold it is? I'm freezing. I'm terribly
cold.

She shivers as if she had a fever. They pull the blankets over them and lie closely together. The wagon canvas flutters and beats in the wind. The roar outside is like a giant bellowing.

The castle is silhouetted like a black boulder against the heavy dawn. Now the storm moves there, throwing itself powerfully against walls and abutments. The sky darkens; it is almost like night.

Antonius Block has brought his companions with him to the castle. But it seems deserted. They walk from room to room. There is only emptiness and quiet echoes. Outside, the rain is heard roaring noisily.

Suddenly the knight stands face to face with his wife. They look at each other quietly.

KARIN: I heard from people who came from the crusade that you were on your way home. I've been waiting for you here. All the others have fled from the plague.

The knight is silent. He looks at her.

KARIN: Don't you recognize me any more?

The knight nods, silent.

KARIN: You also have changed.

She walks closer and looks searchingly into his face. The smile lingers in her eyes and she touches his hand lightly.

KARIN: Now I can see that it's you. Somewhere in your eyes, somewhere in your face, but hidden and frightened, is that boy who went away so many years ago.
KNIGHT: It's over now and I'm a little tired.

KARIN: I see that you're tired.
KNIGHT: Over there stand my friends.
KARIN: Ask them in. They will break the fast with us.

They all sit down at the table in the room, which is lit by torches on the walls. Silently they eat the hard bread and the salt-darkened meat. Karin sits at the head of the table and reads aloud from a thick book.

KARIN: "And when the Lamb broke the seventh seal, there was silence in heaven for about the space of half an hour. And I saw the seven angels which stood before God; and to them were given seven trumpets. And another . . ."

Three mighty knocks sound on the large portal. Karin interrupts her reading and looks up from the book. Jöns rises quickly and goes to open the door.

KARIN: "The first angel sounded, and there followed hail and fire mingled with blood, and they were cast upon the earth; and the third part of the trees was burnt up and all the green grass was burnt up."

Now the rain becomes quiet. There is suddenly an immense, frightening silence in the large, murky room where the burning torches throw uneasy shadows over the ceiling and the walls. Everyone listens tensely to the stillness.

KARIN: "And the second angel sounded, and as it were a great mountain burning with fire was cast into the sea; and a third part of the sea became blood . . ."

Steps are heard on the stairs. Jöns returns and sits down silently at his place but does not continue to eat.

KNIGHT: Was someone there?

Jöns: No, my lord. I saw no one.

Karin lifts her head for a moment but once again leans over the large book.

Karin: "And the third angel sounded, and there fell a great star from heaven, burning as it were a torch, and it fell upon the third part of the rivers and upon the fountains of waters; and the name of the star is called Wormwood . . ."

They all lift their heads, and when they see who is coming toward them through the twilight of the large room, they rise from the table and stand close together.

Knight: Good morning, noble lord.
Karin: I am Karin, the knight's wife, and welcome you courteously to my house.
Plog: I am a smith by profession and rather good at my trade, if I say so myself. My wife Lisa—curtsy for the great lord, Lisa. She's a little difficult to handle once in a while and we had a little spat, so to say, but no worse than most people.

The knight hides his face in his hands.

Knight: From our darkness, we call out to Thee, Lord. Have mercy on us because we are small and frightened and ignorant.
Jöns: (*bitterly*): In the darkness where You are supposed to be, where all of us probably are . . . In the darkness You will find no one to listen to Your cries or be touched by Your sufferings. Wash Your tears and mirror Yourself in Your indifference.
Knight: God, You who are somewhere, who *must* be somewhere, have mercy upon us.

JÖNS: I could have given you an herb to purge you of your worries about eternity. Now it seems to be too late. But in any case, feel the immense triumph of this last minute when you can still roll your eyes and move your toes.

KARIN: Quiet, quiet.

JÖNS: I shall be silent, but under protest.

GIRL (*on her knees*): It is the end.

Jof and Mia lie close together and listen to the rain tapping lightly on the wagon canvas, a sound which diminishes until finally there are only single drops.

They crawl out of their hiding place. The wagon stands on a height above a slope, protected by an enormous tree. They look across ridges, forests, the wide plains, and the sea, which glistens in the sunlight breaking through the clouds.

Jof stretches his arms and legs. Mia dries the wagon seat and sits down next to her husband. Mikael crawls between Jof's knees.

A lone bird tests its voice after the storm. The trees and bushes drip. From the sea comes a strong and fragrant wind.

Jof points to the dark, retreating sky where summer lightning glitters like silver needles over the horizon.

JOF: I see them, Mia! I see them! Over there against the dark, stormy sky. They are all there. The smith and Lisa and the knight and Raval and Jöns and Skat. And Death, the severe master, invites them to dance. He tells them to hold each other's hands and then they must tread the dance in a long row. And first goes the master with his scythe and hourglass, but Skat dangles at the end with his lyre. They dance away from the dawn and it's a solemn dance toward the dark lands, while the rain washes their faces and cleans the salt of the tears from their cheeks.

He is silent. He lowers his hand.

His son, Mikael, has listened to his words. Now he crawls up to Mia and sits down in her lap.

MIA (*smiling*): You with your visions and dreams.

Stockholm
June 5, 1956

WILD STRAWBERRIES

WILD STRAWBERRIES

THE CAST

Professor Isak Borg	Victor Sjöström
Sara	Bibi Andersson
Marianne	Ingrid Thulin
Evald	Gunnar Björnstrand
Agda	Jullan Kindahl
Anders	Folke Sundquist
Viktor	Björn Bjelvenstam
Isak's mother	Naima Wifstrand
Mrs. Alman	Gunnel Broström
Isak's wife	Gertrud Fridh
Her lover	Åke Fridell
Aunt	Sif Ruud
Alman	Gunnar Sjöberg
Åkerman	Max von Sydow
Uncle Aron	Yngve Nordwall
Sigfrid	Per Sjöstrand
Sigbritt	Gio Petré
Charlotta	Gunnel Lindblom
Angelica	Maud Hansson
Mrs. Åkerman	Anne-Mari Wiman
Anna	Eva Norée
The twins	Lena Bergman
	Monica Ehrling

Hagbart	Per Skogsberg
Benjamin	Göran Lundquist
Promoter	Professor Helge Wulff

NOTE: *There are no cast listings for Tiger and Jakob because the scene in which these characters appear (see pp. 277-8) did not appear in the finished film.*

THE CREDITS

Screenplay	Ingmar Bergman
Director	Ingmar Bergman
Assistant director	Gösta Ekman
Director of photography	Gunnar Fischer
Assistant cameraman	Björn Thermenius
Music	Erik Nordgren
Music directed by	E. Eckert-Lundin
Sets	Gittan Gustafsson
Costumes	Millie Ström
Make-up	Nils Nittel
	(of Carl M. Lundh, Inc.)
Sound	Aaby Wedin and Lennart Wallin
Editor	Oscar Rosander
Production supervisor	Allan Ekelund

Running time: 90 minutes

Produced by Svensk Filmindustri; distributed in the United States by Janus Films, Inc., and in Great Britain by Contemporary Films Ltd.

Agda, Professor Isak Borg and Marianne

Sara and Sigfrid

The family at breakfast

Isak Borg, Marianne, Sara, Viktor and Anders

Isak's mother with Marianne

Isak dreams; with Marianne

Isak and Alman

Isak's wife

Evald and Marianne   Isak and Agda

Isak receives his honorary title

With Evald and Marianne

"I dreamed that I stood by the water and shouted toward the bay, but the warm summer breeze carried away my cries, and they did not reach their destination. Yet I wasn't sorry about that; I felt, on the contrary, rather lighthearted."

AT THE AGE of seventy-six, I feel that I'm much too old to lie to myself. But of course I can't be too sure. My complacent attitude toward my own truthfulness could be dishonesty in disguise, although I don't quite know what I might want to hide. Nevertheless, if for some reason I would have to evaluate myself, I am sure that I would do so without shame or concern for my reputation. But if I should be asked to express an opinion about someone else, I would be considerably more cautious. There is the greatest danger in passing such judgment. In all probability one is guilty of errors, exaggerations, even tremendous lies. Rather than commit such follies, I remain silent.

As a result, I have of my own free will withdrawn almost completely from society, because one's relationship with other people consists mainly of discussing and evaluating one's neighbor's conduct. Therefore I have found myself rather alone in my old age. This is not a regret but a statement of fact. All I ask of life is to be left alone and to have the opportunity to devote myself to the few things which continue to interest me, however superficial they may be. For example, I derive pleasure from keeping up with the steady progress made in my profession (I once taught bacteriology), I find relaxation in a game of golf, and now and then I read some memoirs or a good detective story.

My life has been filled with work, and for that I am grateful. It began with a struggle for daily bread and developed into the continuous pursuit of a beloved science. I have a son living in Lund who is a physician and has been married for many years. He has no children. My mother is still living and quite active despite her advanced age (she is ninety-six). She lives in the vicinity of Huskvarna. We seldom see each other. My nine sisters and brothers are dead, but they left a number of children and grandchildren. I have very little contact with my relatives. My wife Karin died many years ago. Our marriage was quite unhappy. I am fortunate in having a good housekeeper.

This is all I have to say about myself. Perhaps I ought to add that I am an old pedant, and at times quite trying, both to myself and to the people who have to be around me. I detest emotional outbursts, women's tears and the crying of children. On the whole, I find loud noises and sudden startling occurrences most disconcerting.

Later I will come back to the reason for writing this story, which is, as nearly as I can make it, a true account of the events, dreams and thoughts which befell me on a certain day.

In the early morning of Saturday, the first of June, I had a strange and very unpleasant dream. I dreamed that I was taking my usual morning stroll through the streets. It was quite early and no human being was in sight. This was a bit surprising to me. I also noted that there were no vehicles parked along the curbs. The city seemed strangely deserted, as if it were a holiday morning in the middle of summer.

The sun was shining brightly and made sharp black

shadows, but it gave off no warmth. Even though I walked on the sunny side, I felt chilly.

The stillness was also remarkable. I usually stroll along a broad, tree-lined boulevard, and even before sunrise the sparrows and crows are as a rule extremely noisy. Besides, there is always the perpetual roar from the center of the city. But this morning nothing was heard, the silence was absolute, and my footsteps echoed almost anxiously against the walls of the buildings. I began to wonder what had happened.

Just at that moment I passed the shop of a watchmaker optometrist, whose sign had always been a large clock that gave the exact time. Under this clock hung a picture of a pair of giant eyeglasses with staring eyes. On my morning walks I had always smiled to myself at this slightly grotesque detail in the street scene.

To my amazement, the hands of the clock had disappeared. The dial was blank, and below it someone had smashed both of the eyes so that they looked like watery, infected sores.

Instinctively I pulled out my own watch to check the time, but I found that my old reliable gold timepiece had also lost its hands. I held it to my ear to find out if it was still ticking. Then I heard my heart beat. It was pounding very fast and irregularly. I was overwhelmed by an inexplicable feeling of frenzy.

I put my watch away and leaned for a few moments against the wall of a building until the feeling had passed. My heart calmed down and I decided to return home.

To my joy, I saw that someone was standing on the street corner. His back was toward me. I rushed up to him and touched his arm. He turned quickly and to my horror I found that the man had no face under his soft felt hat.

I pulled my hand back and in the same moment the entire figure collapsed as if it were made of dust or frail splinters. On the sidewalk lay a pile of clothes. The person himself had disappeared without a trace.

I looked around in bewilderment and realized that I must have lost my way. I was in a part of the city where I had never been before.

I stood on an open square surrounded by high, ugly apartment buildings. From this narrow square, streets spread out in all directions. Everyone was dead; there was not a sign of a living soul.

High above me the sun shone completely white, and light forced its way down between the houses as if it were the blade of a razor-sharp knife. I was so cold that my entire body shivered.

Finally I found the strength to move again and chose one of the narrow streets at random. I walked as quickly as my pounding heart allowed, yet the street seemed to be endless.

Then I heard the tolling of bells and suddenly I was standing on another open square near an unattractive little church of red brick. There was no graveyard next to it and the church was surrounded on all sides by gray-walled buildings.

Not far from the church a funeral procession was wending its way slowly through the streets, led by an ancient hearse and followed by some old-fashioned hired carriages. These were pulled by pairs of meager-looking horses, weighed down under enormous black shabracks.

I stopped and uncovered my head. It was an intense relief to see living creatures, hear the sound of horses trotting and church bells ringing.

Then everything happened very quickly and so frighteningly that even as I write this I still feel a definite uneasiness.

The hearse was just about to turn in front of the church gate when suddenly it began to sway and rock like a ship in a storm. I saw that one of the wheels had come loose and was rolling toward me with a loud clatter. I had to throw myself to one side to avoid being hit. It struck the church wall right behind me and splintered into pieces.

The other carriages stopped at a distance but no one got out or came to help. The huge hearse swayed and teetered on its three wheels. Suddenly the coffin was thrown out and fell into the street. As if relieved, the hearse straightened and rolled on toward a side street, followed by the other carriages.

The tolling of the church bells had stopped and I stood alone with the overturned, partly smashed coffin. Gripped by a fearful curiosity, I approached. A hand stuck out from the pile of splintered boards. When I leaned forward, the dead hand clutched my arm and pulled me down toward the casket with enormous force. I struggled helplessly against it as the corpse slowly rose from the coffin. It was a man dressed in a frock coat.

To my horror, I saw that the corpse was myself. I tried to free my arm, but he held it in a powerful grip. All this time he stared at me without emotion and seemed to be smiling scornfully.

In this moment of senseless horror, I awakened and sat up in my bed. It was three in the morning and the sun was already reflecting from the rooftops opposite my window. I closed my eyes and I muttered words of reality against my dream—against all the evil and frightening dreams which have haunted me these last few years.

Isak: My name is Isak Borg. I am still alive. I am seventy-six years old. I really feel quite well.

When I had muttered these words I felt calmer, drank a glass of water, and lay down to ponder on the day which was ahead of me. I knew immediately what I should do. I got out of bed, pulled open the curtains, found the weather radiant, and breathed in the fine morning air. Then I put on my robe and went through the apartment (where the clocks were striking three) to the room of my old house-keeper. When I opened the door she sat up immediately, wide awake.

AGDA: Are you ill, Professor?

ISAK: Listen, Miss Agda, will you please prepare some break-fast? I'm taking the car.

AGDA: You're taking the car, Professor?

ISAK: Yes, I'll drive down to Lund with my own two hands. I've never believed in airplanes.

AGDA: Dear Professor! Go back to sleep and I'll bring you coffee at nine o'clock and then we'll start at ten, as was decided.

ISAK: Very well then, I'll go without eating.

AGDA: And who's going to pack the frock coat?

ISAK: I'll do that myself.

AGDA: And what will become of me?

ISAK: Miss Agda, you can go with me in the car or take the airplane—that's up to you.

AGDA: For an entire year I've been looking forward to being present at the ceremony when you become a Jubilee Doctor, and everything was perfectly organized. Now you come and tell me that you're going to drive down instead of going by plane.

ISAK: The presentation is not until five o'clock, and if I leave at once I'll have fourteen hours in which to get there.

AGDA: Everything will be ruined that way. Your son will be waiting at Malmö airport. What will he say?

ISAK: You can make some explanation, Miss Agda.

AGDA: If you take the car, I won't be with you at the ceremony.

ISAK: Now listen, Miss Agda.

AGDA: You can take the car and drive there and destroy the most solemn day of my life . . .

ISAK: We are not married, Miss Agda.

AGDA: I thank God every night that we're not. For seventy-four years I have acted according to my own principles, and they won't fail me today.

ISAK: Is that your last word on this matter, Miss Agda?

AGDA: That is my last word. But I'll be saying a lot to myself about mean old gentlemen who think only of themselves and never about the feelings of others who have served them faithfully for forty years.

ISAK: I really don't know how I've been able to stand your immense hunger for power all these years.

AGDA: Just tell me and it can be ended tomorrow.

ISAK: Anyway, I'm going to drive, and you may do whatever the hell you want to. I'm a grown man and I don't have to put up with your bossiness.

Our last words, I must admit, were spoken rather loudly, partly because of Miss Agda's unruly temper and partly because I had gone to the bathroom, where I shaved and completed my morning toilet. When I came out of the bathroom, I found to my surprise that Miss Agda was busy packing my frock coat and other necessities. She seemed to have come to her senses and I tried a friendly pat on the back to make her understand that I had forgiven her.

ISAK: There is no one who can pack like you.

AGDA: Is that so.

ISAK: Old sourpuss.

I was very angry that she didn't answer. True, my last words weren't very well chosen, but Miss Agda has a way of being cross which would try the patience of a saint.

AGDA: Should I boil a couple of eggs to go with the coffee, sir?

Isak: Yes, thank you, that's very kind of you, Miss Agda. Thank you, dear Miss Agda.

Without noticing my efforts to be nice in spite of everything, the old lady disappeared into the kitchen.

Isak: Jubilee Doctor! Damn stupidity. The faculty could just as well make me jubilee idiot. I'm going to buy something for the old sourpuss to sweeten her up a little. I hate people who are slow to forget. I can't even hurt a fly; how could I ever hurt Miss Agda?

Then she appeared in the doorway.

Agda: Do you want toast?
Isak: No, thank you for everything. Don't trouble yourself over me.
Agda: Why are *you* sour?

I didn't have time to answer before the door closed in my face. I dressed and went into the dining room, where my breakfast was waiting. The morning sun threw a bright stripe across the dining-room table. Miss Agda puttered about quietly with a coffee pot and poured steaming coffee into my personal cup.

Isak: Won't you have a cup too?
Agda: No, thanks.

Miss Agda went over to water the flowers in the window and turned her back to me quite naturally but in a very definite way. Then the door of a nearby room opened and my daughter-in-law, Marianne, entered. She was still wearing pajamas and was smoking a cigarette.

Isak: May I ask why my esteemed daughter-in-law is out of bed at this hour of the morning?

MARIANNE: It's a little difficult to sleep when you and Miss Agda are shouting at each other loud enough to shake the walls.

ISAK: Surely no one here has been shouting.

AGDA: Of course not, no one here has been shouting.

MARIANNE: You're going by car to Lund.

ISAK: Yes, I think so.

MARIANNE: May I go with you?

ISAK: What? You want to go home?

MARIANNE: Yes, I want to go home.

ISAK: Home to Evald?

MARIANNE: That's it. You don't have to ask my reasons. If I could afford it, I would take the train.

ISAK: Of course you can go with me.

MARIANNE: I'll be ready in about ten minutes.

Marianne put out her cigarette in an ash tray on the table, went into her room and closed the door. Agda brought another cup but said nothing. We were both surprised but had to remain silent about Marianne's sudden decision to go home to my son Evald. Nevertheless, I felt obliged to shake my head.

AGDA: Good Lord!

Shortly after half past three, I drove my car out of the garage. Marianne came out through the front gate dressed in slacks and a short jacket (she is a stately young woman). I looked up toward the window to see if Agda was standing there. She was. I waved to her but she did not wave back. Angrily I got into the car, slammed the door and started the engine. Silently we left the quiet, sleeping city. Marianne was about to light a cigarette.

ISAK: Please don't smoke.

MARIANNE: Of course.

ISAK: I can't stand cigarette smoke.

MARIANNE: I forgot.

ISAK: Besides, cigarette smoking is both expensive and un-healthy. There should be a law against women smoking.

MARIANNE: The weather is nice.

ISAK: Yes, but oppressive. I have a feeling that we'll have a storm.

MARIANNE: So do I.

ISAK: Now take the cigar. Cigars are an expression of the fundamental idea of smoking. A stimulant and a relaxa-tion. A manly vice.

MARIANNE: And what vices may a woman have?

ISAK: Crying, bearing children, and gossiping about the neighbors.

MARIANNE: How old are you really, Father Isak?

ISAK: Why do you want to know?

MARIANNE: No real reason. Why?

ISAK: I know why you asked.

MARIANNE: Oh.

ISAK: Don't pretend. You don't like me and you never have.

MARIANNE: I know you only as a father-in-law.

ISAK: Why are you going home again?

MARIANNE: An impulse. That's all.

ISAK: Evald happens to be my son.

MARIANNE: Yes, I'm sure he is.

ISAK: So, it may not be so strange that I ask you.

MARIANNE: This is something which really does not con-cern you.

ISAK: Do you want to hear my opinion?

She provoked me with her unshakable calm and re-moteness. Besides, I was very curious and a little worried.

ISAK: Evald and I are very much alike. We have our princi-ples.

MARIANNE: You don't have to tell me.

Isak: This *loan* for example. Evald got a loan from me with which to complete his studies. He was to have paid it back when he became a lecturer at the university. It became a matter of honor for him to pay it back at the rate of five thousand per year. Although I realize that it's difficult for him, a bargain is a bargain.

Marianne: For us it means that we can never have a holiday together and that your son works himself to death.

Isak: You have an income of your own.

Marianne: . . . Especially when you're stinking rich and have no need for the money.

Isak: A bargain is a bargain, my dear Marianne. And I know that Evald understands and respects me.

Marianne: That may be true, but he also hates you.

Her calm, almost matter-of-fact tone startled me. I tried to look into her eyes, but she stared straight ahead and her face remained expressionless.

Isak: Evald and I have never coddled each other.

Marianne: I believe you.

Isak: I'm sorry that you dislike me, because I rather like you.

Marianne: That's nice.

Isak: Tell me, what do you really have against me?

Marianne: Do you want me to be frank?

Isak: Please.

Marianne: You are an old egotist, Father. You are completely inconsiderate and you have never listened to anyone but yourself. All this is well hidden behind your mask of old-fashioned charm and your friendliness. But you are hard as nails, even though everyone depicts you as a great humanitarian. We who have seen you at close range, we know what you really are. You can't fool us. For instance, do you remember when I came to you a month ago? I had some idiotic idea that you would help Evald and me. So I asked to stay with you for a few weeks. Do you remember what you said?

ISAK: I told you that you were most cordially welcome.

MARIANNE: This is what you really said, but I'm sure you've forgotten: Don't try to pull me into your marital problems because I don't give a damn about them, and everyone has his own troubles.

ISAK: Did I say that?

MARIANNE: You said more than that.

ISAK: That was the worst, I hope.

MARIANNE: This is what you said, word for word: I have no respect for suffering of the soul, so don't come to me and complain. But if you need spiritual masturbation, I can make an appointment for you with some good quack, or perhaps with a minister, it's so popular these days.

ISAK: Did I say that?

MARIANNE: You have rather inflexible opinions, Father. It would be terrible to have to depend on you in any way.

ISAK: Is that so. Now, if I am honest, I must say that I've enjoyed having you around the house.

MARIANNE: Like a cat.

ISAK: Like a cat, or a human being, it's the same thing. You are a fine young woman and I'm sorry that you dislike me.

MARIANNE: I don't dislike you.

ISAK: Oh.

MARIANNE: I feel sorry for you.

I could hardly keep from laughing at her odd tone of voice and lack of logic. She herself laughed, by the way, and it cleared the air a bit.

ISAK: I really would like to tell you about a dream I had this morning.

MARIANNE: I'm not very interested in dreams.

ISAK: No, perhaps not.

We drove for a while in silence. The sun stood high in the sky and the road was brilliantly white. Suddenly I had an impulse. I slowed down and swung the car into a small side road on the left, leading down to the sea. It was a twisting, forest road, bordered by piles of newly cut timber which smelled strongly in the heat of the sun. Marianne looked up, a bit surprised, but remained silent. I parked the car in a curve of the road.

IsAK: Come, I'll show you something.

She sighed quietly and followed me down the little hill to the gate. Now we could see the large yellow house set among the birch trees, with its terrace facing the bay. The house slept behind closed doors and drawn blinds.

IsAK: Every summer for the first twenty years of my life we lived out here. There were ten of us children. Yes, you probably know that.
MARIANNE: What a ridiculous old house.
IsAK: It is an antique.
MARIANNE: Do people live here now?
IsAK: Not this summer.
MARIANNE: I'll go down to the water and take a dip if you don't mind. We have lots of time.
IsAK: I'll go over to the wild-strawberry patch for a moment.

I suddenly found that I was speaking without a listener. Marianne was lazily making her way down to the beach.

IsAK: The old strawberry patch. . . .

I went toward the house and immediately found the spot, but it seemed to be much smaller and less impressive than I had remembered. There were still many wild straw-

berries, however. I sat down next to an old apple tree that
stood alone and ate the berries, one by one. I may very well
have become a little sentimental. Perhaps I was a little tired
and somewhat melancholy. It's not unlikely that I began
to think about one thing or another that was associated
with my childhood haunts.

I had a strange feeling of solemnity, as if this were a day
of decision. (It was not the only time that day that I was to
feel that way.) The quietness of the summer morning. The
calm bay. The birds' brilliant concert in the foliage. The
old sleeping house. The aromatic apple tree which leaned
slightly, supporting my back. The wild strawberries.

I don't know how it happened, but the day's clear reality
flowed into dreamlike images. I don't even know if it was
a dream, or memories which arose with the force of real
events. I do not know how it began either, but I think that
it was when I heard the playing of a piano.

Astonished, I turned my head and looked at the house,
a short distance up the hill. It had been transformed in a
strange way. The façade, which only a few moments ago
was so blind and shut, was now alive and the sun glittered
on the open windows. White curtains swayed in the warm
summer breeze. The gaudy awnings were rolled halfway
down; smoke came from the chimney. The old summerhouse seemed to be bursting with life. You could hear the
music of the piano (it was something by Waldteufel),
happy voices echoing through the open windows, laughter,
footsteps, the cries of children, the squeaking of the pump.
Someone started to sing up there on the second floor. It
was a strong, almost Italian *bel-canto* tenor. In spite of all
this, not a human being was in sight. For a few moments
the scene still had a feeling of unreality, like a mirage
which could instantly evaporate and be lost in silence.

Suddenly I saw her. When I turned around after looking
at the strangely transformed house I discovered her where
she was kneeling in her sun-yellow cotton dress, picking

wild strawberries. I recognized her immediately and I became excited. She was so close to me that I could touch her, but my lingering feeling of the evanescence of the situation prevented me from making her notice my presence. (I was amused. Mental image or dream or whatever this was, she looked just as I remembered her: a girl in a yellow summer dress, freckled and tanned and glowing with light-hearted young womanhood.)

I sat for a few minutes and silently looked at her. Finally I couldn't help calling out her name, rather quietly but nevertheless quite audibly. She didn't react. I tried once more, a little louder.

ISAK: Sara . . . It's me, your cousin Isak. . . . I've become a little old, of course, and do not quite look as I used to. But you haven't changed the slightest bit. Little cousin, can't you hear me?

She didn't hear me, but eagerly continued to pick the wild strawberries, putting them into a small straw basket. I understood then that one cannot easily converse with one's memories. This discovery did not make me particularly sad. I decided to keep quiet and hoped that this unusual and pleasant situation would last as long as possible.

Then, a boy came strolling down the hill. He was already growing a small mustache despite the fact that he couldn't have been more than eighteen or nineteen years old. He was dressed in a shirt and trousers and wore his student's cap pushed way back on his head. He stepped right behind Sara, took off his glasses and wiped them with a large white handkerchief. (I recognized him as my brother Sigfrid, one year older than myself. We shared many happy moments and troubles. He died, by the way, relatively young, of pyelitis. He was a lecturer in Slavic languages at Uppsala University.)

SIGFRID: Good morning, sweet cousin. What are you doing?
SARA: Can't you see that I'm picking wild strawberries, stupid?
SIGFRID: And who shall be favored with these tasty berries, plucked in the morning watch by a dulcet young maiden?
SARA: Oh you! Don't you know that Uncle Aron's birthday is today? I forgot to prepare a present for him. So, he gets a basket of wild strawberries. That's good enough, isn't it?
SIGFRID: I'll help you.
SARA: You know, Charlotta and Sigbritt have sewn a sampler for him and Angelica has baked a cake and Anna has painted a really pretty picture and Kristina and Birgitta have written a song which they'll sing.
SIGFRID: That's the best of all, because Uncle Aron is stone deaf.
SARA: He will be very happy and you are stupid.
SIGFRID: And the nape of your neck is deuced pretty.

Sigfrid quickly bent over the girl and rather gallantly kissed her on her downy neck. Sara became rather annoyed.

SARA: You know that you're not allowed to do that.
SIGFRID: Who said so?
SARA: I said so. Besides, you are a particularly unbearable little snot who thinks he's something.
SIGFRID: I'm your cousin, and you're sweet on me.
SARA: On you!
SIGFRID: Come here and I'll kiss you on the mouth.
SARA: If you don't keep away I'll tell Isak that you try to kiss me all the time.
SIGFRID: Little Isak. I can beat him easily with one hand tied behind my back.
SARA: Isak and I are secretly engaged. You know that very well.

SIGFRID: Yes, your engagement is so secret that the whole house knows about it.

SARA: Could I help it if the twins ran around and blabbered everything?

SIGFRID: Then when are you going to get married? When are you going to get married? When are you going to get married? When are you going to get married?

SARA: I'll tell you one thing, of your four brothers I can't decide which is the least vain. But I think it's Isak. In any case, he's the kindest. And you are the most awful, the most unbearable, the most stupid, the most idiotic, the most ridiculous, the most cocky—I can't think of enough names to call you.

SIGFRID: Admit that you're a little sweet on me.

SARA: Besides, you smoke smelly cigars.

SIGFRID: That's a man's smell, isn't it?

SARA: Besides, the twins, who know *everything*, say that you've done *rather* nasty things with the oldest Berglund girl. And she's not a *really nice* girl, the twins say. And I believe them.

SIGFRID: If you only knew how pretty you are when you blush like that. Now you must kiss me. I can't stand it any more. I'm completely in love with you, now that I think about it.

SARA: Oh, that's only talk. The twins say that you're crazy about girls. Is it really true?

Suddenly he kissed her hard and rather skillfully. She was carried away by this game and returned his kiss with a certain fierceness. But then she was conscience-stricken and threw herself down on the ground, knocking over the basket of wild strawberries. She was very angry and began crying with excitement.

SIGFRID: Don't scream. Someone might come.

SARA: Look at the wild strawberries, all spilled. And what

will Isak say? He is so kind and really loves me. Oh, how sorry I am, oh, what you've done to me. You've turned me into a bad woman, at least *nearly*. Go away. I don't want to see you any more, at least not before breakfast. I have to hurry. Help me pick up the strawberries. And look, I have a spot on my gown.

Then the gong suddenly sounded, announcing that breakfast was being served. The sound seemed to bring forth many human beings not far from where I stood, an astonished onlooker.

The flag with the Swedish-Norwegian Union emblem went up and instantly stiffened against the light summer clouds; big brother Hagbart, dressed in his cadet uniform, handled the ropes expertly. From the bathhouse one could hear wild laughter, and through the louvered door tumbled two redheaded girls about thirteen years old, as identical as two wild strawberries. They laughed so hard they could hardly walk, and they whispered things to each other that were apparently both very secret and quite amusing. Sigbritt, tall and lanky, with thick hair in heavy rolls across her forehead, came out carrying the baby's bassinet and placed it in the shadow of the arbor. Charlotta (the diligent, self-sacrificing sister who carried the responsibilities of the household on her round shoulders) rushed out on the veranda and shouted to Sara and Sigfrid to hurry. Seventeen-year-old Benjamin dived out of some bushes, his pimply face red from the sun, and looked around with an annoyed expression. In his hand he held a thick, open book. Angelica (the beauty of the family) came skipping out of the woods, joined the twins, and was immediately made part of some hilarious secret. Finally, fifteen-year-old Anna came running out of the house, asked Hagbart about something, then raised her voice and started to shout for Isak. I arose, surprised and worried, unable to answer her cry.

TWINS (*in unison*): I think that Isak is out fishing with Father and they probably can't hear the gong. And Father said, by the way, that we shouldn't wait to eat. That's what Father said, I definitely remember.

Oh, yes, Father and I were out fishing together. I felt a secret and completely inexplicable happiness at this message, and I stood for a long while wondering what I should do in this new old world which I was suddenly given the opportunity to visit.

The rest of the family had entered the house and something was being discussed quite loudly inside. Only Sigbritt's little child remained on the terrace, sleeping in the shadows of the tall lilac bushes.

Curiosity overwhelmed me. I went slowly up the slope toward the house and soon found myself in the long, dark corridor which was connected with the foyer by glass doors. From there I had a good view into the large, sunlit dining room with its white table already set for breakfast, the light furniture, the wallpaper, the figurines, the palms, the airy summer curtains, the scoured white wooden floor with its broad planks and blue rag rugs, the pictures and the sampler, the large, crownlike chandelier.

There they were now, my nine brothers and sisters, my aunt, and Uncle Aron. The only ones missing were Father, Mother and I.

Everyone was standing behind his chair, with lowered head, and hands clenched together. Aunt recited the prayer "In Jesus' name to the table we go/, Bless You for the food You bestow." After which the whole troop sat down with much chatter and scraping of chairs. My aunt (a stately woman in her best years, endowed with a powerful sense of authority and a resonant voice) demanded silence.

AUNT: Benjamin will immediately go and wash his hands.

How long is it going to take you to learn cleanliness?
BENJAMIN: I *have* washed my hands.
AUNT: Sigbritt, pass the porridge to Angelica and give the twins their portions. Your fingernails are coal-black. Pass me the bread, Hagbart. Who taught you to spread so much butter on the bread? Can you do that at the military academy? Charlotta, the salt shaker is stopped up. How often have I told you that it shouldn't be left out in the open, because the salt gets humid.
BENJAMIN: *I have washed my hands,* but I have paint under my nails.
UNCLE ARON: Who has picked wild strawberries for me?
SARA: I have. (*Louder*) I have.
AUNT: You have to speak up, my child. You know that Uncle Aron is a bit hard of hearing.
SARA (*thunderously*): I have!
ARON: Oh my, you remembered Uncle Aron's birthday. That was really very kind of you.
HAGBART: Couldn't Uncle Aron have a little drink for breakfast in honor of the day?
AUNT: A drink at breakfast when Father isn't home is completely out of the question.
TWINS (*in unison*): Uncle Aron has already had three drinks. I know. I know. We saw him at eight o'clock when we went down to the bathhouse.
AUNT: The twins should hold their tongues and eat. Besides, you haven't made your beds and as punishment you'll have to dry the dinner silverware. Benjamin must not bite his nails. Don't sit and jump on the chair, Anna. You aren't a child any more.
ANNA: I want to give Uncle Aron my picture, please, Auntie. Can't we give him our presents now, right away?
AUNT: Where is your picture?
ANNA: Here under the table.
AUNT: You'll have to wait until we've eaten.
SIGFRID: It's a very advanced work of art, I'd say. It's a pic-

ture of Tristan and Isolde, but you can't tell for sure which one is Tristan.

SARA: Oh, he always spoils things, the little fop! Now he's making Anna unhappy. See if she doesn't start to cry.

ANNA: Not at all. I can overlook Sigfrid's faults.

TWINS (*together*): By the way, what were Sara and Sigfrid up to in the wild-strawberry patch this morning? We saw everything from the bathhouse.

SIGBRITT: Calm down now, children!

CHARLOTTA: Someone should put gags on the twins.

AUNT: Twins, keep still or leave the table.

BENJAMIN: Doesn't a person have freedom of expression, eh?

SIGFRID: Shut up, you snotnoses.

ANGELICA: Sara is blushing, Sara is blushing, Sara is blushing.

TWINS: Sigfrid is blushing, too. Ha-ha! Sigfrid and Sara! Sigfrid and Sara! Sigfrid and Sara!

AUNT (*thunderously*): Quiet! We'll have quiet at the table!

ARON: What did you say? Of course we shall be happy.

The twins snicker in the silence. Sara throws the porridge spoon at her tormentors.

CHARLOTTA: But, Sara!

SARA: They're just lying! They're liars!

Sara rose from the table so violently that her chair turned over. She stood hesitantly for a moment, her face red and tears splashing down her cheeks. Then she ran away furiously, throwing herself at the door and out into the foyer.

She opened the glass door and disappeared out on the porch, where I could hear her sobbing violently. Gentle Charlotta came out of the dining room and went past me on her way to console Sara.

I could hear their voices from the darkness of the foyer and I came closer stealthily. Sara sat on a red stool (which Grandmother once used, when she wanted to take off her rubber boots) while Charlotta stood in front of her, patting her gently on the head. The miserable girl pressed her tear-stained face against Charlotta's skirt over and over again. The tinted light from the stained-glass windows of the outer door painted the whole picture in a strange way.

SARA: Isak is so refined. He is so enormously refined and moral and sensitive and he wants us to read poetry together and he talks about the after-life and wants to play duets on the piano and he likes to kiss only in the dark and he talks about sinfulness. I think he is extremely intellectual and morally aloof and I feel so worthless, and I *am* so worthless, you can't deny that. But sometimes I get the feeling that I'm much older than Isak, do you know what I mean? And then I think he's a child even if we are the same age, and then Sigfrid is so fresh and exciting and I want to go home. I don't want to be here all summer, to be a laughingstock for the twins and the rest of you—*no, I don't want that.*
CHARLOTTA: I'll talk to Sigfrid, I will! If he doesn't leave you alone I'll see to it that he gets a few more chores to do. Father will arrange that without any trouble. He also thinks Sigfrid is nasty and needs a little work to keep him out of mischief.
SARA: Poor little Isak, he is so kind to me. Oh, how unfair everything is.
CHARLOTTA: Everything will work out for the best, you'll see. Listen, now they're singing for Uncle Aron.
SARA: Isn't it crazy to write a song for a deaf man! That's typical of the twins.

Then two girlish voices sang a song that could be heard throughout the house. Charlotta placed her arm around Sara's shoulders, and Sara blew her nose quite loudly. Both girls returned to the dining room, where the mood had become very lively. Uncle Aron had arisen, his round perspiring face lit like a lantern, and he had tears in his eyes. He held a sheet of music before him while the twins stood nearby and sang with all their might. When they had finished everyone applauded, and Uncle Aron kissed them on the forehead and wiped his face with a napkin. My aunt rose from the table and proposed a quadruple cheer. Everyone got up and hurrahed. Suddenly Anna shouted and pointed out the window. Everyone turned to look.

ANNA: Look, here comes Father.
AUNT: Well, finally! Sigbritt, take out the porridge bowl and have it warmed. Charlotta, you bring up more milk from the cellar.

The women fussed around, but Sara ran out of the house, down the slope, and disappeared behind the small arbor which stood on the edge of the birch-tree pasture. I followed her with curiosity, but lost her. Suddenly I stood alone at the wild-strawberry patch. A feeling of emptiness and sadness came over me. I was awakened by a girl's voice asking me something. I looked up.

In front of me stood a young lady in shorts and a boy's checked shirt. She was very tanned, and her blond hair was tangled and bleached by the sun and the sea. She sucked on an unlit pipe, wore wooden sandals on her feet and dark glasses on her nose.

SARA: Is this your shack?
ISAK: No, it isn't.
SARA: It's a good thing you're the truthful type. My old man owns the whole peninsula . . . including the shack.
ISAK: I lived here once. Two hundred years ago.
SARA: Uh huh. Is that your jalopy standing up at the gate?
ISAK: It's my jalopy, yes.

SARA: Looks like an antique.

ISAK: It *is* an antique, just like its owner.

SARA: You've got a sense of humor about yourself, too. That's fantastic. Where are you heading, by the way? In which direction, I mean.

ISAK: I'm going to Lund.

SARA: What a fantastic coincidence. I'm on my way to Italy.

ISAK: I'd feel very honored if you came along.

SARA: My name is Sara. Silly name, isn't it?

ISAK: My name is Isak. Rather silly too.

SARA: Weren't they married?

ISAK: Unfortunately not. It was Abraham and Sara.

SARA: Shall we take off?

ISAK: I have another lady with me. Here she comes. This is Sara, and this is Marianne. We'll have company to Lund. Sara is going to Italy but she has agreed to travel part way with us.

SARA: Now you're being ironic again, but it suits you.

We began walking toward the car. Marianne and I exchanged amused glances, the first contact between us. When we came to the car, two young men with round blond crew-cut heads popped up. They were also wearing checked shirts, shorts, wooden sandals and sunglasses. Each carried a rucksack.

SARA: Hey, fellows. I've got a lift nearly all the way to Italy. This is Anders, and this one with the glasses is Viktor, called Vicke . . . and this is Father Isak.

VIKTOR: Hello.

ISAK: Hello.

ANDERS: How do you do, sir.

ISAK: Hello.

SARA: That cookie you're staring at so hard, her name is Marianne.

MARIANNE: Hello.
BOYS (*together*): Hello.
SARA: It's a pretty big car.
ISAK: Just jump in. There's room for everybody. We can put the baggage in the trunk, if you don't mind.

We packed things away, and then we all got into the car. I drove carefully, leaving my childhood world behind. Sara took off her sunglasses and laughed. She was very much like her namesake of the past.

SARA: Of course I have to tell Isak that Anders and I are going steady. We are crazy about each other. Viktor is with us as a chaperon. That was decided by the old man. Viktor is also in love with me and is watching Anders like a madman. This was a brilliant idea of my old man. I'll probably have to seduce Viktor to get him out of the way. I'd better tell Isak that I'm a virgin. That's why I can talk so brazenly.

I looked at her through the rear-view mirror. She was sitting comfortably with her legs on the backs of the folding seats. Anders had a proprietary arm around her shoulders and looked rather angry, for which I could hardly blame him. Viktor, on the other hand, seemed completely disinterested and stared fixedly at the nape of Marianne's neck —and whatever else he could glimpse of her figure.

SARA: I smoke a pipe. Viktor says it's healthier. He's crazy about everything that's healthy.

No one answered, or considered any comment necessary. We continued our trip in a silence which was by no means unpleasant, just a little shy. The weather had become quite warm, almost oppressive, and we had opened all the windows. The road was broad and straight. I was in a spirited mood. The day had been full of stimulating surprises.

ISAK: I had a first love whose name was Sara.
SARA: She was like me, of course.
ISAK: As a matter of fact, she was rather like you.
SARA: What happened to her?
ISAK: She married my brother Sigfrid and had six children. Now she's seventy-five years old and a rather beautiful little old lady.
SARA: I can't imagine anything worse than getting old. Oh, excuse me. I think I said something stupid.

Her tone was so sincerely repentant that everyone burst into laughter. And then it happened.

We were on a broad, blind right curve. I kept hard to the left and at that moment a little black car came speeding straight toward us. I had time to see Marianne brace her right hand against the windshield and I heard Sara scream. Then I slammed on the brakes with all my strength. Our big car skidded to the left and went off the road into a pasture. The black car disappeared with a squeal, rolled over and fell into a deep ditch to the right of the road. Startled, we stared at one another; we had escaped without a scratch. Some thick black tire tracks and several big marks on the road surface were the only signs of the other car. A short distance away, a couple of rotating front wheels stuck up from the ditch.

All of us began running toward it and then stopped in astonishment. The overturned car's radio sang a morning hymn. Two people crawled out of the ditch, a man and a woman, in the midst of a violent quarrel which was on the verge of coming to blows. When they saw us watching they immediately stopped and the man limped toward me.

ALMAN: How are you? There's nothing for me to say. The

blame is completely ours. We have no excuses. It was my wife who was driving. Are you all right? Everyone safe and sound? Thank God for that.

He mumbled nervously, took off his eyeglasses and put them on again, and looked at us with frightened glances.

ALMAN: The would-be murderers should introduce themselves. Alman is my name. I'm an engineer at the Stockholm electric power plant. Back there is my wife, Berit. She used to be an actress, and it was that fact we were discussing when . . . when . . . when . . .

He interrupted himself with an artificial laugh and waved at his wife. When she remained motionless, he took a few limping steps toward her.

ISAK: How is your leg?
ALMAN: It's not from this. I've been crippled for years. Unfortunately it's not only my leg that's crippled, according to my wife. Come here now, Berit, and make your apologies.

The woman mustered her courage. She moved jerkily in spite of her rotund body.

BERIT: Please, pretty please forgive me, as children say. It was my fault, everything. I was just going to hit my husband when that curve appeared. One thing is obvious: God punishes some people immediately—or what do you think, Sten? You're a Catholic.
ISAK: Perhaps we should take a look at your car and see if we can't put it right side up again.
ALMAN: Please don't trouble yourself over us. I beg of you.
BERIT: Shut up now, Sten darling. Some people do have completely unselfish intentions, even if you don't believe it.

ALMAN: My wife is a little nervous, I think. But we've had a shock. That's the word. A shock.

He laughed once more and tore off his glasses and put them on again. The young men had already jumped down into the ditch and were trying to lift the little car. Marianne ran back to our car and backed it down the road. With the help of a rope which I always carry in the trunk, we succeeded in getting the other car on an even keel. Mr. Alman suddenly cheered up, threw off his jacket and rolled up his shirt sleeves. Then he put his shoulder alongside Sara, Viktor and Anders and began to push.

BERIT: Now watch the engineer closely, see how he matches his strength with the young boys, how he tenses his feeble muscles to impress the pretty girl. Sten darling, watch out that you don't have a hemorrhage.
ALMAN: My wife loves to embarrass me in front of strangers. I let her—it's psychotherapy.

We towed and shoved and pushed and suddenly the little car was standing on the road. By then, of course, its radio had gone dead. Alman sat down behind the wheel of the dented car and got the motor started. The car had gone a few feet when one of the front wheels rolled off abruptly and slid far down into the ravine.

BERIT: A true picture of our marriage.

Alman stood hesitantly on the gleaming white road, perspiring nervously. Marianne, who had stayed out of the whole scene, was still sitting behind the wheel of our car. The youngsters sat down at the edge of the road. All of us were a little upset.

ISAK: I can't see any other way out. The lady and the gen-

tleman must ride with us to the nearest gas station. There
you can telephone for help.

ALMAN: Don't trouble yourself over us. We'll have a refreshing walk. Won't we, Berit?

BERIT: With his leg. Dear Lord, that would be a scream.

ALMAN: In her delightful way my wife has just said thank
you for both of us.

Silently we climbed into the car, which was suddenly
completely filled. (Marianne drove; I sat beside her. Mr.
and Mrs. Alman were on the folding seats. The three
youngsters occupied the back seat.) Alman whistled some
popular tune softly but soon fell silent. No one had any
particular desire to converse. Marianne drove very calmly
and carefully.

Suddenly Berit Alman started to cry. Her husband carefully put his arm around her shoulders, but she drew away
and pulled out a handkerchief, which she began tearing
with her fingernails.

ALMAN: I can never tell if my wife is really crying or putting on an act. Dammit, I think these are real tears. Well,
that's the way it is when you see death staring you in the
face.

BERIT: Can't you shut up?

ALMAN: My wife has unusual powers of the imagination.
For two years she made me believe that she had cancer and
pestered all our friends with all kinds of imaginary symp-
toms, despite the fact that the doctors couldn't find anything the matter. She was so convincing that we believed
her more than the doctors. That's pretty clever, admit it.
It's such stuff that saints are made of! Look, now she's crying about a death scare. It's a pity we don't have a movie
camera around. Lights! Action! Camera! It's a "take," as
they say in the film world.

MARIANNE: It's understandable that you're upset, Mr. Alman, but how about leaving your wife alone for a little while?

ALMAN: A woman's tears are meant for women. Don't criticize a woman's tears; they're holy. You are beautiful, dear Miss whatever your name is. But Berit here is beginning to get a little shabby. That's why you can afford to defend her.

MARIANNE: Allow me to feel compassion for your wife for different reasons.

ALMAN: Very sarcastic! Still, you don't seem to be at all hysterical. But Berit is a genius at hysterics. Do you know what that means from my point of view?

MARIANNE: You're a Catholic, aren't you? That's what your wife said.

ALMAN: Quite right. That is my way of enduring. I ridicule my wife and she ridicules me. She has her hysterics and I have my Catholicism. But we need each other's company. It's only out of pure selfishness that we haven't murdered each other by now.

Berit turned toward her husband and slapped his face. He dropped his glasses, which he had fortunately just taken off. His large nose swelled and began to bleed. His froglike mouth twitched spasmodically as if he were on the verge of tears, but he immediately got control of himself, pulled out a handkerchief and pressed it to his nose, blinked his eyes and laughed. Viktor leaned forward, picked up the glasses and slowly handed them to him.

ALMAN: Right on the beat. It's called syncopation, isn't it? Ha-ha! Isn't it comic? If I had a stop watch, I could have timed the explosion on the nose.

BERIT (screams): Shut up! Shut up! Shut up!

Marianne turned pale. She applied the brakes and slowly stopped the car.

MARIANNE: Maybe this is the terrible truth and maybe it's just what's called letting off steam. But we have three children in the car and for their sake may I ask the lady and the gentleman to get out immediately. There is a house back there; maybe they have a telephone. The walk won't be too strenuous.

All of us were silent after Marianne's speech. Without another word, Sten Alman stepped out of the car. His face was ashen gray and his nose was still bleeding. His wife looked at us and suddenly made a heroic attempt to say something sincere.

BERIT: Forgive us if you can.

Then Berit got out and stood by her husband, who had turned his back on us. He had pulled out a comb and a pocket mirror and was straightening the hair on his white scalp. His wife took his bloody handkerchief and blew her nose. Then she touched his elbow, but he was suddenly very tired and hung his head. They sat down close to each other by the road. They looked like two scolded schoolchildren sitting in a corner.

Marianne started the car, and we quickly drove away from this strange marriage.

The gas station between Gränna and Huskvarna lies on a hill with a wide view over a very beautiful, richly foliaged landscape. We stopped to fill up the tank and decided to have lunch at a hotel some kilometers farther south.

It was with mixed feelings that I saw this region again. First, because I began my medical practice here (incidentally, it lasted for fifteen years; I succeeded the local doctor). Second, because my old mother lives near here in a large house. She is ninety-six now and is generally considered a miracle of health and vitality, although her ability to move around has diminished considerably during the last few years.

The gas-station owner was a big, blond man with a broad face, abnormally large hands and long arms.

ÅKERMAN: Ah ha! So the doctor is out driving. Shall it be a full tank? Well, well, so it is, and those are children and grandchildren, I know. Have you got the key to the gas tank, Doctor?

ISAK: Hello, Henrik. You recognize me.

ÅKERMAN: Recognize! Doctor, you were there when I was born. And then you delivered all my brothers. And fixed our cuts and scratches and took care of us, as you did of everybody while you were a doctor around here.

ISAK: And things are going well for you?

ÅKERMAN: Couldn't be better! I'm married, you know, and I have heirs. (*Shouts*) Eva!

Eva came out of the gas station. She was a young woman, gypsy-like, dark, with long, thick hair and a generous smile. She was in an advanced stage of pregnancy.

ÅKERMAN: Here you see Dr. Borg himself in person. This is the man that Ma and Pa and the whole district still talk about. The world's best doctor.

I looked at Marianne, who was standing to the side. She applauded somewhat sarcastically and bowed. The three youngsters were in the midst of a lively dispute and pointing in different directions. Eva stepped up and shook my hand.

ÅKERMAN: I suggest that we name our new baby for the doctor. Isak Åkerman is a good name for a prime minister.

EVA: But what if it's a girl?

ÅKERMAN: Eva and I only make boys. Do you want oil and water too?

Isak: Yes, thank you. And your father is well, in spite of his bad back?

Åkerman: Well, it's getting a bit hard for the old man, you know, but the old lady is a little bombshell.

The last was said in greatest confidence as we bent over the measuring rod to see if we needed more oil. We did.

Åkerman: And now you'll be visiting *your* mother, eh, Doctor?

Isak: I suppose so.

Åkerman: She's a remarkable lady, your mother, although she must be at least ninety-five.

Isak: Ninety-six.

Åkerman: Well, well, how about that.

Isak: How much is all this?

Åkerman: Eva and I want it to be on the house.

Isak: No, I can't allow that.

Åkerman: Don't insult us, Doctor! We can do things in the grand manner too, even if we live here in little Gränna.

Isak: There isn't the slightest reason you should pay for my gas. I appreciate your kindness, but . . .

Åkerman: One remembers things, you know. One doesn't forget one's gratitude, and there are some things that can never be paid back.

Åkerman became a little serious and I a little sentimental. We looked at each other quite moved. Eva stepped up and stood beside her husband. She squinted in the sun and beamed like a big strawberry in her red dress.

Eva (*like an echo*): No, we don't forget. We don't forget.

Åkerman: Just ask anybody in town or in the hills around here, and they remember the doctor and know what the doctor did for them.

I looked around, but Marianne had disappeared. No, she had got into the car. The youngsters were still busy with their discussion.

ISAK: Perhaps I should have remained here.
ÅKERMAN: I don't understand.
ISAK: What? What did you say, Henrik?
ÅKERMAN: You said that you should have stayed here, Doctor.
ISAK: Did I say that? Yes, perhaps. Thank you anyway. Send me word and I may come to be godfather for the new Åkerman. You know where to reach me.

I shook hands with them and we parted. Marianne called the youngsters and we continued our trip to the inn.

Our lunch was a success. We had a large table on the open terrace and enjoyed a most magnificent view across Lake Vättern. The headwaiter, one of my former patients, did everything to satisfy our slightest wish.

I became very lively, I must admit, and told the young-sters about my years as a country doctor. I told them hu-morous anecdotes which had a great deal of human interest. These were a great success (I don't think they laughed just out of politeness) and I had wine with the food (which was excellent) and cognac with my coffee.

Anders suddenly rose and began to recite with both feeling and talent.

ANDERS: "Oh, when such beauty shows itself in each facet of creation, then how beautiful must be the eternal source of this emanation!"

None of us thought of laughing at him. He sat down immediately and emptied his coffee cup in embarrassment. Sara was the one who broke the silence.

SARA: Anders will become a minister and Viktor a doctor.

VIKTOR: We swore that we wouldn't discuss God or science on the entire trip. I consider Anders' lyrical outburst as a breach of our agreement.

SARA: Oh, it was beautiful!

VIKTOR: Besides, I can't understand how a modern man can become a minister. Anders isn't a complete idiot.

ANDERS: Let me tell you, your rationalism is incomprehensible nonsense. And you aren't an idiot either.

VIKTOR: In my opinion the modern—

ANDERS: In my opinion—

VIKTOR: In my opinion a modern man looks his insignificance straight in the eye and believes in himself and his biological death. Everything else is nonsense.

ANDERS: And in my opinion modern man exists only in your imagination. Because man looks at his death with horror and can't bear his own insignificance.

VIKTOR: All right. Religion for the people. Opium for the aching limb. If that's what you want.

SARA: Aren't they fantastically sweet? I always agree with the one who's spoken last. Isn't this all extremely interesting?

VIKTOR (*angry*): When you were a child you believed in Santa Claus. Now you believe in God.

ANDERS: And you have always suffered from an astonishing lack of imagination.

VIKTOR: What do you think about it, Professor?

ISAK: Dear boys, you would receive my opinion with ironic indulgence, whatever I happened to say. That's why I'm keeping still.

SARA: Then think how very unlucky they are.

ISAK: No, Sara. They are very, very lucky.

Marianne laughed and lit my cigar. I leaned back in my chair and squinted at the light filtering down between the table umbrellas. The boys looked surprised as I began to recite.

ISAK: "Where is the friend I seek everywhere? Dawn is the time of loneliness and care. When twilight comes, when twilight comes . . ." What comes after that, Anders?

MARIANNE: "When twilight comes I am still yearning."

ANDERS: "Though my heart is burning, burning. I see His trace of glory . . ."

SARA: You're religious, aren't you, Professor?

ISAK: "I see His trace of glory and power, In an ear of grain and the fragrance of flower . . ."

MARIANNE: "In every sign and breath of air. His love is there. His voice whispers in the summer breeze . . ." (*Silence*)

VIKTOR: As a love poem, it isn't too bad.

SARA: Now I've become very solemn. I can become quite solemn for no reason at all.

I rose from the table.

ISAK: I want to pay a visit to my mother, who happens to live nearby. You can remain here and enjoy yourselves for a while. I'll be back soon.

MARIANNE: May I come with you?

ISAK: Of course. Goodbye for now, young friends.

I was in a good mood and felt very happy. Marianne suddenly took my arm and walked beside me. In passing, I patted her hand.

The house was surrounded by an ancient, parklike garden and protected from onlookers by a wall as tall as a man. Inside, everything was quiet and somewhat unreal. The sky had clouded over, and the gray light sharpened the contours of the landscape so that it looked like a skillfully painted set in an old theater.

In a little round drawing room filled with storm-gray light and graced by light, delicate furniture, an old nurse in uniform sat embroidering. On the carpet next to her chair a fat white poodle lay looking at us with sleepy, lidded eyes. When the nurse saw us she immediately arose, smiling politely, to greet us and shake our hands. She introduced herself as Sister Elisabet. I asked her quietly how my mother was and if it was convenient for us to visit her. Sister Elisabet answered that Mrs. Borg was quite well and would be happy with our visit because she was usually rather lonely. I pointed out that it was unfortunate that my visits were rather infrequent, because of the difficult journey, and Sister Elisabet said that she understood. After this hushed introduction, the Sister asked us to wait for a few minutes and disappeared into a nearby room. Marianne became a little nervous with all the solemnity and pulled out a cigarette from a crushed pack and was just about to light it.

ISAK: Please don't smoke. Mother hates the smell of tobacco and her senses are as sharp as those of an animal in the woods.

At the same moment, Sister Elisabet returned and told us that we were welcome.

The room was rather small and oddly irregular, but it had a lofty ceiling. On the walls hung many beautiful and expensive paintings. Heavy draperies covered the doors. In a corner stood a tall porcelain stove with a fire burning. At the room's only window stood an incongruous desk which did not harmonize with the other pieces of furniture. My mother was sitting in a big chair. She was dressed entirely in black and wore a small lace cap on her head. She was busy entering figures in a large blue ledger. When she recognized me, she immediately rose from her seat (although with some difficulty) and walked toward us with many small steps; she seemed to be shoving one foot in front of the other without her soles ever leaving the floor. She smiled cordially and stretched forth both her hands. I grasped them and then kissed her with a son's reverence.

MOTHER: I just sent a telegram to tell you that I was thinking about you today. Today is your big day. And then you come here!
ISAK: Well, I had a moment of inspiration, Mother!
MOTHER: Is that you wife standing back there, Isak? You will ask her to leave the room immediately. I refuse to talk with her. She has hurt us too much.
ISAK: Mother, darling, this is not Karin. This is Evald's wife, my daughter-in-law, Marianne!
MOTHER: Well, then, she can come here and greet me.
MARIANNE: How do you do, Mrs. Borg. (*Curtsies*)
MOTHER: I've seen you in a photograph. Evald showed it to me. He was extremely proud of your beauty. By the way, why are you out traveling this way?
MARIANNE: I've been in Stockholm, visiting.
MOTHER: Why aren't you home with Evald and taking care of your child?
MARIANNE: Evald and I don't have any children.
MOTHER: Isn't it strange with young people nowadays? I bore ten children. Will someone please bring me that large box standing over there.

She pointed at a brown cardboard box on a chair. Marianne picked it up and placed it on the desk in front of the old lady. Both of us helped lift the lid.

MOTHER: My mother lived in this house before me. And you children often visited here. Do you remember, Isak?
ISAK: I remember quite well.
MOTHER: In this box are some of your toys. I've tried to think which of you owned what.

Mother looked bewilderedly into the big box, as if she

expected to find all her children there among the toys and things. Then she shook her head and looked up at Marianne.

MOTHER: Ten children, and all of them dead except Isak. Twenty grandchildren. None of them visits me except Evald, once a year. It's quite all right—I don't complain —but I have fifteen great-grandchildren whom I've never seen. I send letters and presents for fifty-three birthdays and anniversaries every year. I get kind thank-you notes, but no one visits me except by accident or when someone needs a loan. I am tiresome, of course.

ISAK: Don't look at it that way, Mother dear!

MOTHER: And then I have another fault. I don't die. The inheritance doesn't materialize according to the nice, neat schedules made up by smart young people.

She laughed sarcastically and shook her head. Then she pulled a doll out of the box. It was an old doll, with fine gold hair and a porcelain face (a little scratched) and a beautiful lace gown.

MOTHER: This doll's name is Goldcrown and it belonged to Sigbritt. She got it when she was eight years old. I sewed the dress myself. She never liked it much, so Charlotta took it over and cared for it. I remember it clearly.

She dropped the doll and picked up a little box of bright-colored tin soldiers and poked in it with a small, sharp finger.

MOTHER: Hagbart's tin soldiers. I never liked his war games. He was shot while hunting moose. We never understood each other.

This she said in a matter-of-fact tone, completely without sentimentality. She threw the tin soldiers into the box and fished up a photograph.

MOTHER: Can you see who this is? This is Sigfrid when he was three years old and you when you were two, and here is Father and me. Good Lord, how one looked in those days. It was taken in 1883.

ISAK: May I see that picture?

MOTHER (*uninterested*): Yes, of course, you can have it. It's only trash. Here is a coloring book. Maybe it belonged to the twins, or perhaps to Anna or Angelica. I really don't know because all of them have put their names in the book. And then it says: "I am Anna's best friend." But Anna has written: "I love Angelica." And Kristina has scribbled: "Most of all in the whole world I love Father best." And Birgitta has added: "I am going to marry Father." Isn't that amusing? I laughed when I read it.

Marianne took the book from her and turned the pages. It was partly scribbled on and partly painted with great vitality and strong colors. The light in the small room grew dimmer as the sky darkened outside. In the distance the thunder was already rumbling in the sky. Mother picked up a toy locomotive and looked at it closely.

MOTHER: I think that this is Benjamin's locomotive because he was always so amused by trains and circuses and such things. I suppose that's why he became an actor. We quarreled often about it because I wanted him to have an honest profession. And I was right. He didn't make it. I told him that several times. He didn't believe me, but I was right. It doesn't pay much to talk. Isn't it cold in here? The fire doesn't really warm.

ISAK: No, it isn't particularly cold.

She turned her head toward the darkened skies outside. The trees stood heavy, as if waiting.

MOTHER: I've always felt chilly as long as I can remember. What does that mean? You're a doctor? Mostly in the stomach. Here.

ISAK: You have low blood pressure.

MOTHER: Do you want me to ask Sister Elisabet to make some tea for us so we can sit down and talk for a while? Wouldn't that be . . .

ISAK: No, Mother, thank you. We don't want to trouble you any more. We've just had lunch and we're rather in a hurry.

MOTHER: Look here for a moment. Sigbritt's eldest boy will be fifty. I'm thinking of giving him my father's old gold watch. Can I give it to him, even though the hands have loosened? It is so difficult to find presents for those who have everything. But the watch is beautiful and it can probably be repaired.

She looked anxiously, appealingly, from Marianne to me and back to Marianne. She had opened the lid of the old gold watch and the blank dial stared at me. I suddenly remembered my early-morning dream: the blank clock face and my own watch which lacked hands, the hearse and my dead self.

MOTHER: I remember when Sigbritt's boy had just been born and lay there in his basket in the lilac arbor at the summerhouse. Now he will be fifty years old. And little cousin Sara, who always went around carrying him, cradling him, and who married Sigfrid, that no-good. Now you have to go so that you'll have time for all the things you must do. I'm very grateful for your visit and I hope we'll see each other some time. Give my best regards to Evald. Goodbye.

She offered me her cheek and I bent down and kissed it. It was very cold but unbelievably soft and full of sharp little lines. Marianne curtsied and my mother answered her gesture with an abstract smile. Sister Elisabet opened the door as if she had been listening to us. In a few minutes we were out in the gray daylight, which hurt our eyes with its piercing sharpness.

Once again Marianne took my arm, and when she did so I was filled with gratitude toward this quiet, independent girl with her naked, observant face.

When we reached the inn the youngsters were no longer there. The waitress told us that the young lady was waiting at the car. The headwaiter stood nearby bowing and looking as if he had just had another of his old ulcer attacks.

Sure enough, Sara was leaning against the car looking as though she were ready to cry.

MARIANNE: Where are Anders and Viktor?

Sara pointed without answering. Down on the slope the boys stood glaring at each other with furious expressions on their faces. Every so often one of them would utter some terrible expletive at the other.

SARA: When you left they were talking away about the existence of God. Finally they got so angry that they began shouting at each other. Then Anders grabbed Viktor's arm and tried to twist it off, and Viktor said that was a pretty lousy argument for the existence of God. Then I said that I thought they could skip God and pay some attention to me for a while instead, and then they said that I could stop babbling because I didn't understand that it was a debate of principles, and then I said that whether there was a God or not, they were real wet blankets. Then I left and they ran down the hill to settle things because each of them insisted that the other had hurt his innermost feelings. So now they're going to slug it out.

Marianne put on a very wise countenance and started off

to calm down the two debaters. I stepped into the car. Sara looked at the departing Marianne with envy.

SARA: Well, which one of the boys do *you* like the most?
ISAK: Which do you like best?
SARA: I don't know. Anders will become a minister. But he is rather masculine and warm, you know. But a minister's wife! But Viktor's funny in another way. Viktor will go far, you know.
ISAK : What do you mean by that?
SARA (*tired*): A doctor earns more money. And it's old-fashioned to be a minister. But he has nice legs. And a strong neck. But how *can* one believe in God!

Sara sighed and we sank into our own thoughts.

Marianne came up the hill bringing with her the two fighting cocks, barely reconciled. She sat down behind the wheel and we continued our trip.

The sun shone white on the blue-black clouds which towered above the dark, gleaming surface of Lake Vättern. The breeze coming from the open side windows did not cool us any longer, and in the south summer lightning cut across the sky with thin, jagged scratches. Because of the approaching storm, and all the food and wine, I became rather sleepy. I silently blessed my luck in having Marianne beside me as a reliable chauffeur. Anders and Viktor sat in sullen silence. Sara yawned again and again and blinked her eyes.

I fell asleep, but during my nap I was pursued by dreams and images which seemed extremely real and were very humiliating to me.

I record these in the order in which they occurred, without the slightest intention of commenting on their possible meaning. I have never been particularly enthusiastic about the psychoanalytical theory of dreams as the fulfillment of desires in a negative or positive direction. Yet I cannot deny that in these dreams there was something like a warning, which bore into my consciousness and embedded itself there with relentless determination.

I have found that during the last few years I glide rather easily into a twilight world of memories and dreams which are highly personal. I've often wondered if this is a sign of increasing senility. Sometimes I've also asked myself if it is a harbinger of approaching death.

Again I found myself at the wild-strawberry patch of my childhood, but I was not alone. Sara was there, and this time she turned her face toward mine and looked at me for a long time. I knew that I sat there looking old, ugly and ridiculous. A professor emeritus who was going to be made a Jubilee Doctor. The saddest thing about it was that although Sara spoke to me in a grieved and penetrating tone, I couldn't answer her except in stammered, one-syllable words. This, of course, increased the pain of my dream.

Between us stood a little woven basket filled with wild strawberries; around us lay a strange, motionless twilight, heavy with dull expectations. Sara leaned toward me and spoke in such a low voice that I had difficulty grasping her words.

SARA: Have you looked at yourself in the mirror, Isak? You haven't. Then I'll show you how you look.

She picked up a mirror that lay hidden under the small strawberry basket and showed me my face, which looked old and ugly in the sinking twilight. I carefully pushed away the looking glass and I could see that Sara had tears in her eyes.

SARA: You are a worried old man who will die soon, but I have my whole life before me . . . Oh, now you're offended.

ISAK: No, I'm not offended.

SARA: Yes, you are offended because you can't bear to hear the truth. And the truth is that I've been too considerate. One can easily be unintentionally cruel that way.

ISAK: I understand.

SARA: No, you don't understand. We don't speak the same language. Look at yourself in the mirror again. No, don't look away.

ISAK: I see.

SARA: Now listen. I'm about to marry your brother Sigfrid. He and I love each other, and it's all like a game. Look at your face now. Try to smile! All right, now you're smiling.

ISAK: It hurts.

SARA: You, a professor emeritus, ought to know why it hurts. But you don't. Because in spite of all your knowledge you don't really know anything.

She threw away the mirror and it shattered. The wind began to blow through the trees, and from somewhere the crying of a child could be heard. She arose immediately, drying her tears.

SARA: I have to go. I promised to look after Sigbritt's little boy.

ISAK: Don't leave me.

SARA: What did you say?

ISAK: Don't leave me.

SARA: You stammer so much that I can't hear your words. Besides, they don't really matter.

I saw her run up to the arbor. The old house was draped in the gray twilight. She lifted the crying child and cradled it in her arms. The sky turned black above the sea and large birds circled overhead, screeching toward the house, which suddenly seemed ugly and poor. There was something fateful and threatening in this twilight, in the crying of the child, in the shrieking of the black birds. Sara cradled the baby and her voice, half singing, was very distant and sorrowful.

SARA: My poor little one, you shall sleep quietly now. Don't be afraid of the wind. Don't be afraid of the birds, the jackdaws and the sea gulls. Don't be afraid of the waves from the sea. I'm with you. I'm holding you tight. Don't be afraid, little one. Soon it will be another day. No one can hurt you; I am with you; I'm holding you.

But her voice was sorrowful and tears ran down her cheeks without end. The child became silent, as if it were listening, and I wanted to scream until my lungs were bloody.

Now I saw that a door had opened in the house and someone was standing there shouting for Sara. It was my brother Sigfrid.

She ran toward him, gave him the child, and they both disappeared into the house and closed the door.

Suddenly I noticed that the wind had died and the birds had flown away. All the windows in the house shone festively. Over the horizon stood a jagged moon, and music from a piano penetrated the stillness of the strawberry patch.

I went closer and pressed my face against the brightly lit dining-room window. An elegantly laid table stood before me and Sara sat behind the piano, playing. She was wearing an expensive but old-fashioned dress and her hair was piled on top of her head, which made her face look womanly and mature. Then Sigfrid entered the room and they both sat down immediately at the table. They laughed and joked and celebrated some kind of event. The moon rose higher in the heavens and the scene inside became obscure. I rapped on the window so that they would hear me and let me in. But they did not notice me; they were too preoccupied with each other.

On the window sill lay many splinters of glass, and in my eager attempt to get their attention I accidentally cut my hand.

Turning away, I was blinded by the moonlight, which threw itself against me with an almost physical force.

I heard a voice calling my name, and then I saw that the door had been opened. Someone was standing in the doorway and I recognized Mr. Alman. He bowed politely though stiffly and invited me inside.

He led me down a short corridor and unlocked a narrow door. We entered a large windowless room with benches arranged like an amphitheater. There sat about ten youngsters, among whom I immediately recognized Sara, Anders and Viktor. On one of the low walls hung a large blackboard, and on a work table in the center of the room stood a microscope.

I realized that this was the hall where I used to hold my polyclinical lectures and examinations. Alman sat down and asked me to take a seat at the short end of the table. For a few moments he studied some papers in a dossier. The audience remained completely still.

ALMAN: Do you have your examination book with you?
ISAK: Yes, of course. Here it is.
ALMAN: Thank you.

I handed him the examination book and he flipped through it distractedly. Then he leaned forward and looked at me for a long time. After that he gestured toward the microscope.

ALMAN: Will you please identify the bacteriological specimen in the microscope. Take your time.

I arose, stepped up to the instrument and adjusted it. But whatever I did, I couldn't find any specimen. The only thing I saw was my own eye, which stared back at me in an absurd enlargement.

ISAK: There must be something wrong with the microscope.

Alman bent over and peered into it. Then he regarded me seriously and shook his head.

ALMAN: There is nothing wrong with the microscope.
ISAK: I can't see anything.
ALMAN: Sit down.

I sank down on the chair and wet my lips. No one moved or said anything.

ALMAN: Will you please read this text.

He pointed to the blackboard which hung behind him. Something was printed on it in large crooked letters. I made a great effort to interpret what was written: INKE TAN MAGROV STAK FARSIN LOS KRET FAJNE KASERTE MJOTRON PRESETE.

ALMAN: What does it mean?
ISAK: I don't know.
ALMAN: Oh, really?
ISAK: I'm a doctor, not a linguist.
ALMAN: Then let me tell you, Professor Borg, that on the blackboard is written the first duty of a doctor. Do you happen to know what that is?
ISAK: Yes, if you let me think for a moment.
ALMAN: Take your time.
ISAK: A doctor's first duty . . . a doctor's first duty . . . a doctor's . . . Oh, I've forgotten.

A cold sweat broke out on my forehead, but I still looked Alman straight in the eye. He leaned toward me and spoke in a calm, polite tone.

ALMAN: A doctor's first duty *is to ask forgiveness.*
ISAK: Of course, now I remember!

Relieved, I laughed but immediately became silent. Alman looked wearily at his papers and smothered a yawn.

ALMAN: Moreover, you are guilty of guilt.
ISAK: Guilty of guilt?
ALMAN: I have noted that you don't understand the accusation.
ISAK: Is it serious?
ALMAN: Unfortunately, Professor.

Next to me stood a table with a water decanter. I poured a glass, but spilled a lot of it on the table and the tray.

ISAK: I have a bad heart. I'm an old man, Mr. Alman, and I must be treated with consideration. That's only right.
ALMAN: There is nothing concerning your heart in my papers. Perhaps you wish to end the examination?
ISAK: No, no, for heaven's sake, no!

Alman arose and lit a small lamp which hung from a cord in the ceiling. Under the lamp (very brightly lit) sat a woman wrapped in a hospital robe and wearing wooden sandals on her feet.

ALMAN: Will you please make an anamnesis and diagnosis of this patient.
ISAK: But the patient is dead.

At that moment the woman arose and began laughing as

if she had just heard a great joke. Alman leaned across the table and wrote something in my examination book.

ISAK: What are you writing in my book?
ALMAN: My conclusion.
ISAK: And that is . . .
ALMAN: That you're incompetent.
ISAK: Incompetent.
ALMAN: Furthermore, Professor Borg, you are accused of some smaller but nonetheless serious offenses. (*Isak remains silent*) Indifference, selfishness, lack of consideration.
ISAK: No.
ALMAN: These accusations have been made by your wife. Do you want to be confronted by her?
ISAK: But my wife has been dead for many years.
ALMAN: Do you think I'm joking? Will you please come with me voluntarily. You have no choice in any case. Come!

Alman placed the examination book in his pocket, made a sign for me to follow him, opened the door and led me into a forest.

The trunks of the trees stood close together. Twilight had almost passed. Dead trees were strewn on the ground and the earth was covered with decaying leaves. Our feet sank into this soft carpet with every step, and mud oozed up around them. From behind the foliage the moon shone steadily, like an inflamed eye, and it was as warm as inside a hothouse. Alman turned around.

ALMAN: Watch out, Professor Borg. You'll find many snakes here.

Suddenly I saw a small, gleaming body which twisted around and disappeared in one of Alman's wet footsteps. I stepped swiftly aside but nearly trod on a large gray creature which slowly pulled away. Wherever I looked, snakes seemed to well forth from the swampy, porous ground.

Finally we arrived at a clearing in the forest, but we halted at the very edge. The moon shone in our eyes and we hid among the shadows of the trees. The clearing stretched out before us. It was overgrown with twisted roots. At one end a black cliff fell away into a body of water. On the sides, the trees stood lofty and lifeless, as if burdened by each other's enormous shadows. Then a giggling laugh was heard and I discovered a woman standing near the hill. She was dressed in a long black gown and her face was averted from us. She made movements with her hands, as if to ward off someone. She laughed continually and excitedly. A man stood half hidden, leaning against a tree trunk. His face, which I glimpsed, was large and flat, but his eyebrows were quite bushy and his forehead protruded over his eyes. He made gestures with his hand and said some unintelligible words, which made the woman laugh uncontrollably. Suddenly she became serious, and a harassed, discontented expression appeared on her face. She bent over and picked up a small purse. The man stretched out his hand and jokingly began to pull the pins out of her skillfully pompadoured hair. She pretended to be very angry and flailed the air around her furiously. This amused the man, who continued his game. When she finally walked away he followed and took hold of her shoulders. Petrified, she stopped and turned her pale, embittered face toward her pursuer. He muttered something and stretched out his other hand toward her breast. She moved away, but couldn't free herself. When she saw that she was caught, she began to twist and squirm as if the man's grip on her shoulders hurt intensely. The man continued to mutter incoherent words, as if to an animal. Suddenly she freed herself and ran with bent knees and a shuffling step in a semicircle. The man remained standing, waiting and breathless. He perspired heavily and wiped his face over and over again with the back of his hand. The woman stopped as if exhausted and regarded the man, wide-eyed and gaping. She was also out of breath. Then she began running again but pretended to trip and fell on her hands and knees. Her large rump swayed like a black balloon over the ground. She lowered her face between her arms and began crying, rocking and swaying. The man knelt at her side, took a firm grasp of her hair, pulled her face upward, backward and forced her to open her eyes. He panted with effort the whole time. She teetered and nearly fell to the side, but the man straddled her and leaned over her heavily. Suddenly she was completely still, with closed eyes and a swollen, pale face. Then she collapsed, rolled over, and received the man between her open knees.

ALMAN: Many men forget a woman who has been dead for thirty years. Some preserve a sweet, fading picture, but *you* can always recall this scene in your memory. Strange, isn't it? Tuesday, May 1, 1917, you stood here and heard and saw exactly what that woman and that man said and did.

The woman sat up and smoothed her gown over her short, thick thighs. Her face was blank and almost distorted in its puffy slackness. The man had got up and was wandering around aimlessly with his hands hanging at his sides.

WOMAN: Now I will go home and tell this to Isak and I know exactly what he'll say: Poor little girl, how I pity you. As if he were God himself. And then I'll cry and say: Do you really feel pity for me? and he'll say: I feel infinitely sorry for you, and then I'll cry some more and ask him if he can forgive me. And then he'll say: You shouldn't ask forgiveness from me. I have nothing to forgive. But he doesn't mean a word of it, because he's completely cold. And then he'll suddenly be very tender and I'll yell at him that he's not really sane and that such hypocritical nobility is sickening. And then he'll say that he'll bring me a sedative and that he understands everything. And then I'll say that it's his fault that I am the way I am, and then he'll look very sad and will say that he is to blame. But he doesn't care about anything because he's completely cold.

She arose with effort and shook out her hair and began combing it and pinning it up in the same careful way that it was before. The man sat down on a stone a little farther away. He smoked quietly. I couldn't see his gaze below the protruding eyebrows, but his voice was calm and scornful.

MAN: You're insane, the way you're carrying on.

The woman laughed and went into the forest.

I turned around. Alman had a strange, wry smile on his face. We stood quietly for a few moments.

ISAK: Where is she?
ALMAN: You know. She is gone. Everyone is gone. Can't you hear how quiet it is? Everything has been dissected, Professor Borg. A surgical masterpiece. There is no pain, no bleeding, no quivering.
ISAK: It is rather quiet.
ALMAN: A perfect achievement of its kind, Professor.
ISAK: And what is the penalty?
ALMAN: Penalty? I don't know. The usual one, I suppose.
ISAK: The usual one?
ALMAN: Of course. Loneliness.
ISAK: Loneliness?
ALMAN: Exactly. *Loneliness.*
ISAK: Is there no grace?

ALMAN: Don't ask me. I don't know anything about such things.

Before I had time to answer, Alman had disappeared, and I stood alone in the complete stillness of the moonlight and the forest. Then I heard a voice quite close to me.

SARA: Didn't you have to go with them to get your father?

The girl stretched out her hand, but when she saw my face she immediately withdrew it.

ISAK: Sara . . . It wasn't always like this. If only you had stayed with me. If only you could have had a little patience.

The girl did not seem to hear what I was saying but began to look restless.

SARA: Hurry up.

I followed her as well as I could, but she moved so much more easily and faster than I.

ISAK: I can't run, don't you understand?
SARA: But hurry up.
ISAK: I can't see you any more.
SARA: But here I am.
ISAK: Wait for me.

She materialized for a moment and then she was gone. The moon disappeared into darkness and I wanted to cry with wild, childish sorrow, but I could not.

At that moment, I awoke. The car stood still and the storm was over, but it was still drizzling slightly. We were in the neighborhood of the Strömsnäs Foundry, where the road wanders between rich forests on one side and river rapids on the other. Everything was completely silent. The three children had left the car and Marianne sat quietly smoking a cigarette and blowing the smoke through the open window. Gusts of strong and pleasant odors came from the wet forest.

ISAK: What is this?
MARIANNE: The children wanted to get out for a moment and stretch their legs. They are over there.

She made a gesture toward a clearing near the river. All three were busy picking flowers.

ISAK: But it's still raining.
MARIANNE: I told them about the ceremony today, and they insisted on paying homage to you.
ISAK (*sighs*): Good Lord.
MARIANNE: Did you sleep well?
ISAK: Yes, but I dreamed. Can you imagine—the last few months I've had the most peculiar dreams. It's really odd.
MARIANNE: What's odd?
ISAK: It's as if I'm trying to say something to myself which I don't want to hear when I'm awake.
MARIANNE: And what would that be?
ISAK: That I'm dead, although I live.

Marianne reacted violently. Her gaze blackened and she took a deep breath. Throwing her cigarette out the window, she turned toward me.

MARIANNE: Do you know that you and Evald are very much alike?
ISAK: You told me that.

MARIANNE: Do you know that Evald has said the very same thing?

ISAK: About me? Yes, I can believe that.

MARIANNE: No, about himself.

ISAK: But he's only thirty-eight years old.

MARIANNE: May I tell you everything, or would it bore you?

ISAK: I'd be grateful if you would tell me.

MARIANNE: It was a few months ago. I wanted to talk to Evald and we took the car and went down to the sea. It was raining, just like now. Evald sat where you are sitting, and I drove.

EVALD: Can't you stop the windshield wipers?

MARIANNE: Then we won't be able to see the ocean.

EVALD: They're working so hard it makes me nervous.

MARIANNE (*shuts them off*): Very well.

They sit in silence for a few minutes, looking at the rain, which streams down the windshield quietly. The sea merges with the clouds in an infinite grayness. Evald strokes his long, bony face and looks expectantly at his wife. He talks jokingly, calmly.

EVALD: So now you have me trapped. What did you want to say? Something unpleasant, of course.

MARIANNE: I wish I didn't have to tell you about it.

EVALD: I understand. You've found someone else.

MARIANNE: Now don't be childish.

EVALD (*mimicking her*): Now don't be childish. What do you expect me to think? You come and say in a funereal voice that you want to talk to me. We take the car and go down to the sea. It rains and it's hard for you to begin. Good Lord, Marianne, let's have it. This is an excellent moment for the most intimate confidence. But for heaven's sake, don't keep me dangling.

MARIANNE: Now I feel like laughing. What do you really think I'm going to say? That I've murdered someone, or embezzled the faculty funds? I'm pregnant, Evald.

EVALD: Oh, is that so.

MARIANNE: That's the way it is. And as careless as we've been recently, there isn't much to be surprised about, is there?

EVALD: And you're sure?

MARIANNE: The report on the test came yesterday.

EVALD: Oh. Oh, yes. So that was the secret.

MARIANNE: Another thing I want to tell you. I shall have this child.

EVALD: That seems to be clear.

MARIANNE: Yes, it is!

MARIANNE (*voice over*): We sat quietly for a long time and I felt how the hatred grew big and thick between us. Evald looked out through the wet window, whistled soundlessly and looked as if he were cold. Somewhere in my stomach I was shivering so hard that I could barely sit upright. Then he opened the door and got out of the car and marched through the rain down to the beach. He stopped under a big tree and stood there for a long while. Finally I also stepped out and went to him. His face and hair were wet and the rain fell down his cheeks to the sides of his mouth.

EVALD (*calmly*): You know that I don't want to have any children. You also know that you'll have to choose between me and the child.

MARIANNE (*looks at him*): Poor Evald.

EVALD: Please don't "poor" me. I'm of sound mind and I've made my position absolutely clear. It's absurd to live in this world, but it's even more ridiculous to populate it with new victims and it's most absurd of all to believe that they will have it any better than us.

MARIANNE: That is only an excuse.

EVALD: Call it whatever you want. Personally I was an unwelcome child in a marriage which was a nice imitation of hell. Is the old man really sure that I'm his son? Indifference, fear, infidelity and guilt feelings—those were my nurses.

MARIANNE: All this is very touching, but it doesn't excuse the fact that you're behaving like a child.

EVALD: I have to be at the hospital at three o'clock and have neither the time nor the desire to talk any more.

MARIANNE: You're a coward!

EVALD: Yes, that's right. This life disgusts me and I don't think that I need a responsibility which will force me to exist another day longer than I want to. You know all that, and you know that I'm serious and that this isn't some kind of hysteria, as you once thought.

MARIANNE (*voice over*): We went toward the car, he in front and I following. I had begun to cry. I don't know why. But the tears couldn't be seen in the rain. We sat in the car, thoroughly wet and cold, but the hatred throbbed in us so painfully that we didn't feel cold. I started the car and turned it toward the road. Evald sat fiddling with the radio. His face was completely calm and closed.

MARIANNE: I know that you're wrong.

EVALD: There is nothing which can be called right or wrong. One functions according to one's needs; you can read that in an elementary-school textbook.

MARIANNE: And what do we need?

EVALD: You have a damned need to live, to exist and create life.

MARIANNE: And how about you?

EVALD: My need is to be dead. Absolutely, totally dead.

I've tried to relate Marianne's story as carefully as possible. My reaction to it was very mixed. But my strongest feeling was a certain sympathy toward her for this sudden confidence, and when Marianne fell silent she looked so hesitant that I felt obliged to say something even though I wasn't very sure of my own voice.

ISAK: If you want to smoke a cigarette, you may.
MARIANNE: Thank you.
ISAK: Why have you told me all this?

Marianne didn't answer at once. She took her time lighting a cigarette and puffed a few times. I looked at her, but she turned her head away and pretended to look at the three youngsters, who had picked up some kind of soft drink which they shared in great amity.

MARIANNE: When I saw you together with your mother, I was gripped by a strange fear.
ISAK: I don't understand.
MARIANNE: I thought, here is his mother. A very ancient woman, completely ice-cold, in some ways more frightening than death itself. And here is her son, and there are light-years of distance between them. And he himself says that he is a living death. And Evald is on the verge of becoming just as lonely and cold—and dead. And then I thought that there is only coldness and death, and death and loneliness, all the way. Somewhere it must end.
ISAK: But you are going back to Evald.
MARIANNE: Yes, to tell him that I can't agree to his condition. I want my child; no one can take it from me. Not even the person I love more than anyone else.

She turned her pale, tearless face toward me, and her gaze was black, accusing, desperate. I suddenly felt shaken in a way which I had never experienced before.

ISAK: Can I help you?
MARIANNE: No one can help me. We are too old, Isak. It has gone too far.
ISAK: What happened after your talk in the car?
MARIANNE: Nothing. I left him the very next day.
ISAK: Haven't you heard from him?
MARIANNE: No. No, Evald is rather like you.

She shook her head and bent forward as if to protect her face. I felt cold; it had become quite chilly after the rain.

MARIANNE: Those two wretched people whom I made leave the car—what was their name again?
ISAK: I was just thinking about Alman and his wife. It reminded me of my own marriage.
MARIANNE: I don't want Evald and I to become like . . .
ISAK: Poor Evald grew up in all that.
MARIANNE: But we love each other.

Her last words were a low outburst. She stopped herself immediately and moved her hands toward her face, then stopped again. We sat quietly for a few moments.

ISAK: We must get on. Signal to the children.

Marianne nodded, started the motor and blew the horn. Sara came laughing through the wet grass, closely followed by her two cavaliers. She handed me a large bouquet of wild flowers wrapped in wet newspapers. All three of them had friendly, mocking eyes. Sara cleared her throat solemnly.

SARA: We heard that you are celebrating this day. Now we want to pay our respects to you with these simple flowers and to tell you that we are *very* impressed that you are so old and that you've been a doctor for fifty years. And we know, of course, that you are a *wise* and *venerable* old man. One who regards us youngsters with *lenience* and gentle irony. One who knows *all* about life and who has learned all the prescriptions by heart.

She gave me the flowers with a little mock curtsy and kissed my cheek. The boys bowed and laughed, embarrassed. I couldn't answer. I only thanked them very briefly and rather bluntly. The children probably thought that I had been hurt by their joke.

After a few more hours' travel, we reached Lund. When we finally stopped at Evald's house, a small round woman ran out and approached us quickly. To my surprise and pleasure I discovered that it was Miss Agda.

AGDA: So you did come. Evald and I had just given up hope. It's relaxing and convenient to drive, isn't it? Now, Professor, you'll have to put on your frock coat immediately. Hello, Marianne. I've prepared Evald for your arrival.

ISAK: So, Miss Agda, you came after all.

AGDA: I considered it my duty. But the fun is gone. There's nothing you can say that will make me feel different. Who are these young people? Are they going to the ceremony too?

MARIANNE: These are good friends of ours, and if there is any food in the kitchen, invite them in.

AGDA: And why shouldn't there be? I've had a lot of things to arrange here, believe me.

Evald met us in the foyer. He was already dressed in evening clothes and seemed nervous. Everything was extremely confused, but Miss Agda was a pillar of strength in the maelstrom. Without raising her voice, and dressed in her best dress (especially made for the occasion), she sent the children, the married couple, servants and an old professor in different directions. Within ten minutes, everything was in order.

Just before that, Evald, Marianne and I had a chance to say hello. I wouldn't want to give the impression that our reunion was marked by overwhelming cordiality. This has never been the case in our family.

EVALD: Hello, Father. Welcome.
ISAK: Hello, Evald. Thank you. As you can see, I brought Marianne with me.
EVALD: Hello, Marianne.
MARIANNE: Can I take my things upstairs?
EVALD: Do you want to stay in the guest room as usual, Father?
ISAK: Thank you, that would be just fine.
EVALD: Let me take your suitcase. It's rather heavy.
ISAK: Thank you, I'll take it myself.
EVALD: Did you have a nice trip?
MARIANNE: Yes, thanks, it's been pleasant.
EVALD: Who were those youngsters you had with you?
MARIANNE: Don't know. They're going to Italy.
EVALD: They looked rather nice.
ISAK: They are really very nice.

We had come to the second floor. Evald politely opened the door to the guest room and I entered. Agda came after us as if she were rolling on ball bearings, forced her way in and took the suitcase, putting it on a chair.

AGDA: I bought new shoelaces, and I took the liberty of bringing the white waistcoat to your evening dress if you should want to go to the banquet after the ceremony. And you forgot your razor blades, Professor.

She unpacked, murmuring sounds of worried concern. I didn't listen. Instead I listened to the conversation between Marianne and Evald outside the half-closed door. Their voices were formal and faultlessly polite.

MARIANNE: No, I'll go tomorrow, so don't worry.
EVALD: Do you intend to stay in a hotel?
MARIANNE (gay): Why? We can share a bedroom for another night, if you have no objection. Help me to unpack.
EVALD: It was really nice to see you. And unexpected.
MARIANNE: I feel the same way. Are we going to the dinner afterward, or what do you want to do?
EVALD: I'll just call Stenberg and tell him that I'm bringing a lady. He arranges such things.

The door was closed, so I couldn't hear any more of the conversation. I had sat down on the bed to take off my shoes. Miss Agda helped me, but she wasn't very gracious.

Oddly enough, there were three Jubilee Doctors that year. The dean's office had thoughtfully placed us three old men in a special room while the procession was arranged out in the large vestibule of the university hall. I happened to know one of the other two who were going to be honored. He was an old schoolmate, the former Bishop Jakob Hovelius. We greeted each other cordially and embraced. The third old man seemed rather atrophied and declined all conversation. It turned out that he was the former Professor of Roman Law, Carl-Adam Tiger (a great fighter in his time and a man who, according to his students, really lived up to his name).

ISAK: How comforting it is to meet another old corpse. How are you nowadays, dear Jakob?
JAKOB: I enjoy my leisure. But don't ask me if I do it *cum dignitate*.
ISAK: Do you know the third man to be honored?

JAKOB: Of course. It's Carl-Adam Tiger, Professor of Roman Law.

ISAK: The Tiger! Good Lord!

JAKOB: He has three interests left in life. A thirty-year-old injustice, a goldfish, and his bowels.

ISAK: Do you think that we are like that?

JAKOB: What's your opinion? As Schopenhauer says somewhere, "Dreams are a kind of lunacy and lunacy a kind of dream." But life is also supposed to be a kind of dream, isn't it? Draw your own conclusion.

ISAK: Do you remember how in our youth we fought with each other on what we called the metaphysical questions?

JAKOB: How could I forget?

ISAK: And what do you believe now?

JAKOB: I'll tell you, I've ceased thinking about all that. One of these days, knowledge will be achieved.

ISAK: My, how surprised you'll be.

JAKOB: And you. But one has a right to be curious.

TIGER: Gentlemen, do you think I'd have time to make a small secret visit before the great farce begins?

ISAK: I don't know, Professor Tiger.

TIGER (sighs): *In dubio non est agendum.* When in doubt, don't, as the old Romans used to say. I'll stay here.

The Festivities

What should I describe? Trumpet fanfares, bells ringing, field-cannon salutes, masses of people, the giant procession from the university to the cathedral, the white-dressed garland girls, royalty, old age, wisdom, beautiful music, stately Latin sentences which echoed off the huge vaults. The students and their girls, women in bright, magnificent dresses, this strange rite with its heavy symbolism but as meaningless as a passing dream.

Then I saw Sara with her two boys among the onlookers outside the cathedral. They waved to me and suddenly looked childishly happy and full of expectations. Among the lecturers was Evald, tall and serious, disinterested and absent. Inside the church, I saw Marianne in her white dress and next to her sat Miss Agda, pale and with her lips pressed tightly together. The ceremonial lecture was dull (as usual). The whole thing went on endlessly (as usual) and the garland girls had to go out and relieve themselves in the little silver pot in the sacristy. But we adults unfortunately had to stay where we were. As you know, culture provides us with these moments of refined torture. Professor Tiger looked as if he were dying, my friend the Bishop fell asleep, and more than one of those present seemed ready to faint. Even our behinds, which have withstood long academic services, lectures, dusty dissertations and dull dinners, started to become numb and ache in silent protest.

I surprised myself by returning to the happenings of the day, and it was then that I decided to recollect and write down everything that had happened. I was beginning to see a remarkable causality in this chain of unexpected, entangled events. At the same time, I couldn't escape recalling the Bishop's words: "Dreams are a kind of lunacy and lunacy a kind of dream, but life is also supposed to be a dream, isn't it . . ."

After the ceremony there was a banquet, but I really felt too tired to go. I took a cab home and found Miss Agda in my room busy making my bed the way I like (very high under my head and folded neatly at my feet). A heating pad was already connected and my sleeping pills stood on the table. Almost at once, Miss Agda began helping me with my shoes and evening dress, and I felt a great warmth toward this extraordinary, faithful, thoughtful old woman. I would really have liked to become friends with her again, and I repented the morning's thoughtless utterances (which, I noticed, she had by no means forgotten).

ISAK: Did you enjoy the ceremony?

AGDA: Yes, thank you.

ISAK: Are you tired, Miss Agda?

AGDA: I won't deny it.

ISAK: Take one of my sleeping pills.

AGDA: No, thanks.

ISAK: Oh, Miss Agda, I'm sorry for this morning.

AGDA: Are you sick, Professor?

ISAK: No. Why?

AGDA: I don't know, but that sounds alarming.

ISAK: Oh really, is it so unusual for me to ask forgiveness?

AGDA: Do you want the water decanter on the table?

ISAK: No, thanks.

We puttered about for a while, silently.

AGDA: Thanks anyway.

ISAK: Oh, Miss Agda.

AGDA: What do you want, Professor?

ISAK: Don't you think that we who have known each other for two generations could drop formality and say "*du*" to each other?

AGDA: No, I don't really think so.

ISAK: Why not, if I may ask?

AGDA: Have you brushed your teeth, Professor?

ISAK: Yes, thanks.

AGDA: Now, I'll tell you. I beg to be excused from all intimacies. It's all right the way it is between us now.

ISAK: But, dear Miss Agda, we are old now.

AGDA: Speak for yourself, Professor. A woman has to think of her reputation, and what would people say if the two of us suddenly started to say "*du*" to each other?

ISAK: Yes, what would people say?

AGDA: They would ridicule us.

ISAK: Do you always act correctly?

AGDA: Nearly always. At our age one ought to know how to behave. Isn't that so, Professor?

ISAK: Good night, Miss Agda.

AGDA: Good night, Professor. I will leave the door ajar. And you know where I am if you should want something. Good night, Professor.

ISAK: Good night, Miss Agda.

I was just going to lie down in bed (I had been sitting on the edge in my old robe) when I heard singing and music from the garden. I thought I recognized the voices and walked over to the window and lifted the blinds. Down there under the trees I recognized my three companions from the trip. They sang to their heart's delight, and Anders accompanied them on his guitar.

SARA: Hey, Father Isak! You were fantastic when you marched in the procession. We were real proud that we knew you. Now we're going on.

ANDERS: We got a lift all the way to Hamburg.

VIKTOR: With a fifty-year-old deaconess. Anders is already sweet on the old girl.

ANDERS: Stop babbling!

VIKTOR: We came to say goodbye.

ISAK: Goodbye, and thank you for your company.

SARA: Goodbye, Father Isak. Do you know that it is really you I love, today, tomorrow and forever?

ISAK: I'll remember that.

VIKTOR: Goodbye, Professor.

ISAK: Goodbye, Viktor.

ANDERS: Goodbye, Professor. Now we have to run.

ISAK: Let me hear from you sometime.

Those last words I said to myself, and rather quietly. The children waved to me and were swallowed up by the summer night. I heard their laughter, and then they were gone.

At the same moment, I heard voices out in the foyer. It was Evald and Marianne. They whispered out of consideration to me and I heard the rustle of Marianne's evening gown. I called to Evald. He entered the room, but stopped at the door.

ISAK: Are you home already?
EVALD: Marianne had to change shoes. Her heel broke.
ISAK: So you are going to the dance?
EVALD: Yes, I suppose so.
ISAK: A-ha.
EVALD: How are you otherwise?
ISAK: Fine, thanks.
EVALD: How's the heart holding up?
ISAK: Excellently.
EVALD: Good night, and sleep well.

He turned and went through the door. I asked him to come back. He looked very surprised. I felt surprised myself, and confused. I didn't really know what to say.

ISAK: Sit down a moment.
EVALD: Is it something special?

He sat obediently on the chair near the bed. His starched shirt rustled and his hands hung a little tiredly across his knees. I realized that my son was becoming middle-aged.

ISAK: May I ask you what's going to happen between you and Marianne? (*Evald shakes his head*) Forgive my asking.
EVALD: I know nothing.
ISAK: It's not my business, but . . .
EVALD: What?
ISAK: But shouldn't . . .

EVALD: I have asked her to remain with me.

ISAK: And how will it . . . I mean . . .

EVALD: I can't be without her.

ISAK: You mean you can't live alone.

EVALD: I can't be without *her*. That's what I mean.

ISAK: I understand.

EVALD: It will be as she wants.

ISAK: And if she wants . . . I mean, does she want?

EVALD: She says that she'll think it over. I don't really know.

ISAK: Regarding that loan you had from me . . .

EVALD: Don't worry, you'll get your money.

ISAK: I didn't mean that.

EVALD: You'll get your money all right.

Evald rose and nodded to me. Just then Marianne appeared in the door. She had on a very simple but extraordinarily beautiful white dress.

MARIANNE: How are you, Father Isak?

ISAK: Fine, thanks. Very well.

MARIANNE: I broke a heel, so we had to come home to change. Can I wear these shoes instead?

ISAK: They look fine.

Marianne came up to me. She smelled good and rustled in a sweet, womanly way. She leaned over me.

ISAK: Thanks for your company on the trip.

MARIANNE: Thank *you*.

ISAK: I like you, Marianne.

MARIANNE: I like you too, Father Isak.

She kissed me lightly on the cheek and disappeared. They exchanged a few words outside the door. I heard their steps on the stairs and then the door slamming in the foyer. I heard my heart and my old watch. I heard the tower clock strike eleven, with the light tones designating the four quarter hours and the heavier sounds marking the hour.

Now it began to rain, not very hard, but quietly and evenly. A lulling sound. The street lamp swung on its cord and threw shadows on the light-colored window blinds.

Whenever I am restless or sad, I usually try to recall memories from my childhood, to calm down. This is the way it was that night too, and I wandered back to the summerhouse and the wild-strawberry patch and everything I had dreamed or remembered or experienced during this long day.

I sat under the tree by the wild-strawberry patch and it was a warm, sunny day with soft summer skies and a mild breeze coming through the birches. Down at the dock, my sisters and brothers were romping with Uncle Aron. My aunt went by, together with Sara. They were laden with large baskets. Everyone laughed and shouted to each other and applauded when the red sail went up the mast of the old yacht (an ancient relic from the days of my parents' childhood; a mad impulse of our grandfather, the Admiral). Sara turned around and when she caught sight of me she put down her baskets and ran toward me.

SARA: Isak, darling, there are no wild strawberries left. Aunt wants you to search for your father. We will sail around the peninsula and pick you up on the other side.
ISAK: I have already searched for him, but I can't find either Father or Mother.
SARA: Your mother was supposed to go with him.
ISAK: Yes, but I can't find them.
SARA: I will help you.

She took me by the hand and suddenly we found ourselves at a narrow sound with deep, dark water. The sun shone brightly on the opposite side, which rose softly into a meadow. Down at the beach on the other side of the dark water a gentleman sat, dressed in white, with his hat on the back of his head and an old pipe in his mouth. He had a soft, blond beard and pince-nez. He had taken off his shoes and stockings and between his hands he held a long, slender bamboo pole. A red float lay motionless on the shimmering water.

Farther up the bank sat my mother. She wore a bright summer dress and a big hat which shaded her face. She was reading a book. Sara dropped my hand and pointed to my parents. Then she was gone. I looked for a long time at the pair on the other side of the water. I tried to shout to them but not a word came from my mouth. Then my father raised his head and caught sight of me. He lifted his hand and waved, laughing. My mother looked up from her book. She also laughed and nodded.

Then I saw the old yacht with its red sail. It cruised so smoothly in the mild breeze. In the prow stood Uncle Aron, singing some sentimental song, and I saw my brothers and sisters and aunt and Sara, who lifted up Sigbritt's little boy. I shouted to them, but they didn't hear me.

I dreamed that I stood by the water and shouted toward the bay, but the warm summer breeze carried away my cries and they did not reach their destination. Yet I wasn't sorry about that; I felt, on the contrary, rather lighthearted.

Stockholm
May 31, 1957

THE

MAGICIAN

(THE FACE)

A COMEDY

THE MAGICIAN

(THE FACE)

THE CAST

Vogler	Max von Sydow
Manda (Aman)	Ingrid Thulin
Vergérus	Gunnar Björnstrand
Grandmother	Naima Wifstrand
Spegel	Bengt Ekerot
Sara	Bibi Andersson
Ottilia	Gertrud Fridh
Simson	Lars Ekborg
Starbeck	Toivo Pawlo
Egerman	Erland Josephson
Tubal	Åke Fridell
Sofia	Sif Ruud
Antonsson	Oscar Ljung
Henrietta	Ulla Sjöblom
Rustan	Axel Duberg
Sanna	Birgitta Pettersson

THE CREDITS

Screenplay	Ingmar Bergman
Director	Ingmar Bergman

Assistant director	Gösta Ekman
Director of photography	Gunnar Fischer
Music	Erik Nordgren
Music directed by	E. Eckert-Lundin
Sets	P. A. Lundgren
Costumes	Manne Lindholm and Greta Johansson
Make-up	Börje Lundh and Nils Nittel
Sound	Aaby Wedin and Åke Hansson
Editor	Oscar Rosander
Production supervisor	Allan Ekelund

Running time: 102 *minutes*

Produced by Svensk Filmindustri; distributed in the United States by Janus Films, Inc., and in Great Britain as The Face *by Contemporary Films Ltd.*

Vogler
and Spegel

The coach.
Its passengers:
Vogler and Manda;
Tubal and Grandmother

Vergérus, Starbeck and Egerman confront . . .

Simson and Sara

Manda, Vogler and Tubal

Sanna and Grandmother

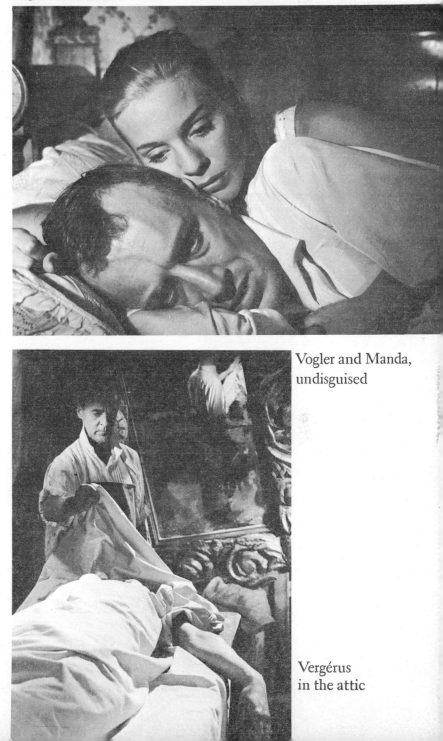

Vogler and Spegel

Vogler and Manda, undisguised

Vergérus in the attic

Tubal and Sofia

"The rain has suddenly stopped. Sara and Simson climb up on the coach box....The coach turns the corner slowly and climbs the hilly streets, which glisten in the afternoon sunshine.
In this way the mesmerizer Albert Emanuel Vogler makes his triumphant entrance into the Royal Palace."

ON A SUMMER EVENING pregnant with thunder in July of the year 1846, a large coach stops beside a road just south of Stockholm. The hot sun slants down mercilessly on the marshes, the forest and the black clouds in the eastern sky.

Four travelers sit around the coach. The fifth—a small, bent old woman—walks around poking in the ground, as if searching for something.

The coachman, who is the youngest in the group, has just returned from the forest with water for the horses. Near the coach step sits a big red-haired man, eating ham. His lunchbox is open beside him.

A little to the side, by themselves, the other two sit. One is a tall, thin man with a pale face, straight black hair, a beard and black eyebrows. Bareheaded, he is dressed in a dusty traveling suit and smokes a short pipe, which he lights continuously. The other, smaller in height, rather delicate, also dressed in a traveling suit, seems more a boy than a man.

The coach is heavily laden with boxes and crates; it looks comfortable enough but has seen better days. The horses are strong but not very well groomed. Now the little old woman has dug a hole in the ground with a stick. She kneels and searches in the hole with her hand, looks rather satisfied, fishes up something which can best be described as a black stone. She looks carefully over her shoulder to see if the others are watching, but when no one seems to be taking notice she puts her find in a small leather bag she carries.

A remarkably large magpie stares at the old woman. She becomes angry and holds the bag close to her. The magpie remains there and sneers scornfully. The old woman spits on the ground and rushes away.

The sun burns down on the edge of the forest and it is very quiet. The travelers step into the coach while the coachman climbs up to the coach box and shouts at the horses. The coach springs creak and sigh as the heavy vehicle slowly sways up onto the narrow, rutted road.

In the forest, sunbeams tremble in the trees like hurled spears, but the twilight is heavy.

The big man—the one who was eating—grins good-humoredly as he picks his teeth. The old woman draws her breath and coughs for a moment.

TUBAL: Well.
GRANDMOTHER: What?
TUBAL: Did you find what you were digging for?
GRANDMOTHER: No.
TUBAL: You mistook the place.
GRANDMOTHER: I know very well where the gallows were. It was right here, it was. Just before the toll house on the edge of the forest.
TUBAL: You with your mandrake roots, chopped-off fingers and other deviltry. (*Grins kindly*)
GRANDMOTHER: And in this forest the spirits went about, howling or sighing, depending on their mood. There was such a racket that people were afraid to go into the forest after sundown. I remember well.

TUBAL: You and your spirits.

He laughs in a friendly way, folds his hands over his vest and belches discreetly. But Grandmother becomes extremely angry.

GRANDMOTHER: Listen, Albert. Why do you keep that Tubal as your assistant? You should get rid of him. Do you hear what your grandmother says?

Albert (who has apparently heard his grandmother's opinions on previous occasions) pretends to be deaf. But Tubal's mood seems to get better and better.

TUBAL: How could Vogler's Magnetic Health Theater get along without Tubal, I'd like to know. For example, who was it that bailed us out of our last booking in Copenhagen? At night. At the risk of my own life. After our Danish tour had gone to hell. I'm asking, but no one answers.
GRANDMOTHER (angry): And who is it that brews our medicines?
TUBAL: Who is it that sells them?
GRANDMOTHER: After all, the medicines are our steady income.
TUBAL: You would have been finished off long ago if people knew what you put into your medicines.
GRANDMOTHER (very angry): "What is good for you is not always tasty"—that's what my mother used to say.
TUBAL: In any case, I'm the one who takes the responsibility.
GRANDMOTHER: And the profits.
TUBAL: Don't try that, Granny. I know something, I do.
GRANDMOTHER (a little humbler): The Lord will punish you, Tubal, on Judgment Day.
TUBAL: You who have sold yourself to the devil, you shouldn't take God's name in your sinful mouth.

GRANDMOTHER: In my father's house there are many mansions, the Bible says.

TUBAL: If that's so, it's because the devil already has a grandmother.

GRANDMOTHER: Do you hear, Albert? Should that big red ox be allowed to insult Grandmother like that? Slap him on his snout, or at least give me my chest medicine. I have a cough.

Grandmother coughs convincingly and takes a sip from a small silver flask. Then she huddles in her corner. Her eyes gleam watchfully in the twilight.

Tubal scratches his nose and looks at his traveling companions with friendly scorn.

Albert makes a few unsuccessful attempts to light his pipe. The young man seems to be asleep in his corner.

The coach sways and creaks; the springs and the axles squeal.

The trees lean out of the forest at them. The road is wet and muddy after the rains.

A light fog rises from the water's surface. The day sinks toward night.

Grandmother opens her eyes.

GRANDMOTHER: Do you hear?

TUBAL: Maybe it's a ghost.

GRANDMOTHER: It was a scream. I heard it quite clearly.

Everyone listens. Through the stillness and the sounds of the coach, a wailing cry is indeed heard. It is prolonged and terrifying, but still distant.

TUBAL: It's a fox.

GRANDMOTHER (*mimics him*): It's a fox! A fox on two wasted legs, bloody, with his head hanging by a few sinews perhaps. A fox without eyes, but with a rotten hole for a mouth. . . . I have seen them, I have. And I know what I know.

The coach stops with a jolt.

The coachman, Simson, comes leaping through the door which he slams shut violently. His legs are covered with mud and his face is pale.

SIMSON: Why don't you get the devil to sit on the coach box in this forest and have ghosts and ghouls howling in *his* ears?

He falls silent and points toward the forest.

A phantom gleams among the trees, clutching at their trunks with haggard arms. Once in a while it utters a dull, inhuman howl.

GRANDMOTHER (*mumbles*): "Wound in the eye, blood in the mouth, fingers gone, neck broken, he calls you down, he calls you forth, beyond the dead, the living, the living dead, beyond the raised hands . . ."

Suddenly the phantom is gone—swallowed up by the darkness of the forest, the thin fog over the marshes.

Albert Vogler steps out of the coach and walks into the forest, searching.

He finds the ghoul sitting in a puddle grinning at him. He is half naked; his clothing hangs in rags on his lean bones. He is a tall man and his back sways as if it were broken.

SPEGEL: Good evening, sir! My name is Johan Spegel. As you can perceive, I am very ill. Will you mitigate my suffering and offer me a little brandy? Although brandy is my infirmity, it is also my solace.

He rises with difficulty, stands swaying and breathing heavily in front of Vogler.

SPEGEL: I am an actor and actually I belong to the renowned Stenborg troupe. But my illness has put an end to my career.

Vogler offers him a small silver flask containing Grandmother's chest medicine. The actor begins to tremble as if he had a fever, but manages to bring the flask to his mouth and drink. The inflamed whites of his eyes are turned upward. He bends forward, stands crouched for a few moments and then straightens up. He returns the flask with an attempt at a polite bow, but nearly collapses. Vogler quickly grabs him around the waist and leads him to the coach. Spegel stops.

SPEGEL: Are you an actor too?

Vogler shakes his head.

SPEGEL: Why, then, are you disguised, sir? You are wearing a false beard and your eyebrows and hair are dyed. Are you a swindler who must hide his real face?

Vogler suddenly laughs.
The dying man opens his eyes and presses his lips together in a shrewd smile. He pulls Vogler close to him.

SPEGEL: Let us rest for a moment and breathe. Now the twilight falls, and this is the last day of life.

Vogler wants to move on, but the actor stops him with unexpected strength and puts his hand on his shoulder.

SPEGEL: I have always yearned for a knife. A blade with

which to lay bare my bowels. To detach my brain, my heart. To free me from my substance. To cut away my tongue and my manhood. A sharp knife blade which would scrape out all my uncleanliness. Then the so-called spirit could ascend out of this meaningless carcass.

He mumbles something indistinguishable and looks around. Vogler leads him gently toward the coach. Tubal comes to meet them and together they help the actor up and place him on the coach floor.

Grandmother protests dully, but moves her feet to make way for him.

Simson, the coachman, climbs up onto the box and sets the horses in motion.

The coach sways through the mud and the pale streaks of fog.

The actor is dying, but peacefully and without pain. Once in a while he takes a deep sip from the silver flask.

Tubal has begun to eat again, chewing calmly and rhythmically. Grandmother stares watchfully from her corner. Vogler lights his pipe. Aman has opened a book and pretends to read.

SPEGEL (*politely*): What kind of book are you reading, sir?
AMAN: It is a novel. It's about cardsharps.
SPEGEL: Colleagues, then?
TUBAL: There are no cardsharps here.
SPEGEL: None. (*Laughs*)
AMAN: Nevertheless it's an interesting book. (*Reads*) "Swindling is so prevalent that those who speak the truth are usually branded as the worst liars."
SPEGEL: The author thus assumes that there is some great general thing called truth somewhere upstage. This is an illusion.
AMAN: Illusion?

SPEGEL: Of course. Truth is made to order; the most skillful liar creates the most useful truth.

TUBAL: That's what you get for your book-reading, Mr. Aman!

AMAN: Mr. Tubal should chew his words before he speaks them.

TUBAL: That business about truth interests me too damn much, I think.

SPEGEL: Yes, it's a beautiful passion.

TUBAL: Naturally there are truths. For instance, if I say: "The rump is behind and the head is on the neck," that is an absolute truth and I like such truths.

SPEGEL: "The rump is behind and the head is on the neck." This is a dubious truth.

TUBAL: Why do you say that?

SPEGEL: Indeed, because on you it seems to be the reverse.

TUBAL: You are an amusing man, sir, and it's almost sad that you have to die.

SPEGEL: So will you, even though you don't believe it now.

TUBAL: A matter for the future, sir! And the future worries me as little as the past. I am a "lily of the field," I live for today. Can't you see that?

Spegel starts to answer, but a violent tremor goes through his body.

TUBAL: Now he's going to die.

Vogler leans over the actor. Spegel's face is closed and nearly lifeless.

SPEGEL: If you want to register the moment itself, look closely, sir. I'll keep my face open to your curiosity. What do I feel? Fear and well-being. Now death has reached my hands, my arms, my feet, my bowels. It climbs upward, inward. Observe me closely. Now the heart stops, now my

consciousness becomes extinguished. I see neither God nor angels. Now I cannot see you any longer. I am dead. You wonder. I will tell you. Death is . . .
TUBAL: That was interesting. (*Eats*)

Vogler lowers the actor to the floor and covers him with a large cloth.

TUBAL: Ruined, wanted by the police, and us with a corpse in the coach! (*Chews*) We could have made a bet ter entrance into the capital.

Tubal sighs and belches, brushes the bread crumbs off his vest, folds his hands over his belly and closes his eyes.

At the southern toll house, the road barrier has been lowered and the coachman reins in the horses.

A uniformed man comes out of the toll house and opens the coach door. Tubal hops out and begins a lively conversation with him. The man shakes his head.

Tubal tries bribing him. To no avail.

Two more uniformed men come out of the house. One of them climbs into the box and takes the reins; the other pushes Tubal into the coach, slams the door and mounts the coach step.

Tubal sinks down in his corner and makes a helpless gesture with his hands.

The coach is set in motion and rolls rather quickly through winding streets bordered by low houses and gardens.

There are not many people outdoors; lamps have already been lighted in the windows.

In the distance, a church bell is heard striking the quarter-hour and then the hour.

The coach rolls cautiously down a short hill, around a two-story stone house and into a court yard.

The travelers get out and look around. The yard is large,

paved with stones and enclosed on two sides by the main house, a massive but handsome building. On the opposite side are wagon sheds, storerooms and a laundry. The fourth side consists of a high fence which borders on a garden.

The window of the ground-floor kitchen is illuminated and the maids of the house look out.

A man in livery comes through the door, hangs up a lantern and begins to unharness the horses.

The uniformed man has gone into the house but returns almost immediately. Quietly and politely he asks the travelers to follow him.

The maids talk and giggle with one another and the cook presses her round body against the window frame.

Tubal sends her an appreciative glance which makes her catch her breath.

The coachman and the man in livery, who is tall and gangling, with an evil face and a long mustache, lead the horses into the stables.

Vogler, his taciturn assistant, Tubal and Grandmother are led through a hallway, up a stone staircase, and into a small, square room with walls completely paneled in oak and sparsely furnished. The man in uniform asks them to be seated, then he departs.

Grandmother suddenly gets a coughing attack, but no one pays attention to her. Everyone is filled with his own thoughts.

Tubal stands at the window and rocks on his toes several times, which makes his shoes squeak. Vogler has pulled out his short pipe, but sucks on it without lighting it. His young assistant sits with crossed legs and looks around rather uninterestedly.

TUBAL: All of you keep quiet and I'll do the talking. Above all, I want Granny to keep her mouth shut.

Grandmother coughs.

TUBAL: Another thing. Granny can make things jump. Granny knows what I mean.
GRANDMOTHER: Oh my, oh my.
TUBAL: Tables fly, chairs fall over, the candles and lamps go out and so on. We know Granny's tricks. Will Granny please be good now and control herself?
GRANDMOTHER: Oh, oh.
TUBAL: For all our sakes.
GRANDMOTHER (*giggles*): Yes, I understand. Perhaps.
TUBAL: Dear Jesus, this old woman makes me nervous. Do you remember what happened in Ostende?
GRANDMOTHER: No, I don't remember.

Grandmother remembers quite well and giggles maliciously. Tubal looks at her thoughtfully but not without respect.

TUBAL: Granny's tricks are passé. They're no fun any more because they can't be explained. Granny, you ought to be dead.
GRANDMOTHER: It was wonderful at Ostende. The mayor's wife got a mouse under her skirt, which she never had before, and the mayor grew a cuckold's horns.
TUBAL: And I was slapped into jail and Vogler got fined and Granny was flogged in the market place. Yes, it was wonderful in Ostende.

Tubal clears his throat. Grandmother's good humor has, despite everything, stimulated him. He pats the old woman on the cheek. Then the door is opened and the uniformed man asks them to enter the next room.

The library is a dark, rectangular room, its walls filled with books from floor to ceiling. Behind the desk sits the Royal Counselor on Medicine, Anders Vergérus. He is about fifty years old, but looks older. He has steel-gray hair cut very short, black eyebrows and a short, heavy beard. His face is pale, irregular. He is dressed in dark, faultless, almost elegant clothes. He is extremely near-sighted and wears thick glasses which often hide his eyes. Beside the desk sits another man, somewhat younger and rather fat. He wears the uniform of an official. This is the chief of police, Frans Starbeck. From time to time he moves his hand over his wavy hair in a coquettish gesture. His face wears a sarcastic expression which changes occasionally to one of sudden insecurity.

In a comfortable armchair sits Consul Abraham Egerman, the young master of the house. He has a soft, child-like face with a winning smile. His look is curious and inquiring. When the strangers enter, he rises politely.

The footman pulls forward several chairs. The uniformed man speaks in whispers to the police chief. Egerman turns to Vergérus.

EGERMAN: What do you say? Perhaps we ought to introduce ourselves.
VERGÉRUS (*rises*): Of course.
EGERMAN: My name is Consul Abraham Egerman and I want to welcome you to my house. I—my wife, too—am greatly interested in the spiritual world. We therefore asked Police Chief Starbeck to arrange this meeting in my home.
STARBECK (*smiling*): Frans Starbeck, chief of police. I arranged this meeting and I hope that my men have treated you with proper courtesy.
VERGÉRUS (*short*): Vergérus. Royal Medical Counselor.

There is a long pause. Nervous glances. Anticipation. Tubal clears his throat.

TUBAL: On behalf of my master, my traveling companions

and myself, may I thank you for this distinguished recep-
tion.

Pause. Tubal gathers courage from somewhere.

TUBAL: It is no more than proper that we in turn introduce ourselves.

The three gentlemen at the desk laugh lightly, but none
of them moves to shake hands with the strangers.

TUBAL: First and foremost, this is the company's leader
and director, Albert Emanuel Vogler, a great name on the
European continent, where for many years he has been
considered the foremost of Mesmer's students. (*Vergérus
looks closely at Tubal*) Mr. Vogler has developed and
perfected the science of animal magnetism in a brilliant
way. The sickness which Mr. Vogler cannot alleviate by
his magnets is not yet known. Everything is completely
scientific! Naturally.
VERGÉRUS: I am very glad to make your acquaintance,
Mr. Vogler.

The men bow. Vogler returns the salutation.

TUBAL: This, gentlemen, is Mr. Vogler's young ward and
foremost pupil, Mr. Aman. He has shown himself to possess the most remarkable gifts.

The men bow. Aman returns the salutation.

TUBAL: The venerable old lady is Mr. Vogler's grandmother, once a celebrated opera singer. Who doesn't remember the Countess Agata de Macopazza?

The chief of police lets slip an "Ah!" and kisses Grandmother's hand. The old lady returns the greeting with great dignity.

TUBAL: I myself am of little importance in this group. My humble self has found a lifetime career in serving the great spirit who bears the name of Albert Emanuel Vogler. Regard me only as the obedient hand, the silent tool.

The three men exchange glances but maintain their correct, opaque behavior. Consul Egerman turns toward Vogler with an obliging smile.

EGERMAN: Would Dr. Vogler mind sitting down for a few minutes to discuss certain general questions concerning his activities?

Vogler shakes his head. Egerman asks the visitors to be seated as he himself sits down in his chair. Starbeck sits at the large desk. The medical counselor remains standing, but takes off his glasses and rubs his face. Suddenly he meets Vogler's glance.

STARBECK: Dr. Vogler! You have advertised, in the town's newspapers, a performance promising all kinds of sensations.

The police chief leans across the table and reads aloud from an open newspaper.

STARBECK (reads): "Sensational marvels never shown before. Magic acts based on the philosophies of the Orient. Health-giving magnets. Spine-tingling thrills of the senses." (Looks up) Is this Mr. Vogler's announcement?
TUBAL: Sir! These wild phrases, the wording of which would be offensive to any educated mind, are not the work of Dr. Vogler's hand.

VERGÉRUS (*interrupts*): We would be grateful if "Doctor" Vogler would answer the police chief's questions himself.
TUBAL: Mr. Vogler is unfortunately deprived of the gift of speech. He is mute, sirs.

The medical counselor seems to ponder this answer. He crosses his hands behind him and regards his shoes seriously. Consul Egerman lights a cigar. The chief of police looks up from his papers with a sarcastic expression on his face.

STARBECK: Mr. Aman . . . (*Aman looks up*) Perhaps Mr. Aman is also deprived of the gift of speech.
AMAN: No.
STARBECK: I haven't heard you say anything up to now.
AMAN: I haven't been asked to, sir.

Aman speaks with scorn. Vergérus is suddenly attentive and turns smilingly toward the young man.

VERGÉRUS: So you devote yourselves to magic séances.
AMAN: We haven't said that.
VERGÉRUS: Your friend, Mr. Tubal . . .
AMAN: A game, nothing else. We use various kinds of apparatus, mirrors and projectors. It is very simple and entirely harmless.
VERGÉRUS: Another question. Does Mr. Vogler heal the sick?
AMAN: This we have not said.
VERGÉRUS: He uses Mesmer's animal magnetism. I know the method rather well. It is completely worthless.

Aman doesn't answer, but looks at the medical counselor with an absent expression. Vergérus takes a step forward.

VERGÉRUS: We happen to know that Mr. Vogler recently, but under another name, made a tour of Denmark. There he posed as a physician and arranged consultations at the inns. The patients were placed in a dimly lit room and were magnetized according to the principles of Mesmer. This treatment led to trembling and nervous attacks of all kinds. Some of them became unconscious.

AMAN: Why do you ask about things which you already know?

VERGÉRUS: As far as I can see, there seems to be a most remarkable division in Mr. Vogler's activities.

STARBECK: How do you mean, sir?

VERGÉRUS: First we have the idealistic *Doctor* Vogler who practices as a physician according to Mesmer's rather doubtful methods. Then we have a somewhat less than idealistic *magician* who arranges all kinds of hocus-pocus according to entirely home-made recipes. If I've grasped the facts correctly, the activities of the Vogler troupe range unscrupulously between these two extremes.

Egerman, who has been sitting quietly puffing on his cigar, enters the conversation. His tone is still extremely polite.

EGERMAN: Tell me one thing. Does Mr. Vogler claim to possess supernatural powers?

Tubal steps forward and raises his hand in a parrying gesture.

TUBAL: This cross-examination is painful both for you and for us, gentlemen. Hold us responsible if we have done anything unlawful . . .

STARBECK: That is exactly what we intend to find out.

The chief of police turns his head. A very pale, very thin

and delicate woman has entered the room, stopping at the door. It is Ottilia Egerman.

OTTILIA: Excuse me, I didn't know . . .
EGERMAN: My dear, sit down! Gentlemen, may I introduce my wife.

The men bow. Mrs. Egerman takes her husband's out-stretched hand and sits down beside him. Starbeck smiles sarcastically, strokes his mouth and then pats his hair in an affected manner.

STARBECK: What we have heard in this matter hardly in-spires confidence.
VERGÉRUS: Mr. Tubal, will you be kind enough to bring me that lamp standing on the table over there?

Tubal holds the lamp. Vergérus takes him gently by the arm and leads him over to Vogler, who sits with his head bowed and his hands resting on his knees.

VERGÉRUS: Look at me, Mr. Vogler.

Vogler raises his head and looks at Vergérus. *The face of the mesmerizer is twisted with rage.* Mrs. Egerman, who sits closest to Vogler, turns her head away in sudden fear.

VERGÉRUS: Why do you look so furious, Mr. Vogler? (*Vogler looks at him*) You have no reason to hate me. I only want to find out the truth. That should be your wish as well. (*Vogler doesn't answer*) Open your mouth. (*Vogler obeys*) Stick out your tongue. (*Vogler obeys*)

Vergérus leans over Vogler and carefully squeezes his throat and windpipe.

VERGÉRUS: I regret to say, Mr. Vogler, that I find no reason for your muteness.

Vergérus takes the lamp from Tubal and sets it on the table. Vogler has tears in his eyes. He wipes them away with the back of his hand.

STARBECK: Moreover, your advertisement states that you *"can provoke terrible visions among your audience."*
TUBAL: Sir! It's our *laterna magica*. A ridiculous and entirely harmless toy.
VERGÉRUS: I am not so sure that it is a toy you are referring to. (*To Vogler*) Do you possess the power to provoke visions, Mr. Vogler?
TUBAL: I protest!
STARBECK: And why, if I may ask?
TUBAL: Mr. Vogler is a great man, Mr. Starbeck. A great man and a distinguished scientist. You treat him as if he were a charlatan.
VERGÉRUS: It's rather the company he keeps that throws a certain shadow over Mr. Vogler's scientific merits. (*To Vogler*) Do you provoke visions, sir?
TUBAL (*angrily*): I protest even more.
STARBECK (*sharply*): If you don't keep quiet, I'll ask you to leave.
VERGÉRUS: Well, Mr. Vogler. Yes or no?

Everyone looks intently at Vogler.

VERGÉRUS: Yes or no. (*Vogler nods*) So it's yes. Can you bring about this state in anyone? (*Vogler nods; Tubal sighs*) Perhaps in me? (*Tubal sinks down and shakes his head*) Let us immediately make an experiment, Mr. Vogler. I am at your disposal.
OTTILIA (*crying out*): No, not that!
VERGÉRUS: And why not, Mrs. Egerman?

OTTILIA: Excuse me, excuse me.

Aman puts a chair in the center of the room and makes a sign to Vergérus to sit down.

VERGÉRUS: No additional arrangements? No magnets? No dark mysterious lights? No secret music behind the draperies?

The chief of police and Egerman have placed themselves so that they can clearly see Vergérus' face, which is lit up by the table lamp. Aman places himself behind Vergérus' back, puts his hands on his shoulders.
Vogler sits calmly, expectantly. He leans forward a little and fixes his eyes on Vergérus, who returns his glance. The others in the room remain immobile. The clock on the wall clicks and strikes once, quickly. There is a long silence.

VERGÉRUS (calmly): What do you want me to see, Mr. Vogler? Something frightening or exciting?

He becomes silent and continues to look calmly at the mesmerizer. Vogler's glance is absolutely fixed and almost expressionless.

VERCÉRUS: It must be weak vessels! Weak vessels and weak souls. You are bursting yourself. Be careful and end your experiment. (Pause) You think that I hate you, but that's not true. There is only one thing which interests me. Your physiology, Mr. Vogler. I would like to make an autopsy of you. (Pause) Weigh your brain, open your heart, explore a little of your nerve circuits, lift out your eyes.

Vergérus has turned pale and his eyes widen. He sits

with his arms crossed. Although his posture is tense, his voice remains completely controlled.

EGERMAN (*suddenly*): Stop now. Before it's too late.
VERGÉRUS: Too late? Too boring, you mean. (*Rises*) Mr. Vogler, you have failed, but you ought to be grateful for your fiasco. You are harmless.
OTTILIA: Why do you lie?

Vergérus turns around and stares at her. Then he takes off his glasses.

VERGÉRUS: I don't understand you, Mrs. Egerman.
OTTILIA: But we saw that you lied. You experienced something that frightened you terribly, but you don't dare tell us what it was.
VERGÉRUS: Pardon me, Mrs. Egerman, but I have nothing to hide, and no prestige to protect. Who knows? Perhaps I regret that I was incapable of experiencing anything.

Vogler leans back and holds one hand over his eyes. He seems exhausted. Vergérus turns toward him with a smile.

VERGÉRUS: You'll surely forgive my little joke, Mr. Vogler. I'm convinced that your magic lantern provokes the most amazing visions.

The chief of police rises behind the desk and gathers his papers. He looks flustered and harried.

STARBECK: Everything all right? Then only the permit of the chief of police is needed for you to hold your magnetic performances.
TUBAL: Sir!
STARBECK (*raises his head*): Calm down! You will have your permit. (*Pause*) On one condition.

TUBAL: Of course! (*Worried*) And that is?

STARBECK: That Mr. Vogler give a private performance of his program tomorrow at ten o'clock in the large hall.

TUBAL (*in despair*): Mr. Starbeck!

STARBECK: Just as a check. In full daylight. Have you any objections, Mr. Tubal?

Tubal remains silent.

STARBECK: Excellent.

Mr. and Mrs. Egerman have risen.

EGERMAN: Supper will be served in an hour.

TUBAL (*bewildered*): It's too great an honor . . .

EGERMAN (*smiling*): Forgive me. Mr. Vogler and his troupe will eat in the kitchen. Mrs. Garp will show you to your rooms. (*To the footman*) Rustan, show our guests to the kitchen.

TUBAL: Perhaps we'd prefer to stay in town.

EGERMAN (*politely*): It is the wish of the chief of police that Mr. Vogler and his troupe be the guests of this house.

Egerman turns his back to Tubal. Rustan makes a sign for the strangers to follow him. On their way upstairs they can hear peals of laughter behind them.

The three men eventually recover from their hilarity and sit down in front of the open fireplace. Ottilia remains standing at the desk.

OTTILIA: Yes, it was a rather humorous game.

EGERMAN: What do you mean, dearest?

OTTILIA: Isn't it amusing to humiliate people who cannot defend themselves?

EGERMAN: You don't understand, my child! The medical

counselor and I had made a wager on a question of great scientific interest.

OTTILIA: A wager?

VERGÉRUS: Indeed, Mrs. Egerman. Your husband holds the opinion that intangible and inexplicable forces really exist.

OTTILIA: And you deny that possibility.

VERGÉRUS: It would be a catastrophe if scientists were suddenly forced to accept the inexplicable.

EGERMAN: Why a catastrophe?

VERGÉRUS: It would lead to the point where we would have to take into account a . . . that we would be suddenly forced to . . . logically we would have to conceive of . . .

EGERMAN: A God.

VERGÉRUS: A God, if you like.

STARBECK: A grotesque thought, and besides it's not modern. Science today is better equipped than ever to penetrate all the obvious mysteries.

EGERMAN: Obvious?

VERGÉRUS: Everything can be explained.

EGERMAN: You seem very optimistic.

STARBECK: Optimistic! Just think of electricity! The steam engine!

EGERMAN: The fact is, at any rate, that the mesmerizer made an impression on you.

VERGÉRUS: On my word of honor, he didn't influence me the least bit.

STARBECK: That wager still stands? No one has won.

EGERMAN: We'll see tomorrow. Shall we have a glass before supper?

Mrs. Egerman brings some port wine and serves it. Then she walks quietly out of the room. Vergérus looks after her.

VERGÉRUS: Your wife seems a little agitated, Egerman. Is it the child's death which still . . .

EGERMAN: We're going abroad this coming fall, and then I hope . . . (*Pause*) Skoal, gentlemen!
STARBECK: Skoal to Dr. Vogler and his magnetic troupe.
VERGÉRUS: A troupe with an extremely bad conscience, it seems.

The three men drink and laugh contentedly.

The Egerman kitchen is large, and like a farm kitchen. It is situated on the ground floor and follows the angular shape of the house. On one side there is an exit leading to the stone staircase and the hallway. On the other side, two doors lead to the pantry and the servants' quarters. The entrance door leads directly out into the courtyard. In the corner of the room stands a large table on which a great deal of food, beer and brandy have been placed.

Sara and Sanna have put the last touches on the preparations. Sara is twenty, Sanna about sixteen. At a little table somewhat to the side sit Vogler and Aman. They are just finishing their meal.

SANNA (*whispers*): I think they are dangerous people and we must guard ourselves against them. I think they look ghastly.
SARA (*whispers*): You don't understand, Sanna dear, because you're still so young.
SANNA: The magician himself is completely mute. Isn't that ghastly? He hasn't said a word during the entire meal.
SARA: Rustan says that he's pretending.
SANNA: That's even worse. You know, I'm really afraid.

Now Vogler and Aman rise from the table and walk out through the door to the hallway. Sanna and Sara look after them with curious respect.

SARA: Anyway, they haven't got any money. You only have to be afraid of rich people.

SANNA: I think it's ghastly that they're poor. Imagine, they might kill us and steal all the master's money.

The door opens and Tubal enters in high spirits. Grandmother follows on his heels.

TUBAL: Good evening, little maids. My name is only Tubal; it is as simple as a folk song. Now let us see! This one is Sara, and that one is Sanna.

SANNA AND SARA (*giggle*): Oh, is that so?

TUBAL: Now I know. This here is Sanna, and that is Sara.

SANNA AND SARA (*giggle*): Do you think so?

TUBAL: I'll find out! In short, we are invited for supper. There are the makings and here are the guests! Shall we sit down?

Tubal turns around. Sofia Garp comes out from her quarters. Tubal steps forward and manages to kiss her hand.

SOFIA: Sofia Garp, the cook of the house.

TUBAL: My lady! I am enchanted! Flattered! Overwhelmed! Not to say *infatuated!*

Sofia's eyes take on a peculiar expression. She frees her hand, smoothes her apron and points toward the table.

SOFIA: Good appetite, as we say in this house.

Rustan, Egerman's footman, has suddenly appeared from some corner. He is a thickset, shapeless boy, endowed with high spirits and a certain animal energy. He is accompanied by Simson, Vogler's coachman, who has changed his clothes and is thereby transformed into a handsome young man.

Everyone sits down at the table and begins to eat in silence. The beer foams, the brandy glitters, the pies rustle and the big slices of bread fall softly. There is much chewing and swallowing; the glasses and dishes tinkle, faces blush. No one speaks, but the silence is filled with friendly curiosity. Tubal belches discreetly.

SOFIA: Bless you.

TUBAL: When I see these beautiful women with curvaceous figures, rosy lips and sparkling eyes, when I see these young men, fiery as young stallions, when I see our table sagging under all this abundance, then I'm inspired to say something about life.

He throws an enthralling glance at Sofia, who draws her breath so sharply that her corset creaks audibly.

SARA: How beautiful you speak, Mr. Tubal. Tell us more.

TUBAL: It's coming, my child. It's coming. (*Drinks*) Life, I want to say, is a perfect performance of magic, with continually new and surprising effects.

SARA: Can you perform magic, Mr. Tubal?

TUBAL: Little child, let us not speak of supernatural things. Let us instead enjoy reality, which is considerably more natural, not to say more wholesome. That which is secret, that which is hidden, the ghosts of the dead, the vision of the future which hangs over us with its threatening dark face, all this we ought to leave be, my child.

SARA: Can you tell fortunes, Mr. Tubal?

TUBAL: Mr. Tubal *can* tell fortunes.

SARA: Read my hand, Mr. Tubal.

TUBAL: No, my dear child. You are much too young and full of hope. I don't want to destroy your curiosity, your joy in life, your naïve faith!

Tubal's voice takes on a clerical tone. The others at the table regard him with respect, all except Grandmother, who seems to have dozed off in the warmth of the stove and the steaming food. Tubal looks around and his glance touches that of Simson.

SOFIA: I'd say that one can really *feel* your supernatural powers, Mr. Tubal.
TUBAL: They are felt, they are felt.
SOFIA: A wonderful gift!
TUBAL: But heavy to bear, Sofia. And dark. He who has once sold himself becomes very lonely.
SOFIA: Oh my, Mr. Tubal, you make one feel both cold and hot under the corset at the same time. (*Blushes*)
TUBAL: One becomes lonely, Sofia. Hungering after tenderness and such things.
SARA: It's as if I heard our minister speaking. But more frightening.
SANNA (*cries*): I get so afraid.
SARA: What are you crying about?
TUBAL: Cry, my child! Her tears are like salve on the cancerous sores of an outcast from society.
SARA: Dear Mr. Tubal, tell my fortune anyhow.

Sara leans forward over the table, blushing with excitement. Tubal grasps her small hand and looks at her for a long while. She breathes heavily. Then the door opens and a large, heavy man enters. He is dressed in livery and has a pale, oval face, a drooping mustache and sinister eyes.

SOFIA: Sit down, Antonsson, and take your fill. This is Antonsson, Mr. Egerman's coachman.
TUBAL: At your service, Antonsson. We have already met.
ANTONSSON (*curtly*): 'Evening.

He takes off his livery coat, sits down at the short end of the table and pulls the brandy jug over to him.

SARA: Quiet now. Mr. Tubal is going to talk about the future.

Tubal holds the girl's hand and closes his eyes. At the same time he lets his other hand sink under the table and, as if by coincidence, fall on Sofia's thigh. Cautiously his hand makes an indiscreet investigation. Sofia Garp stops breathing and opens her mouth, but remains silent. In the meantime, Tubal has begun to prophesy with swelling pomposity.

TUBAL: I see a light. Now it is extinguished. It is dark. I hear sweet words of love. No, I cannot repeat them. My sense of decency forbids it. I think I see . . . I . . . Now it is beautiful . . . who can talk about decency at such a moment? Oh, it's stimulating. A young man. He rides at full gallop. It is beautiful! Nature itself.

Sofia puts her hands in front of her face, which is flushed with excitement. Grandmother has awakened and mumbles like a counterpoint to Tubal's melody. Sara is breathless; her cheeks are burning. Sanna cries quietly, leaning against Rustan, who sits with a sagging jaw and breathes heavily for the first time in his life. Simson, a handsome young man with moist lips and gleaming hair, searches Sara's face but she hasn't noticed him yet.

TUBAL: Glittering tears of a maiden. Oh my child. The heaving breast of the turtle dove. Pardon me for lingering on this vision, but I see nothing else. It goes on for a long time. (*Pause*) A long time!

Tubal's left hand caresses the lower half of Sofia, who becomes more and more excited in her upper half. His right hand still holds Sara fast, but he falls silent. He merely nods rather seriously.

TUBAL: Yes, yes. (*Sighs*) I see no more. But something came to mind: Sara, my child, before you go to celebrate your love feast, take a few drops of our love potion and you'll delight in it sevenfold.

Out of a carrying case which he always has at hand Tubal takes an unusual-looking flask. He offers it to Sara.

TUBAL: A gift from Mrs. Aphrodite Venus, the goddess of love. Tubal is only the humble delivery man.
SANNA (*excited*): A love potion.
SOFIA: Is it expensive, Mr. Tubal?
TUBAL: It is costly, Madame Sofia, because its ingredients are almost impossible to procure and they are gathered under the greatest hardship.
SOFIA: That you dared!
TUBAL: In the name of science! And that of love!
SOFIA: May I buy a bottle, Mr. Tubal?
TUBAL (*shakes his head*): That is impossible. Your means are much too small, Madame Sofia. These potions can only be bought by countesses, princesses and certain successful actresses.
SOFIA: Oh!
TUBAL: But for you, Sofia—well, because of your beauty and your great hospitality and courtesy, let us say thirteen shillings.* Two bottles for twenty.

Sofia nods wanly but determinedly. She rises from the table and staggers to her room.

SARA: It has a strong smell.

Sara has opened the bottle and sniffed the contents. She looks up bright-eyed at the others.

SARA: So strong, so strong.

* The shilling (skilling) was a coin used in Sweden up to 1855.

TUBAL: It is *fluidum* itself, my child. Materialized stimulation, if I may be allowed to express myself scientifically.

Sara suddenly offers the bottle to Simson. Their hands touch. He sniffs the bottle, pours a few drops into his brandy glass and drinks, emptying it.

SARA: Is it good for men?
TUBAL: Not merely good! Mrs. Aphrodite Venus touches their hearts with her finger tips. And then there's the devil to pay!
SARA: God in heaven, if only Mother were here!
SANNA (*cries*): I'm so scared, so scared.

Sofia Garp comes out of her room quickly, puts twenty shillings on the table and stands at Tubal's side, steaming. He leans under the table, but Grandmother is equally fast.

TUBAL (*whispers*): The love potion is finished. What do we use now?
GRANDMOTHER: Take this one, against the colic and bunions. The most important thing is what the bottle looks like and how it tastes.

Tubal fishes out two small bottles and places them on the table. The lanky Rustan has risen with a coin in his hand and stutters bewilderedly.

RUSTAN: What can I get for this shilling?
TUBAL: A night of love which you'll never forget, you lanky bumpkin. (*Picks up a bottle*)
GRANDMOTHER (*whispers*): But that's rat poison.
TUBAL (*whispers*): This one won't kick the bucket just yet. (*Aloud*) Drink the whole bottle in one swallow and you'll feel a bliss greater than King Solomon's when he enjoyed himself with his thousand concubines.

Rustan immediately pulls the cork out of the bottle, empties it, breathes heavily and rolls his eyes. Sanna cries even harder. Sofia sits down beside Tubal and looks at him soberly while she fills his glass.

SOFIA: Of course you are a swindler, Tubal.

TUBAL: Of course, Madame Sofia. But I'm something special, don't you agree?

She empties her beer glass and puts it down on the table with a bang.

SOFIA: You're also poor?

TUBAL: My capital is not of this world.

SOFIA: I was just thinking that. You would make a good preacher.

TUBAL: My faith is wavering. . . .

SOFIA: You may be right. This subject requires a private discussion. (*Whispers*) I'm going to my room. In a few minutes, walk out into the yard and around the house to your right. There is a little door there, and I'll let you in.

TUBAL (*enthusiastically*): You are a real woman, Sofia!

SOFIA: Perhaps. My husband died eight years ago.

TUBAL: My condolences!

SOFIA: He was fragile. But he was a great preacher in our parish. He fired our souls. He had a spiritual storm in his heart.

TUBAL: That is a wonderful thing.

SOFIA: Perhaps, perhaps not.

She looks at him sharply, but her bosom heaves. Tubal is burning with brandy and hell-fire.

TUBAL: Won't you take the flasks with you?

SOFIA (*calmly but without scorn*): Keep your bottles. You can sell them again.

Sofia's behind sways in a stately fashion as she walks un-
hurriedly from the room. Tubal becomes nervous, bites
his nails and looks around with watchful eyes. Simson and
Sara sit, bashful and mute, on opposite sides of the table.
Simson has stretched out his hand toward the girl and her
hand is halfway stretched out toward his. Sanna cries
quietly and persistently. Rustan gets up and staggers toward the door but lands on a stool beside the water barrel.
He seems badly muddled. Antonsson sits immobile.

TUBAL (*raps on the table*): Marry Sofia. (*Drinks*) Halle-
luja, brothers—*and* sisters! It's conceivable. The main
thing is not faith but power. Sofia felt the power. (*Gets
up*) Peace be with you, my children. Now brother Tubal
goes to sister Sofia and finds salvation. Peace be with you.

No one has heard his statement, nor did he expect
them to. Tubal simply felt a bursting need to clarify his
situation. He goes out into the yard, closing the door carefully. He can be seen for a moment in the window before
he turns the corner and is gone. Simson looks after him
slightly distracted, and suddenly grips Sara's hand. At first
she pulls back but then remains completely still, her head
turned away from him. Sanna cries in confused anguish.

Grandmother, who has eaten as much as she can hold,
is oblivious to what has happened around her. She moves
to the chair next to Sanna and nudges her arm.

GRANDMOTHER: Why do you cry, little ant?
SANNA: Are you a witch?
GRANDMOTHER: Perhaps.
SANNA: I'm so frightened of everything that's happened
tonight. (*Quietly*) And you are so old and ugly.
GRANDMOTHER: When you are almost two hundred years
old, you'll be ugly too, little ant.
SANNA: Are you really *that* old?

GRANDMOTHER: Yes, of course.

SANNA: Can you also perform magic?

GRANDMOTHER: It's happened. (*Quietly*) But nowadays nobody believes in my secrets, so I have to be careful. One must not offend the new faith, because then one might be put in a madhouse. That's what Tubal says.

SANNA: How did you become a witch?

GRANDMOTHER: Shh! I can't tell you that.

SANNA: Have you sold your soul?

GRANDMOTHER: Yes. Perhaps I have.

SANNA (*cries again*): Oh, I'm becoming so frightened again.

GRANDMOTHER: Now go along to bed and the witch will give you a gift. Do what I say, little ant. I only want the best for you. There, there.

Sanna gets up hesitantly and walks out of the kitchen. Grandmother remains seated, a little thoughtful. She chatters to herself and happens to catch sight of Antonsson. They exchange black looks.

ANTONSSON: What are you staring at?

GRANDMOTHER: I have been present at a number of executions, especially in my earlier years. (*Antonsson stares at her*) I have seen the hanged ones looking down at me. I have met glances from the eyes of beheaded men. I have known several hangmen, especially in past years.

ANTONSSON: So?

GRANDMOTHER: So I know how a criminal looks.

ANTONSSON: I have never offended anyone.

GRANDMOTHER: No, no.

ANTONSSON: But to crack your neck would almost be a good deed.

GRANDMOTHER (*rises*): When I passed the laundry, I looked into the darkness. In a corner a corpse was hanging from a rope. I went closer to see who it was. And I recognized him.

ANTONSSON: I'm not afraid of you!

GRANDMOTHER: It was a murderer hanging from that hook.

ANTONSSON: Oh.

GRANDMOTHER: Yes, that's how it is. One sees what one sees and one knows what one knows. It just doesn't pay to talk about it.

Grandmother leaves the kitchen, but she doesn't forget to take along Tubal's case. Antonsson remains seated at the table, engrossed in his thoughts.

SARA: What a life you must lead, Mr. Simson.

SIMSON: Exciting, you mean. Well, one gets accustomed to it.

SARA: All of us stay here, day in and day out. Everything is the same all week long. Sometimes my whole body tingles so that I want to laugh and cry at the same time.

SIMSON: Our life! Oh, how can you describe it! Performances, travels, great parties, a life of luxury.

SARA: Naturally you meet beautiful women, Mr. Simson.

SIMSON: The magic attracts women, you know. Especially beautiful, hot-blooded women with instincts. Sometimes we actually have to fight them off.

SARA: Oh!

SIMSON: I just remembered a Russian princess with green eyes and a lily-white bosom . . . Oh, well, let's talk about something else.

SARA: Oh!

SIMSON: I can say that I've come to know women well. Only a glance, and everything is revealed.

SARA: And just think, I'm sitting here with you, Mr. Simson.

SIMSON: But you're cute.

SARA: Do you think so?

SIMSON: And I'm a man of experience, I'd say. So I know

what I'm talking about. You've got a sweet mouth, beautiful eyes, and a really neat figure.

SARA: Mama, help!

SIMSON: What are you shouting for!

SARA: I don't know. But I feel so strange. Particularly in the stomach. Maybe I'm sick.

SIMSON: It's the love potion, of course.

SARA: But I didn't swallow any.

SIMSON: It doesn't matter. (*Quickly*) You smelled it.

SARA: Do you think *that* could be the reason? What are you doing!

Simson dives under the table and comes up next to Sara. He sits down beside her and puts his arm around her waist.

SIMSON: Now let's each of us take a swallow. And then Mrs. Venus Aphrodite will come and touch us. She's the goddess of love, you know. And then everything will be lovely. One does what one does and one knows what one knows, as Granny says.

SARA: I think you're teasing me, Mr. Simson.

SIMSON: No, my child, I'm not teasing you, I'm preparing a wonderful amusement for us both.

SARA: And the Russian princess?

SIMSON: Is your bosom less white?

SARA: I don't think so. But her eyes were green.

SIMSON: She used to close her eyes. You can do that too.

SARA (*happily*): Then let's drink.

They clink glasses and drink the love potion which Simson has poured. To make sure, they drink again and empty the bottle. Sara puts her glass down and sighs.

SARA: What will happen now?

SIMSON: Now we'll just wait.

SARA: Here?

SIMSON (*unsure*): No, not exactly here.

SARA: Let's go to the laundry.

SIMSON: The laundry?

SARA: Of course! (*Happy*) There are big baskets full of soft, clean clothes there.

SIMSON: Perhaps we should wait awhile, though. (*Becomes pale*)

SARA: Wait for what?

SIMSON: Mr. Vogler may want me for something, I think . . .

SARA: How pale you look all of a sudden. What's wrong?

SIMSON: I just remembered that the medicine can have very different effects on different people. For example, some men turn into raging lions. It's happened that I've almost ripped my women apart.

SARA (*attracted*): How terrible!

SIMSON: I'm afraid of hurting you, dear Sara.

SARA: Oh, I'll stay in one piece.

SIMSON: It works differently, as I said. One can also become nauseous. I've heard of people who died.

SARA: And I think that Mrs. Venus Aphrodite has just touched me in the right way. (*Giggles*)

SIMSON: Yes, that's possible. But I'm much more sensitive.

SARA: Come now and don't be silly. (*In giggling whispers*) I won't eat you, little Simson.

She takes him by the hand and runs out. They can be seen for a moment in the yard. Sara's light-colored dress is silhouetted against the coach, which stands high and dark in the twilight. Antonsson sits immobile, raises his head and looks at poor Rustan, who, half dazed, has crouched on the stool near the water barrel.

ANTONSSON: Drink something and you'll feel better.

RUSTAN: Just think! He just walked off with her. And she's always been so standoffish.

Sanna has her own little room under the big stairs. A triangular window looks out on the garden. The girl has crept into her narrow bed. Grandmother, who has followed her into the room, searches in her black bag. Finally she comes up with something which gleams faintly in the night light. She tiptoes up to Sanna and lays the object on the girl's breast. It is an ornament shaped like an ear. In the ear is a ring and a sparkling stone. Attached to the ring is a thin gold chain.

GRANDMOTHER: Hush, hush. You shouldn't be sad, little ant. You'll soon be in the game. First Grandmother gives you a gift to console you. Hush, hush. Now I'll sit here and sing to you so that you'll fall asleep.
SANNA: Is it an ear?
GRANDMOTHER: It's an ear. And if you whisper your wishes into this ear, you'll get what you ask for. But only on one condition.
SANNA: What kind of condition?
GRANDMOTHER: You can only wish for things that live, are living, or can become alive.
SANNA: I don't understand what you mean.
GRANDMOTHER: No, not now, but it doesn't matter. Hush, hush, little nose, I'm going to sing for you. What do you want to hear? I know all kinds of songs, you know.
SANNA: Nothing scary.
GRANDMOTHER (sings):
    A soldier with his rifle did stand
    While the enemy fought his fatherland,
    And dreamed of his lass while he followed command.
    The sun was hot and the wind was cold,
    The weary soldier marched so bold;
    From the wood the screaming enemy came

And the soldier fought on murmuring her name.
The soldiers battled hand to hand,
And every foray he did withstand.
The blood ran in the bayonets' flash
And many brave men died in that clash.
And under the mountain sank the sun,
Covered by night the foe did run.
The soldier rejoiced that the battle had ceased
As his comrades prepared for the victory feast.
But our soldier sat to the side
And wrote a letter of love to his bride:
"I felt your thoughts of me through the strife;
It is this which surely spared my life.
And now I stand on watch this night,
Knowing that your love has heavenly might."

SANNA (*sighs*): That was a beautiful song and now I feel much better, I think.

GRANDMOTHER: There is one stanza left.

> Love is trust and love is rest,
> Love gives strength to the cowardly breast;
> Love is one and never two,
> Love is for every lover new.

GRANDMOTHER (*whispers*): Did you hear, little ant?

SANNA: Now I'm almost asleep.

GRANDMOTHER: Yes, yes. (*Mumbles incomprehensible words*) Yes, yes.

Suddenly the room is filled by a white light which disappears almost immediately. Sanna reawakens.

SANNA: Now it will thunder.

GRANDMOTHER (*listens*): Far away.

SANNA: I'm not afraid of thunder. (*Sleeps*)

Grandmother listens tensely for something else, something which had sounded frightening in the stillness.

She patters noiselessly out into the large hallway. The door to the courtyard stands ajar, but the lamp over the portal has gone out. She stands, a small figure in the grayish light, listening tensely. Now there is a soundless flash; Grandmother waits, immobile and expectant. She hears a moaning nearby, a few shuffling footsteps and then silence again.

GRANDMOTHER (*mumbles*): "He calls you down, he calls you out, beyond the dead, the living, the living dead, beyond the raised hands."

She moistens her finger, scribbles a sign on the wall and starts upstairs, a gray shadow without substance in the immobile gray light.

Next to the laundry with its large vats and smell of cellar dampness is the ironing room. A mangle stands in the center of the floor, bulging and monstrous. A huge washbasket lies nearby, filled with fresh-smelling, newly washed clothes. There is also a box of old winter apples in a corner, and in the narrow, high-ceilinged window is a bird's nest.

SIMSON: It's very hot in here.
SARA: Doesn't it smell nice? It's the newly ironed linen with its lavender scent from the linen closet, and the winter apples in a box over there. In the window is a bird's nest.
SIMSON: It's still damned warm, anyhow.
SARA: You're trembling.
SIMSON: It's so hot.
SARA: Then take off your coat.

Sara giggles and disappears into the darkness. Then she pushes open the door to the courtyard. Just then the third flash comes, this time followed by a faint clap of thunder.

SIMSON: Close the door.
SARA: No, I want to see you.
SIMSON: I've lost a shoe.

Sara giggles, then becomes serious. Simson searches around in the darkness.

SARA (*standing quietly at the door*): I can see that Rustan and Antonsson are still sitting in the kitchen. And there is a light in the guest room where Mr. Aman and Mr. Vogler are staying.
SIMSON: Sara.
SARA: Where are you? I can't see you.
SIMSON: In the washbasket. Where you said we should be.

Simson has sat in the huge washbasket and made himself comfortable. Sara jumps in with him.

SARA: Well.
SIMSON: Of course it would be easy for me to seduce you, little Sara.
SARA: Do you think so?
SIMSON: I'm quite sure. But one becomes older with the years and more considerate, if you know what I mean.
SARA: If I try very hard, I think I might understand.
SIMSON: One learns not to trample on things just like that. Not to pick every flower by the side of the road.
SARA: Well, you can at least smell it.
SIMSON: I merely lean over the fragile petals and then go my way.
SARA: Why do you talk so much?

Now there is another flash of lightning, but this time the thunder comes faster and louder.

SARA: Oh, I'm afraid of thunder.

She puts her arms around Simson's neck and moans.

SIMSON: Just be calm. You have me.
SARA: It's very, very calming.
SIMSON: Oh!
SARA (*whispers*): What!
SIMSON: The love potion.
SARA: Do you feel it very strongly?
SIMSON: Oh, yes! I'm perspiring like a camel.

Lightning and soft thunder in the distance.

SARA: Now it's thundering again. Hold me tight.
SIMSON: There's a hard knot!
SARA: I'll help you. No, don't look.
SIMSON: Oh, should that button be unbuttoned? This is very difficult.

The cloth rustles and the basket squeaks. Flashes of smiles and heavy breathing. Two tender sighs.

SARA: You don't seem very experienced, dear Simson.
SIMSON: I've been abroad most of the time, you know.
SARA (*laughs*): Oh, I have to laugh.
SIMSON: Why are you laughing?
SARA: Now Mrs. Venus Aphrodite touches me with her finger tips. Isn't it true? Wasn't it so?
SIMSON: Hush, hush.

They fail to see a pale figure staggering around in the courtyard, nor do they hear a dull groaning which seems to come from purgatory.

The large basket squeaks in an unaccustomed manner.

The lamps flicker in the kitchen. Uneasy shadows rebound off the walls and the utensils. Rustan leans against the water barrel, gripped by the double pain of a stomach-ache and melancholy.

Antonsson pours some brandy.

ANTONSSON: That man Vogler.

RUSTAN: His kind ought to be flogged. There's something special about swindlers. One is provoked by their faces.

ANTONSSON: Faces?

RUSTAN: Exactly. Seeing a face like Vogler's makes me furious. It makes me want to hit him.

ANTONSSON: Vogler's face?

RUSTAN: There is something special about those faces. Do you understand what I mean, Antonsson? One ought to trample them. Faces like Vogler's and Aman's and the old woman's . . .

Rustan emits a cry of horror and tumbles backward as he tries to get up. The water barrel collapses and a flood bursts over the floor. Antonsson reaches out with his arms in a sudden movement but doesn't have time to rise. The door has been thrown open, the lamp is blown out by the sudden draft, and a huge, flickering figure with inhuman features fills the whole room for a moment. An ax lands in the table with a dull thud next to Antonsson's shoulder. Rustan howls like a lunatic and throws himself on the floor.

The giant figure vanishes as fast as it appeared. After a few moments of dumb · horror, Antonsson manages to light a candle.

Rustan sits in a lake. His eyes are glassy with fear. Antonsson takes hold of the ax and rushes out into the hallway, but it is empty.

RUSTAN: A ghost.

ANTONSSON: Or the devil himself.

RUSTAN: Where is the brandy?

ANTONSSON: Where is the brandy?
RUSTAN: The jug is gone.
ANTONSSON: On the floor?
RUSTAN: No.
ANTONSSON: Where?
RUSTAN: The ghost took the brandy!

The large hall is a rectangular room on the second floor with a rather low ceiling, paneled in dark maple and painted lintels. The windows face the street. On the opposite wall hang family portraits, a long row of warriors, bishops, officials, matrons and merchants. The floor is covered with an expensive parquet, and from the ceiling hangs a heavy, ancient chandelier. A few candles burn, but they light up the large room only partially.

Vogler and Aman are busy setting up the next day's performance. Grandmother patters in and sits down on a long black casket.

GRANDMOTHER: What are you doing?
AMAN: We're preparing for tomorrow morning's performance.
GRANDMOTHER: One sees what one sees and one knows what one knows. It doesn't smell good in here. Today smells sour, but tomorrow smells rotten, and then it's best to withdraw.
AMAN: We still can't escape from here.
GRANDMOTHER: Well, someone will be killed, maybe you, maybe me.

She clutches her black bag to her and looks scornful.

AMAN: Don't sit there cackling.
GRANDMOTHER: Albert is an idiot, and you, poor child, behave like a fool, despite your good sense. No one listens to Grandmother. Blame yourselves.

The old lady disappears, swallowed up by the darkness.

Aman looks after her, but returns to work. They have unpacked part of their apparatus and stood up several simple sets and screens. On the room's short wall hangs a dark drapery, painted with astrological signs. The whole thing has a shabby look, even in the sparse light.

Occasionally during the following scene a flashing light suddenly fills the room—the thunderstorm of the summer night.

A door is opened and Mrs. Ottilia Egerman comes in carrying a lamp. Through the door Egerman, Vergérus and Starbeck can be seen at the supper table.

Mrs. Egerman closes the door, stops, somewhat bewildered, and puts the lamp down on the table.

OTTILIA: I hope they gave you a good meal in the kitchen. (*Pause*) I thought that you might need a little more light.

She remains standing and looks steadily at Vogler. Aman stops working and turns to him.

AMAN: I'm going to unpack in the guest room.

Aman takes his coat and departs. Vogler is now preoccupied with a small square tin box in which a lamp is mounted. Suddenly a leering face flashes onto one of the screens.

OTTILIA: Oh!

The picture is transformed, becomes romantic.

OTTILIA: How beautiful.

The picture wavers and disappears, and the strange leering face returns.

OTTILIA (*suddenly*): Perhaps you wonder why I'm dressed in black, Mr. Vogler. My daughter died last spring.

Vogler leans over the magic lantern. A tiny coil of smoke rises from the funnel on the tin box.

OTTILIA: Mr. Vogler!

Vogler rises and stands, listening respectfully. Mrs. Egerman takes a step.

OTTILIA: You must forgive those people. I mean, for humiliating you. They cannot understand you, and that's why they hate you.

Vogler is silent.

OTTILIA: *I* understand you!

She takes still another step toward him.

OTTILIA: Who are you, really?

Neither Vogler nor Mrs. Egerman sees that a door has been opened behind the drapery. On the thin cloth a rectangle of light and a shadow suddenly appear. Then the light moves, the shadow dances away. It becomes dark again, but a hand carefully lifts up a corner of the cloth and a face becomes visible. It is Mr. Egerman, listening to his wife.

OTTILIA: I recognized you immediately when I saw you. I became terribly excited. Pardon me for being so frank. But I almost never speak.

She presses her hand against her mouth, and tears

stream from her eyes. She turns away for a moment, but continues to speak.

OTTILIA: No, I shouldn't cry. We haven't got time for tears. I have longed for you. My thoughts have been with you perpetually. I have lived your life! Yet I saw you for the first time today. (*Smiles*)

Vogler remains immobile. Mrs. Egerman puts her hand on his. Now she stands quite close and speaks in a barely audible voice.

OTTILIA: Perhaps you're laughing at me silently. It doesn't matter. My love is strong enough for both of us.

Mrs. Egerman sighs heavily and presses Vogler's hand against her heart.

OTTILIA: Now I understand why you have come. Feel how my heart beats.

Vogler looks at her.

OTTILIA (*strongly*): You will explain why my child died. What God meant. That's why you have come. To soothe my sorrow and lift the burden from my shoulders.

She sinks down on a chair and covers her face with her hands. Vogler sits silently on the black casket. He lowers his head and looks at his hands. Then he clenches his fist so that his nails puncture his skin and drops of blood emerge.

OTTILIA: My poor husband doesn't know anything. How could *he* understand!

Her agony mounts while she enjoys the sweetness of be-
trayal.

OTTILIA: Isn't it terribly warm tonight? It has been an
oppressing day. I felt such pain.

She leans toward Vogler and whispers breathlessly but
without looking at him.

OTTILIA: My husband will go to bed in about an hour. He
sleeps very heavily and I gave him a sleeping potion in his
last drink. You'll come to me at two o'clock. I sleep on the
other side of the corridor, opposite the guest rooms.

She gets up and is just about to go, but stops. She falls
on her knees and presses her mouth against Vogler's hand.

OTTILIA: Let me kiss your hands. No, I want to. Just be
still. Oh! You've hurt yourself!

She rises, staggering.

OTTILIA: My husband and I have had separate bedrooms
ever since our daughter died.

The drapery moves slightly as Mrs. Egerman disappears
through the door. Vogler remains seated on the casket,
staring at his hand. The magic lantern flickers and smokes,
and the twisted face still shimmers on the screen.

Suddenly a shape frees itself from the room's forest of
shadows. It is the actor Johan Spegel, who stands there
swaying with Antonsson's brandy jug under his arm.

SPEGEL: I haven't died, but I have already started to haunt.
Actually, I think that I'm a better ghost than I am a human
being. I have become *convincing*. I never was, as an actor.

He holds out his hand against the beam of light from the magic lantern. It forms a shadow on the screen.

SPEGEL: A shadow of a shadow. (*To Vogler*) Don't worry about me, sir. I am already in a state of decomposition.

He disappears among the shadows as silently as he came. Vogler takes a few quick steps to follow him. They meet behind the screen where the shadows are deepest, close to the drapery with its zodiac and secret signs. Spegel's face is turned toward the darkness.

SPEGEL: I have prayed just one prayer in my life. Use me. Handle me. But God never understood what a strong and devoted slave I had become. So I had to go unused. (*Pause*) Incidentally, that is also a lie. (*Pause*) One walks step by step into the darkness. The motion itself is the only truth.

He suddenly sways and comes out on the other side of the screen. For a moment his shadow hovers giant-like. Then he collapses against the black casket. It is a hard, numbing fall.

SPEGEL: When I thought that I was dead, I was tormented by horrible dreams . . .

Vogler opens the lid and lets the lifeless body glide down into the box. The false bottom opens like dark water and swallows up the dead man. Vogler then begins to extinguish the lights of the chandelier and the magic lantern.

Egerman returns to the supper table which is set in the dining room, a smaller room on the second floor. Vergérus and Starbeck have lingered over the excellent cognac of the Egerman house.

STARBECK (to Egerman): You're a little pale, I think. Have you seen a ghost?
EGERMAN: I'm only somewhat tired.
VERGÉRUS: Of course. I wish you a good night. My best to Mrs. Egerman.
EGERMAN: Can you find the way to your room?
VERGÉRUS: This is not the first time that I have the pleasure and honor of being a guest in your house.

Starbeck remains at the table, intoxicated, his eyes watery and his face slack. His sneering expression has disappeared and been replaced by a kind of bloated stupidity.

STARBECK: Egerman, come and sit down. Let's have another glass.
EGERMAN: Just what I was thinking.
STARBECK: The only thing to do when the chief of police gives an order is to obey.

The three guest rooms are in a row along a narrow corridor which in its turn leads to the large staircase. Just as Vergérus is about to walk into his room, he discovers that one of the other doors is ajar. He tiptoes up to the beam of light and stops, hidden by the darkness of the corridor.

Aman, Vogler's assistant, is inside but very changed. Dressed in a stay and a long petticoat, she walks around the room as if awaiting someone. Now and then she stops and listens.

Vergérus puts his cane against the door and lets it slide open. The woman turns to him.

VERGÉRUS: What a strange magnetic miracle. Dr. Vogler's talents have my greatest esteem.
MANDA: I am his wife.
VERGÉRUS: And why this masquerade?

MANDA: We are wanted by the police and have to disguise ourselves so as not to be recognized.

VERGÉRUS: Why don't you leave the whole business?

MANDA: Where should I go?

VERGÉRUS: Let me tell you a secret. Throughout this whole evening I have been struggling with a strange feeling of sympathy for you and your husband.

MANDA: That doesn't seem likely.

VERGÉRUS: When you first came into the room, I immediately liked you. Your face, your silence, your natural dignity. This bias on my part is very deplorable and I wouldn't be telling you if I weren't slightly intoxicated.

MANDA: If you feel like that you should leave us in peace.

VERGÉRUS: I can't do that.

MANDA: Why?

VERGÉRUS: Because you represent something which I most abhor.

Manda looks questioningly at him.

VERGÉRUS: The unexplainable.

MANDA: Then you can immediately stop your persecution, Mr. Vergérus, because our activities are a fraud from beginning to end.

VERGÉRUS: A fraud?

MANDA: Pretense, false promises, and double bottoms. Miserable, rotten lies throughout. We are the most ridiculous scoundrels you can find.

VERGÉRUS: Is your husband of the same opinion?

MANDA: He doesn't speak.

VERGÉRUS: Is that true?

MANDA: *Nothing is true!*

This comes in a sudden, suppressed outburst. She quickly gains control of herself and strokes her face with her hands. Vergérus looks at her. He is inwardly excited, but his face remains calm.

VERGÉRUS: Your husband has no secret power. No, perhaps not. I remained uninfluenced at his first attempt. I just felt a certain cold excitement. He failed.
MANDA: It is meaningless.
VERGÉRUS: So I ought to feel at ease.
MANDA: Yes, of course, feel at ease. We can prove our inability as many times as you like.
VERGÉRUS: It seems to me that you regret this fact. (*Manda is silent*) As if you wished for something else. (*Manda doesn't answer. Vergérus laughs*) But miracles don't happen. It's always the apparatus and the spiel which have to do the work. The clergy have the same sad experience. God is silent and people chatter.
MANDA: If just once . . .
VERGÉRUS: That's what they all say. If just once. For the faithless, but above all for the faithful. If just once.
MANDA: If just once—that's true.
VERGÉRUS: You say that you are afraid.
MANDA: Yes.
VERGÉRUS: Of me too?
MANDA: Of you especially.
VERGÉRUS: That is flattering.
MANDA: One can tolerate your voice and your sharp mind.
VERGÉRUS: But what are you afraid of then?
MANDA: Your sympathy, your smile.

Vergérus laughs. It almost sounds like a coughing attack. He takes off his glasses and looks at them nearsightedly.

VERGÉRUS: You are probably the only sensible person in the troupe. Why do you continue on a road which can only lead to disgrace and prison? (*Manda doesn't answer*) Has it always been this way?

MANDA: No.

VERGÉRUS: Perhaps you believed once?

Manda nods silently.

VERGÉRUS: Because you felt you were useful and your activity had meaning.

MANDA: That was a long time ago.

VERGÉRUS: Why don't you stop while you still have time, Mrs. Vogler?

MANDA: It's useless.

VERGÉRUS: You mean that your husband . . .

MANDA: I mean that it's useless. There is no way back or to the side. (*Quietly*) Not for us.

VERGÉRUS: In spite of this, I have a proposition. When you tire of your magnets, you can look me up. I promise to help you in one way or another.

MANDA: And my husband?

Vergérus shrugs his shoulders.

MANDA: I am very grateful.

They turn around. Vogler stands in the doorway.

VERGÉRUS: I'll go at once.

He takes his cane and walks past Vogler into the corridor, then stops and smiles.

VERGÉRUS: One last question. Can we expect any more exposés, or has Dr. Vogler's magnetic theater exhausted its resources?

Vogler suddenly puts his palm against Vergérus' chest and turns him around into the room. He gives him a strong push so that he tumbles backward and lands on the bed. Then Vogler closes the door and takes a step forward. Vergérus reaches for his cane, but Vogler is faster. He takes it in his hands, breaks it across his knee and throws the pieces at Vergérus.

MANDA (*demanding*): Don't touch him.

Furious and breathless, Vogler stares at Vergérus, who gets up from the bed.

VERGÉRUS: You pay me altogether too much honor, Mr. Vogler. Your wife's faithfulness borders on madness.
MANDA: Go now, for God's sake!
VERGÉRUS: You think that your husband wants to kill me. Do you want to kill me, Mr. Vogler?
MANDA: Just go!
VERGÉRUS: Do you hate me? And I like you. This is really quite stimulating.
MANDA: Won't you please go?
VERGÉRUS: I shall go. (*Bows*) Good night, Madame. (*To Vogler*) Good night, Mr.—Doctor!

He departs.
Vogler slams the door behind him, paces the room like a caged animal, stops, leans against the wall, bangs the back of his head several times against the doorpost. Manda leaves him alone and sits motionlessly with her face turned away.
Eventually the attack is over, the tension eases. Vogler becomes calm.
Manda begins to undress. Vogler sits down at the mirror and carefully loosens his beard, his eyebrows and his wig. When Manda has put on her nightgown, she walks up to

Vogler and stands behind him, looks into the mirror. He sits, shrunken, with a naked, blank face.

MANDA: Do you remember that summer in Lyon when we earned lots of money, bought a country house and intended to stop traveling? (*Vogler nods*) Then we sold the farm and bought the coach and the horses. In Kiel we sold all my jewelry and nearly all our clothes. You said that it would be practical for me to dress in man's clothes. No one would recognize us. And it would be warmer too. You also began to act mute.

VOGLER: It was Tubal who—

MANDA: Do you remember the Grand Duke at the court of Köten who became so infatuated with me that he promised to recommend us to His Majesty the King of Sweden? You thought that I had betrayed you and gave the duke a whipping. (*Vogler nods*) Then we had to sit in jail for two months before the duke forgave us. He was very magnanimous and promised to recommend us to the Swedish Court anyway. Do you think that he did? (*Vogler shakes his head*) Neither do I. Do you remember when the Catholics engaged us to perform miracles in Ascona? We invented seven new miracles and cured pilgrims for three weeks. When Tubal came with the bill, the priest called us heretics and threatened us with damnation, banishment and eternal persecution.

Manda walks over to the bed. Vogler puts on his nightshirt and lies down at her side. She blows out the candle on the night table. There is a long silence.

VOGLER: I hate them. I hate their faces, their bodies, their movements, their voices. But I am also afraid. Then I become powerless.

Manda turns her head toward him.

VOGLER: I want to shout at them, or beat them, or beseech them. But nothing helps. It's only empty and silent.

MANDA: And if I leave you?

VOGLER (*without bitterness*): Indeed.

MANDA: The time when we really believed that we healed people. That there was some meaning in it.

VOGLER: Then Tubal came. And we earned money.

MANDA: Then Tubal came. People started to laugh at us. Found us suspicious. (*Pause*) As swindlers we were not very successful. There were others more skillful. (*Pause*) Are you asleep?

Vogler rises on one elbow and leans over his wife.

VOGLER (*furious*): Listen, I know all that. And I've heard it before. But I'm tired of your damn complaints. Go your own way, if you want to. It doesn't matter anyhow.

MANDA (*calmly*): Albert Emanuel Vogler!

Vogler presses his head against her shoulder. She turns her head toward the window.

Mrs. Egerman has lain down on top of the bed. The curtains sway slightly in the night breeze. A church clock somewhere strikes two. The clock on the writing desk echoes it with a light chime. A night lamp gives off a soft light. The door opens slowly and the lamp flickers. Someone enters the room soundlessly, but stops back in the darkness.

OTTILIA (*whispers*): So you came after all.

She rises on one elbow and offers her hand. The man approaches. She sinks back on the pillows and closes her eyes. When a shadow falls over her face, she looks up.

Husband and wife regard each other silently.

OTTILIA: What are you going to do?
EGERMAN: It depends.
OTTILIA: I'm not guilty. It was he who seduced me.

Egerman's face is suddenly twisted with rage.

OTTILIA: You intend to beat me.
EGERMAN: Yes, I do.
OTTILIA: You wouldn't dare . . .

He raises his hands to beat her, but stops. She looks at him with sudden scorn.

OTTILIA: You don't dare beat me. You're a wretch.

Then he hits her. She falls back and brings her hand to her mouth. Her lips widen, tears tremble in her eyelashes, a faint smile is on her face. Egerman sits down on the bed heavily. He wipes his forehead with a handkerchief.

OTTILIA: It's bleeding.
EGERMAN (*heavily*): Forgive me.

He gets up to go. She remains seated on the bed.

OTTILIA: No, don't go.

Egerman turns around.

OTTILIA: Stay with me . . .

Sunday morning at ten o'clock, Albert Emanuel Vogler displays his Magnetic Health Theater in the large hall of the Egerman house. The performance takes place in dazzling sunlight and in front of a carefully chosen audience.

Mrs. Egerman is sitting in a comfortable armchair. Consul Egerman stands leaning against the back of her chair. Ottilia has a small bruise at her temple.

Also present are the Royal Medical Counselor, Vergérus, who has sat down in a shaft of light with his arms folded, the sun reflecting from his thick glasses. On the other side of Mrs. Egerman sits the wife of the police chief. She is a rosy matron with puffy, slack features. The chief of police himself stands like a statue behind her chair, fat but erect, with signs of last night's drinking bout still on his face. At the door to the stairs, the servants are gathered: Sara, Sanna, Rustan and Antonsson the coachman.

In front of the drapery with the astrological symbols, which looks patched and worn in the sunlight, the mesmerizer Vogler and his wife appear, dressed in fantastic costumes. Tubal talks incessantly, like a barker at a carnival. Simson dives forward every so often from behind the painted screens.

TUBAL: The power which flows from our magnets meets the power which radiates from Mr. Vogler's aura, as we call it. At the point of intersection between these twin forces, that of nature and the ego, Mr. Vogler's assistant will float free in the air.

In the meantime, Manda lies down on a platform which is supported by four swaying legs. Tubal covers her with a dusty, stained cloth. Vogler strikes a pose of concentration. He wrinkles his forehead, covers his face with his hands, stretches out his arms as if in benediction and lowers his head.

TUBAL: At this moment Mr. Vogler is reaching back through thousands of years, searching for the fundamental power which the sages once used for the benefit of mankind. Silence, ladies and gentlemen! Your serious attention is requested!

He gestures dramatically for silence. Sofia Garp quivers secretly and clenches her hands.

Sanna starts to cry, but Sara reaches out a hand and pulls her close.

TUBAL: It has happened that Mr. Vogler's assistant fell on the floor. Once—it was before the Duke of Naples—he was hurt very badly.

Tubal breathes deeply and looks around. Vogler seems to be at the climax of his concentration. Tubal leans forward and carefully loosens the platform from under Manda's body. With a magicianlike sweep of his hand, Vogler pulls away the black cover and for a moment it seems to the audience as if Manda is floating in the air. Then Starbeck leans forward and with his cane pushes away the nearest screen. It swings aside on its hinges and reveals Simson, perspiring and red-faced, energetically counter-balancing four black ropes which are in turn affixed to a narrow black board on which Manda rests. When Simson sees himself exposed, he is so bewildered that he releases the ropes.

Manda falls to the floor and the audience bursts into ringing laughter. Tubal bows deeply and holds up his hand, demanding silence.

TUBAL: Ladies and gentlemen, we thank you for your applause and we hope that our small tricks really please you. We are now going to show you something far more fabulous. A performance which has attained world fame, in which the strange powers of Mr. Vogler and his assistant give even more tangible proof of the diabolical aspects of our world order.

He points with his forefinger toward the audience.

TUBAL: Will one of the ladies present step forward? A woman of pure heart and beautiful thoughts?

Mrs. Starbeck rushes forward with a loud laugh. She curtsies deeply to Tubal and Vogler. The chief of police reaches out his hand after her, but it is already too late.

Tubal brings forward a strangely carved armchair and asks Mrs. Starbeck to be seated. Then he fastens a couple of magnets to her wrists. Mrs. Starbeck finds it all very funny and giggles continuously. But her husband is not amused. The other spectators encourage her with shouts.

TUBAL: This is *the moment of absolute truth*. Through the magnet's powers Mrs. Starbeck is freed from all pretense and each word she says will be the purest truth.

Vogler has sat down on Mrs. Starbeck's right and Manda on her left. The mesmerizer touches her very lightly with his finger tips. Mrs. Starbeck is still giggling.

MANDA: Mrs. Starbeck, how much pin money does your husband give you?
STARBECK (*furious*): I protest against this prank.
VERGÉRUS: Just a moment, sir. Don't forget that you are sacrificing yourself for science. (*Laughs*)
MANDA: When did you get married, Mrs. Starbeck?
MRS. STARBECK: I'm not married. (*Giggles*) Oh, no, how terrible. I'm much too young!
MANDA: Aren't you married to Mr. Starbeck?
MRS. STARBECK (*laughs*): Mr. Starbeck is a carrot.
STARBECK: Stop this disgraceful performance!
MRS. STARBECK: Every Saturday Mr. Starbeck goes to a whorehouse. He eats like a pig and farts at the table.

STARBECK: Don't you hear me! (*To Vogler*) Stop her! (*To Manda*) Stop her!

MRS. STARBECK: Mr. Starbeck wears a wig. Mr. Starbeck stinks. Mr. Starbeck is unsavory.

STARBECK: At least think of our poor children!

MRS. STARBECK (*giggles*): I have often wondered how many of them are really Starbeck's. Although a few of them are both ugly and stupid. Mr. Starbeck is a pig!

Suddenly Mrs. Starbeck stops laughing and looks around wide-eyed. A blush mounts in her fat face and her mouth begins to tremble.

MRS. STARBECK (*seriously*): I have to go home at once. I have a roast in the oven. No, please remain, dear Starbeck. You really need a little diversion.

She shakes her fat shoulders lightly as if she were cold, walks backs to her chair with dignity and picks up her wrap.

MRS. STARBECK: I haven't said anything silly, have I? (*Laughs*) Just think how amazing these tricks are. Goodbye, Starbeck. You'll be home for dinner, I suppose. No, no, my friend, I'm not revengeful. You mustn't think that!

She giggles and curtsies quickly to those present. Vergérus bows deeply and Egerman follows her to the door.

Starbeck stares straight ahead with a fixed expression of fury.

TUBAL: Our last number is called "The Invisible Chain." Will one of the gentlemen step up? The stronger the better. Step up, you Goliath, wherever you are!

EGERMAN: Antonsson!

ANTONSSON: I don't want to, sir.
EGERMAN: That's an order.

Antonsson walks up to Vogler sulkily. Tubal pats him on the shoulder and makes cheery, pacifying noises.

TUBAL: Bravo, my good man. Nothing dangerous, nothing painful. Just breathe calmly. Ladies and gentlemen, Antonsson is a brute! But his physical strength is small compared to Mr. Vogler's spiritual power! Assistant, will you tie this man with "The Invisible Chains"?

Manda pretends to lift heavy chains from a table and to fetter Antonsson, both at his hands and feet. Vogler has sat down. He doesn't even look at Antonsson, who stands quiet and witless, with head bowed.

MANDA: Your hands are chained together and your feet are also linked. The chain is fastened to the wall.

Antonsson looks at Manda. Then he turns his glance toward Vogler. The hall is filled with a tense, almost frightened silence. Antonsson lifts his hands and tries to jerk them apart but fails, then tries again. His face turns pale, he pants with effort and his mouth becomes a gaping hole. He takes a few steps, but the invisible chains stop him and he collapses on the floor. He writhes about, he thrashes, he tenses himself like a bow. Then he raises his arms like clubs and rushes at Vogler to crush him but is pulled back by the chain which binds him to the wall. Foam forms around his mouth and his eyes become bloodshot.

After a few minutes of fruitless struggle, he sags to the floor like a slaughtered animal, stretches his neck and bends his head backward. He is immobile and gasping; his eyes bulge widely. Vogler sits quite still throughout. He

seems almost absent. The audience stares quietly, fasci-
nated by the horrible show. Vogler lifts his head and looks
at the clock on the wall. The minute hand points at six and
the hour hand is between ten and eleven. The sunlight is
dazzling against the whiteness of the curtains.

Finally the clock strikes a light ringing tone. Antonsson
loosens his fetters and lies still. Vogler leans over him.
Then Antonsson raises his hands imploringly. Vogler does
not pull away, but leans still closer. Suddenly Antonsson's
hands close around Vogler's neck and quick as lightning he
drags him down. Vogler tries to free himself but fails. Before anyone has time to take a step or make a move, Vogler
lies motionless. With ponderous speed Antonsson jumps
up and rushes out the door.

Mrs. Egerman screams and falls unconscious.

That is the signal for general turmoil. Vergérus and
Egerman carry Mrs. Egerman from the room. Sofia takes a
firm grip on Sanna and pushes her out on the stairway.
Starbeck shouts to Rustan that he should follow the murderer, but Rustan is hesitant. Within a few moments the
room is empty.

After about five minutes, Egerman, Vergérus and Starbeck return to the hall. Rustan is posted at the door, still
pale and trembling.

Starbeck sits down at the table. The medical counselor
makes a quick examination of the dead man, who lies on
the floor where he has fallen. Tubal sits panting on the
long, black casket, which stands at the wall. Simson sniffs
sadly in a corner and Manda sits on the floor at Vogler's
side.

VERGÉRUS: There is no doubt that the man is dead.

He throws a cloth over Vogler's body and turns toward
Starbeck, who, with an important air, writes something
on a paper.

STARBECK: In my report I intend to present Antonsson's responsibility for what has occurred as none at all or almost negligible. Nor can any penalty be expected since no person related to Mr. Vogler has pressed charges. If, contrary to all expectations, this should be the case, the matter will be carefully examined and special measures will be taken to investigate the debts which Vogler has accrued during his activities. Claims which may amount to considerable sums. Are there any objections from anyone?

No one answers.

STARBECK: If no one finds reason to challenge the aforementioned report, the case will be closed.
TUBAL: What does that mean, if I may ask?
STARBECK: That means that you can go to hell, if it amuses you, Mr. Tubal.
TUBAL: I thank you for the advice, sir. What happens to Vogler?
STARBECK: Pursuant to the ordinance about autopsies in private and public places, the aforementioned Albert Emanuel Vogler will in due order be dissected in accordance with the decision of the medical counselor, Anders Vergérus, and the chief of police, Frans Starbeck. The autopsy will be performed immediately at the expense of the municipal authorities, for scientific purposes.
TUBAL (bows): We are very grateful.
STARBECK: I thought so.

Tubal bows again.

STARBECK: Then it's time to carry Mr. Vogler up to the attic, where the autopsy will take place. For scientific reasons, the medical counselor wants to examine the cadaver as soon as possible.
TUBAL: Just like at executions?

STARBECK (*smiling*): Perhaps. We can carry him in that black casket on which you are sitting, Mr. Tubal.

Starbeck gets up and collects his papers. Then he walks over to Manda.

STARBECK: If you expect to have financial difficulties, Mrs. Vogler, I can recommend an excellent "house" on Luntmakare Street where I have some influence.
MANDA: I'm grateful for your consideration.
STARBECK: My wife has rather strange moods, don't you think?

He turns his back to her. In the meantime, Tubal and Simson have placed Vogler's body in the black casket.

There is something ominous in the afternoon silence, in the sunlight and the ticking of the clocks. It is good to be in the kitchen with Sofia. She sits at the table and holds a guitar in her arms. Tubal has sat down next to her.

A little to the side, but still close by, Sara and Simson are huddled together. At the other corner of the table sit Rustan and Sanna.

RUSTAN (*whispers*): . . . and then we had to carry the casket up to the attic. And then the medical counselor came with the police chief and lifted up Vogler's body on a large table and began undressing it.
SARA (*whispers*): What are they really going to do?
SIMSON: Cut up the body and pick out all the guts, saw off the head and peek into the brain. And the blood gushes and gushes.
SARA: Just imagine if he should awaken and get up while under the knife and get down from the table and walk downstairs. Just think if he came in here and looked at us with bloody eye sockets.

SANNA: You shouldn't talk like that! (*Begins to weep*)
RUSTAN (*shaken*): Don't be afraid, Sanna. I'll protect you.
SOFIA: The best we can do is to sing a song about trust in the Lord.
TUBAL: You are so right, Sofia. What shall we sing?

Tubal's manner is fawning. Sofia gives him a thoughtful nod and tunes her instrument. Then she begins to sing in a clear, firm voice. Simson searches for Sara's hand, but she withdraws.

SIMSON: Have you changed your mind?
SARA: Changed my mind? I've never promised one thing or another.
SIMSON: I'll tell you one thing—last night you were hot on the porridge.
SARA: Be quiet. Do you want to embarrass me? Last night was last night and today is Sunday.

Sara looks at Rustan, who puts his arm around Sanna's shoulder. Sanna leans trustfully against Rustan's narrow chest. Sara sighs sentimentally. Simson is drooping. Tubal has his hands clasped over his stomach and looks thoughtfully at the ceiling. Sofia interrupts her song.

SOFIA: What are you staring at?
TUBAL: I?
SOFIA: You. Is the ceiling dirty, or what's wrong with you? Are you uneasy about something . . . ?
TUBAL: Everything is in vain, Sofia. (*He smiles wryly*)
SOFIA: I mean now that your swindling days are over.
TUBAL: It's the Lord's will.
SOFIA: Don't talk rubbish, Tubal! You are caught. that's the whole thing. The Lord has let Sofia arrest you.
TUBAL (*frightened*): Arrest!

Sofia: Were you frightened? It's better to be caught by the heavenly police than one of the worldly kind.

Tubal (*carefully*): You say that, Sofia?

Sofia: Tonight you'll come along to the parish and stand witness.

Tubal (*even more carefully*): Isn't that rather quick?

Sofia: Come into my room, Tubal. We have to think about your testimony. It ought to be private and soul-searching.

Tubal sighs.

Sofia: Well, how do you want it? (*She gets up*)

Tubal (*gives in*): Yes, yes.

Sofia goes to her room and Tubal hurries after her. They lock the door. Simson sighs. Sara rests her head in her hands. Sanna and Rustan have closed their eyes and are not in this world.

The church bells announce that it is Sunday.

The attic is rather large and stretches over the entire house. The mansard roof's beams shimmer in the dim light. The floor is made of rough-hewn planks. Most of the space is taken up by furniture and miscellaneous articles piled against the walls and roof. Chests, chandeliers, old statues, paintings, books, toys. Leaning against a tall floor clock stands a huge baroque mirror, which reflects and enlarges the dimensions of the room. In the middle of the floor is a simple wooden table. On the table lies a body covered by a sheet. Under the table stands the large black casket in which the dead man has been transported.

Vergérus and Starbeck stand leaning over a small writing desk strewn with papers and pens. The sunlight streaming through the attic window frames the two men and the autopsy table in a burning white rectangle. Starbeck reads from a document, hurriedly and half-aloud. He perspires in the heat and wipes his forehead from time to time with a large handkerchief. Vergérus listens thoughtfully.

STARBECK (*reads*): . . . and the undersigned has after the autopsy of the aforementioned Vogler been unable to find any physiological peculiarities or abnormalities and must therefore characterize the phenomena which have occurred involving the aforementioned Vogler as incidental and therefore of no consequence and at any rate of such slight importance that they hardly claim science's further attention. Stockholm, the fourteenth of July, in the year 1846.

VERGÉRUS: That's all?

STARBECK: That's all.

VERGÉRUS: Thanks for all your help. I'll send you a copy of the report as soon as I've completed the original.

STARBECK: Are you coming? I want to have your signature on my report.

VERGÉRUS: I'll see you tomorrow morning.

STARBECK: Good afternoon.

VERGÉRUS: Good afternoon.

During the conversation they have walked together down the attic stairs and now stand in the hallway of the top floor. The doors to the large hall are still open.

Within, Manda can be seen packing the apparatus and props of the Vogler troupe.

When she hears the conversation, she listens intently for a moment but immediately continues her work.

The gentlemen separate. Vergérus returns to the attic, while Starbeck continues on downstairs and out into the courtyard.

The coach still stands there. On the footstep of the coachbox sits Grandmother, perched like a black bird.

STARBECK (*friendly*): Well, what will become of old Granny now?

GRANDMOTHER: Small fat pigs shouldn't grunt too loud. They might lose their hams.

STARBECK (*slowly*): I'm not resentful, but I have a good memory, especially for faces.

GRANDMOTHER: "It was the first time the fly farted and didn't lose its rump"—that's what my grandmother used to say.

STARBECK: You're impudent, old woman.

GRANDMOTHER: Your most humble servant.

STARBECK: Watch out! There are institutions and establishments for such people as you and your rabble.

GRANDMOTHER: You can't be mean to a feeble-minded old woman.

STARBECK: I only said that you should watch out.

GRANDMOTHER: Of course. Give my best to your wife, by the way.

Starbeck intends to answer, but finds it wisest to swallow his words. He turns and marches away, but suddenly stumbles. His hat falls off, as well as his wig.

GRANDMOTHER: Oh my, I think he lost his head. (*Cackles*)

Starbeck looks at the old woman furiously. He steps quickly into his carriage and departs.

Grandmother remains seated and giggles to herself. An unusually large magpie comes flying down and lands in the yard right in front of the coach. The old woman is annoyed and spits carefully at the magpie, which ignores her and hops up onto a shaft of the coach. Grandmother mumbles something inaudible and crawls down to the ground. She patters quickly across the yard, into the laundry, and closes the door. She presses her black bag close to her body.

Suddenly she catches sight of something. It is Antons-son, who has hanged himself in a dark corner.

The old woman stands for a moment and peeks fear-lessly through the doorway. Then she climbs up on a bar-rel, searches for Antonsson's dagger and cuts him down.

Mrs. Egerman has gone to bed. Her face, swollen by the effects of the emotional shock, is completely open, and de-fenseless. She has placed one hand over her heart in a stiff, dramatic gesture. The window is open on the summer afternoon and the thin curtains sway in the breeze. To the left of her bed sits Consul Egerman with his face in his hands. Long silence.

OTTILIA: Do you want to do me a favor?

Egerman looks up.

OTTILIA: Stop the clock, please.

Egerman obeys.

OTTILIA: Do you hear how quiet it is?
EGERMAN: Yes, it's very quiet.
OTTILIA: What are they doing with him?
EGERMAN: Try to rest a bit.
OTTILIA: Why did you allow it to happen?
EGERMAN: I!
OTTILIA: Did you want revenge?
EGERMAN: I don't know what you're talking about. Ver-gérus surprised me with his suggestion about immediate autopsy. I said neither yes nor no.
OTTILIA: You wanted revenge.
EGERMAN: In that case, it's a strange kind of revenge.
OTTILIA: Yes, it's very strange.
EGERMAN: Revenge. (*Quietly*)

OTTILIA: I can't bear it any longer.

Ottilia's voice breaks in a convulsive sob. Then she lies still again with her eyes closed.

Manda stands in the big hall, listening to the silence and the ticking of the clocks. Then she steals quickly and cautiously out into the hallway, pushes the attic door closed and soundlessly turns the key.

Vergérus is still up in the attic and does not react when the door is shut. He sits bent over his papers, signing his name to the report with a rasping goose quill. When he is about to put the pen back into the inkwell, he stops.

A human eye stares at him from the top of the inkwell.

He is more surprised than frightened, and after a few moments' hesitation he lifts up the inkwell containing the quivering thing.

At the same moment, the autopsy report falls to the floor. He puts down the inkwell and tries to gather together his papers. Then the clock behind the mirror begins to strike quickly and repeatedly, but falls silent just as suddenly. Vergérus whispers something to himself, tries to arrange the papers, squints at the page numbers. His right hand holds the papers firmly, and his left hand rests on top of the table.

Another hand lays itself quietly over his left hand.

Vergérus looks long and thoughtfully at this strange phenomenon.

The hand which rests upon his own is cut off, amputated. He frees himself carefully and rises.

VERGÉRUS (to himself): Very hot up here under the roof . . . a momentary nausea . . .

He walks down the small staircase to the attic door. It is locked.

He begins to perspire. He moves the door handle up and down, but without effect. He stands there, thoughtful.

VERGÉRUS (*mumbles*): . . . some kind of tool . . .

The large baroque mirror shines dully in the dimness. He approaches and meets his own image, strongly lit by the sunlight.

He strokes his hair and straightens his glasses, tries to focus his image in the mirror, but sees something else deep in the room behind him. It is a face, floating formlessly above the body of the dead man. A glaring face, lit from inside, with pale, tense features and a look of hatred. When he turns around, the vision disappears immediately. He runs over to the dead man and rips away the sheet, but everything is unchanged—dead and tangible.

VERGÉRUS: . . . just a momentary . . .

Then his glasses are ripped off and thrown into the darkness. He cannot suppress a cry of pain, puts his hands over his face and steps back. After several moments he has calmed down, removes his hands and tries to orient himself with nearsighted glances.

VERGÉRUS: This is either a dream, or I'm going crazy. But it's entirely out of the question that I'm losing my reason. I'll sit down here and wait until I wake up.

The large clock behind the mirror has begun ticking slowly and unevenly. The door to the pendulum opens on a dark emptiness. Vergérus looks around with great curiosity.

VERGÉRUS: This is really very interesting . . .

He peers into the mirror. Once again he sees the face floating behind him in the dim light. A hand stretches out suddenly toward his neck, but he steps back and gasps for air. At the same moment, a sharp report is heard and the mirror shatters into whirling slivers. The face disappears immediately.

Vergérus staggers backward toward the table, holds his breath and listens in the heavy silence. He hears someone breathing close to his ear, then light, quick steps across the floorboards. It becomes quiet. The silence is immense, overwhelming. He stands motionless and tries to peer through the dimness.

VERGÉRUS: It is only the silence. And the face . . .

He takes several staggering steps away from the table. A hand stretches out again from the darkness and touches his throat. Then fear flares up in him, overpowering and irresistible. He runs toward the staircase, stumbles on the top step, rolls down the stairs, throws himself against the door, pounds and cries. Finally he sinks down and crouches at the threshold like an animal.

Now he hears light steps behind him. An enormous, formless shadow leans over him and again he sees the face, pale and hateful. Again the hand approaches and touches his throat.

Then the door glides open. The first thing he sees is Mrs. Vogler, who stands there half concealed by the doorpost.

MANDA: Let him alone.

She says this to Vogler, who is unmasked and dressed in the actor Spegel's rags. He grasps Vergérus by the hair, turns his face toward the light and looks at him closely.

VERGÉRUS: You only gave me a scare, a slight fear of death. Nothing more. Nothing else.
MANDA: Leave him alone, I tell you.

Vogler releases him.

It has clouded and darkened. The rain returns, murmuring and monotonous. Vogler and his wife begin to pack their apparatus and the sets. They tear down screens and draperies, magnets and props. Everything is packed into the large boxes.

MANDA: I'll get Tubal.

She leaves. Vogler continues the dismantling, kicks over a support, stares in disgust at a box full of broken glass pictures, throws them on the pile of torn and dented objects.
The rain beats against the windows and it is gray in the large hall.
In the kitchen, however, it is rather pleasant. Rustan and Simson play cards. Sofia Garp peels potatoes into a large pot. Sanna and Sara are busy at the stove and Tubal is sitting half asleep in the rocking chair, minding the house cat. Everyone looks up when Manda opens the door.

MANDA: Simson, will you go out and harness the horses? We are leaving now.
SIMSON: But I . . .
MANDA: Do as I say.

Simson gets up sadly, his head hanging. Sara tries to pretend that she's more interested in the roast in the oven than in Simson's decision to obey.

MANDA: Will you be good enough to help us with the packing, Mr. Tubal?

Sofia clears her throat.

TUBAL: I'm staying here. My road is another. (*Sofia peels*) One should live for the *hereafter*, as Sofia says. For a higher goal, you understand, more meaning and less apparatus.

He rocks cautiously in the chair, searching for words in a soft voice as he continues to stroke the cat's back. Sofia peels her potatoes without favoring him with a glance.

MANDA: Goodbye, Mr. Tubal, and good luck. (*To Sofia*) May I congratulate you on your acquisition.

Sofia looks Manda up and down.

Vogler lifts one of the large boxes and carries it to the stairs. Mrs. Egerman is just on her way up to the top floor and stops as if petrified, staring with fright at this figure that she knows but does not recognize. Behind her comes Egerman. He is about to say something to his wife but his mouth remains open in amazement and fear. Long silence.

VOGLER: May I ask for some money? (*Pause*) We have nothing, not a shilling. We are destitute! You can at least give us something for our performance this morning.

He sets the box down on the stairs and stretches out his hand toward Mrs. Egerman, who backs away.

VOGLER: You stare at me as if you had never seen me! And yet you thought we were "twin souls," Mrs. Egerman. You wanted me to explain your life. Isn't that so?
OTTILIA (*shakes her head*): I have never seen you before. I don't know you. Get out of here!
VOGLER: I was in disguise then. Does that make any differ-

ence? Mrs. Egerman, please ask your husband to help us. We don't need very much.

OTTILIA (*backs away*): No, don't touch me.

She runs down the stairs and throws herself into her husband's arms for protection. At this moment, Mr. Vergérus comes out on the upper landing.

VOGLER: Mr. Vergérus! Please help me! Talk to your friend, police chief Starbeck, so that we can leave the city. I promise that we'll never come here again. I beg you. Help us!

VERGÉRUS: It would interest me to know whom I've actually dissected.

VOGLER: A poor actor who wished for nothing better than to be dissected and scraped clean.

VERGÉRUS: And you lent him your face. Changed places on the floor in the hall. You were never dead. Not even unconscious, perhaps?

VOGLER (*humble*): It was a cheap trick.

VERGÉRUS: But you are nevertheless positive that you are the mesmerizer Vogler.

VOGLER: I think so.

VERGÉRUS: Not the actor or any third or fourth person?

VOGLER: All right, you may scorn me, sir, but help me. You said that you felt sympathy . . .

VERGÉRUS: I liked *his* face more than I like yours. Go up and get your false beard and your eyebrows and disguise yourself so that I can recognize you. Then perhaps we can discuss your problems.

VOGLER: You are ungrateful, sir. Haven't I exerted myself beyond my usual powers in order to give you an experience?

Vergérus pulls out a coin from his pocket and offers it to the mesmerizer.

VERGÉRUS: It was a miserable performance, but of course you must be paid.

He drops the coin at Vogler's feet, continues down the stairs and walks up to Egerman.

VERGÉRUS: Look carefully at that beggar on the stairs and then tell me if I haven't won our bet!
EGERMAN: You are right. I have lost.

Vogler rises and lifts up his box.
The rain pours over the yard. Simson has just harnessed the horses and Manda comes out dragging several large bags.
Vogler hoists up his crate and places it under the coach box.
Manda steps into the coach and stops in surprise.
Grandmother has ripped up the padding inside the coach with a knife and is busy pulling out many small leather bags which she carefully places in the black sack she always carries. She is in a great hurry and talks while she works.

GRANDMOTHER: What? No. I won't go along. You look at my bags and then perhaps you wonder? Very well, look. It's six thousand riksdalers which Granny has collected over the years and buried here and there. Don't you believe me?

She opens one of the small bags and a pile of glistening gold coins pours out into her hand. She holds them up to Manda.

GRANDMOTHER: Granny's medicines! People will pay anything for love, didn't you know that, eh?
MANDA: And what are you going to do with all this money?
GRANDMOTHER: It doesn't concern you. But if you want to

know, I'm going to buy respectability with it. (*Whispers*) An apothecary, for example. (*Whispers*) An apothecary for specialties.

She has gathered her bags and counted them. She nods to Manda and opens up her large umbrella. She walks up to Vogler, who is just about to leave the house.

GRANDMOTHER: Goodbye, Albert. I'm going now. You are stupid and careless. I've always said that. One should know one's limits.

Tubal gets out of the rocking chair and goes over to the window. Sara is already standing there. Both sigh, each in his own way.

TUBAL: Yes, now they go their way.
SARA (*near tears*): Yes, now he goes his way.
TUBAL: Without apparatus, without money, without Granny and without Tubal. The troupe is going to hell.
SARA: Of course.
TUBAL: And the police will be after them before they can blink. Oh, oh, it's lucky that I got away in time.
SARA (*cries*): I think so too.
TUBAL: "One should take care of one's lice so they don't catch cold"—that's what my aunt said, and she was right.

Sara turns her head and looks toward the kitchen. Sanna and Rustan stand behind the stove, thinking that no one can see them. They kiss.

SARA (*sad*): Oh, dear mother! This is crazy.
TUBAL: Sofia says this world is vain. The devil knows, maybe it was meant to be that way.

Sofia has finished her potato peeling. With her strong arms she lifts the large kettle onto the stove and wipes her hands on her apron. She throws a quick glance at the window and wipes her hands again, unnecessarily.

SOFIA: Now the rabble are leaving. I won't miss them.
TUBAL: Nor I.
SARA: Nor I.

Sofia goes to the door of her room and turns around.

SOFIA: Come, Tubal.
TUBAL: *Again*, Sofia! I . . .

Sofia looks at him.

TUBAL: I'm coming, Sofia. I'm coming.

The door closes. Sara looks around at Sanna and Rustan. The cat meows. The rain streams down on the courtyard and against the windowpanes.

Simson climbs up into the coach box.

Vogler and Manda have stepped into the coach, which creaks and sways.

Then Sara rushes out into the rain, jumps over a puddle and jerks open the coach door. She stands there, soaked and beseeching.

SARA: Dear, kind people, may I come along? (*Pause*) I don't know what's happened to me, but I've probably lost my mind. (*Pause*) It must be the love potion. (*Cries*) Because I can't think the way I decided I *should* think.

Simson sits up in the coach box like a wooden soldier and doesn't dare look at Sara. The rain drips down from his big hat.

MANDA: Run and get your things. Hurry.
SARA (*yells*): Simson darling, I'm coming with you.
SIMSON (*yells*): I'll help you.

He jumps down from the box and rushes after the girl.

The rain bounces off the pavement, streams over the roof and the sides of the coach, finds its way into cracks and holes, gushes across the floor, runs down the padding and walls.

Manda bites her knuckles. Vogler sits reclined with closed eyes; he seems exhausted and indifferent.

MANDA: If we can only get out of the city, then we can escape. Sit somewhere in a God-forsaken hole and invent new tricks. If we can just get away.

She looks out. Sara and Simson are not to be seen.

Mrs. Egerman stands with a pale face in the bedroom window. The figure of her husband appears dimly behind her.

In the staircase window, medical counselor Vergérus can be seen. His expression is one of calm indifference.

Sanna and Rustan stand at the kitchen window in shimmering outline.

In the cook's room are Tubal and Sofia. But they disappear after a few moments.

MANDA: Why don't they come? We have to get away. If we can only get out of this town. Oh, it's too late. It's too late.

Now a loud noise is heard in the streets—the rattle of horses' hoofs and the thunder of wagon wheels.

Three black carriages drive up and block the driveway. From two of them pours a swift stream of uniforms. Suddenly the entire yard is filled with police. Finally Frans Starbeck rolls up, dressed in parade uniform and cape.

Sara and Simson come out on the stairs, but stop, petrified.

A uniformed man salutes Mr. Starbeck, who immediately walks into the house. The coach door is pulled open and the uniformed man gives a sign to Vogler and his wife to step out immediately. Vogler wraps himself in an old blanket, because he is still dressed in the actor's rags. Four policemen stand guard around the coach. Some guard the driveway.

Two constables accompany Vogler and his wife up the stone stairs to the top floor, followed by surprised and curious glances. They enter the large hall.

A number of people have already gathered there. Mr. and Mrs. Egerman, the chief of police, the medical counselor, Tubal and Sofia, Sanna and Rustan, Sara and Simson, and several policemen at the doors.

Starbeck clears his throat noisily and then becomes silent.

SOFIA: You were lucky, Tubal.

Tubal draws his breath and glances at the ceiling; it's difficult to say whether he is expressing gratitude. Starbeck frowns and points at Vogler.

STARBECK: Who are you, sir?

Vogler doesn't answer.

VERGÉRUS: It's the mesmerizer, Albert Emanuel Vogler, whom we thought we had dissected a few hours ago. But Mr. Vogler cheated us in his own special way. It is probably —and I'm careful to say probably—Mr. Vogler who stands there wrapped in a blanket.

STARBECK (*pale*): Is that true?

VERGÉRUS: As far as we know. As far as we know!

Starbeck takes a step backward and falls down on a chair. He pulls out a large handkerchief and wipes his forehead. A general and amazed silence follows.

STARBECK (*hoarsely*): I am saved!

He controls his emotions and immediately gets up. Searching his pockets he soon finds a paper, which he unfolds. He immediately begins to read in a trembling voice.

STARBECK: By His Majesty's command, I have the pleasure to inform you as follows. His Majesty the King has made it understood that he wishes to witness one of Mr. Vogler's magnetic performances. I therefore command you to conduct the aforementioned Vogler to the Royal Palace in order to have the required arrangements made for tonight's entertainment, which is expected to take place immediately following the royal dinner. Issued at the Royal Palace, Stockholm, the fourteenth of July A.D. 1846, by the Grand Marshal of the Royal Court.

Starbeck is silent and wipes his forehead again. He makes an energetic gesture with the document and clears his throat.

STARBECK: Hurry up, Dr. Vogler. Everyone is waiting for you. It's high time to leave.

Vogler, who has been sitting with his head bowed, rises slowly and looks from one to another. Then he walks toward the door. Starbeck rushes ahead of him and opens it. The policemen snap to attention. The atmosphere is charged but solemn. Vogler stands at the door and looks around.

VOGLER: Gather the rest of the apparatus and send it to the palace. Be careful; they are expensive objects.

STARBECK: Of course, Doctor. Of course!
VOGLER: Then let's go.

They march down the stairs as in a procession. Starbeck
runs ahead, half backward. The people of the house are
gathered at the windows to watch the departure.

The rain has suddenly stopped and the sun flashes down
between black clouds. Sara and Simson climb up on the
coach box.

Simson whips the horses ceremoniously. The coach door
slams.

SARA (*lustful*): My sweetest little Simson.
SIMSON: Not now, for God's sake. (*Whispers*) Tonight!

The coach sways through the gate, turns the corner
slowly and climbs the hilly streets, which glisten in the
afternoon sunshine.

The other carriages follow.

In this way the mesmerizer Albert Emanuel Vogler
makes his triumphant entrance into the Royal Palace.

Stockholm
June 4, 1958

❊ A CHRONOLOGY OF FILMS
DIRECTED BY INGMAR BERGMAN

ABBREVIATIONS: P, Producer; Sc, Screenplay; Ph, Director of photography; A, Leading actors

NOTE: The English titles used are either a direct translation from the Swedish, or the titles used in the United States and Great Britain. The Swedish title follows within parentheses.

1945 CRISIS (KRIS)
P, Svensk Filmindustri. Sc, Ingmar Bergman, from a play by Leck Fischer, The Mother Animal. Ph, Gösta Roosling. A, Inga Landgré, Dagny Lind, Marianne Löfgren, Stig Olin.

1946 IT RAINS ON OUR LOVE (DET REGNAR PÅ VÅR KÄRLEK)
P, Nordisk Tonefilm. Sc, Ingmar Bergman and Herbert Grevenius from Oskar Braathen's play Decent People. Ph, Hilding Bladh and Göran Strindberg. A, Birger Malmsten, Barbro Kollberg.

1947 A SHIP TO INDIA (SKEPP TILL INDIALAND)
P, Nordisk Tonefilm. Sc, Ingmar Bergman, from Martin Söderhjelm's play. Ph, Göran Strindberg. A, Birger Malmsten, Gertrud Fridh.
MUSIC IN THE DARK (MUSIK I MÖRKER)
P, Terrafilm. Sc, Dagmar Edqvist from her own novel. Ph, Göran Strindberg. A, Birger Malmsten, Mai Zetterling.

1948 PORT OF CALL (HAMNSTAD)
P, Svensk Filmindustri. Sc, Ingmar Bergman, from a story by Olle Länsberg. Ph, Gunnar Fischer. A, Nine-Christine Jönsson, Bengt Eklund, Berta Hall, Mimi Nelson.
PRISON (FÄNGELSE)
P, Terrafilm. Sc, Ingmar Bergman. Ph, Göran Strindberg. A, Doris Svedlund, Birger Malmsten, Eva Henning, Hasse Ekman, Stig Olin.

1949 THREE STRANGE LOVES (TÖRST)
P, Svensk Filmindustri. Sc, Herbert Grevenius from Birgit Tengroth's short story. Ph, Gunnar Fischer. A, Eva Henning, Birger Malmsten, Birgit Tengroth, Mimi Nelson.
TO JOY (TILL GLÄDJE)
P, Svensk Filmindustri. Sc, Ingmar Bergman. Ph, Gunnar Fischer. A, Maj-Britt Nilsson, Victor Sjöström, Stig Olin.

1950 THIS CAN'T HAPPEN HERE (SÅNT HÄNDER INTE HÄR)
P, Svensk Filmindustri. Sc, Herbert Grevenius. Ph, Gunnar
Fischer. A, Alf Kjellin, Signe Hasso, Ulf Palme.
ILLICIT INTERLUDE (British title: SUMMER INTERLUDE)
(SOMMARLEK)
P, Svensk Filmindustri. Sc, Ingmar Bergman and Herbert Gre-
venius. Ph, Gunnar Fischer. A, Maj-Britt Nilsson, Birger
Malmsten, Alf Kjellin.

1951 No Swedish feature films were produced during this year because of an industry shut-down in protest against the heavy
entertainment tax. Ingmar Bergman made only a short film for
commercial advertising.

1952 SECRETS OF WOMEN (British title: WAITING WOMEN)
(KVINNORS VÄNTAN)
P, Svensk Filmindustri. Sc, Ingmar Bergman. Ph, Gunnar
Fischer. A, Eva Dahlbeck, Anita Björk, Maj-Britt Nilsson,
Gunnar Björnstrand, Jarl Kulle, Birger Malmsten.
MONIKA (British title: SUMMER WITH MONIKA) (SOM-
MAREN MED MONIKA)
P, Svensk Filmindustri. Sc, Ingmar Bergman and Per-Anders
Fogelström, from the latter's novel. Ph, Gunnar Fischer. A,
Harriet Andersson, Lars Ekborg.

1953 THE NAKED NIGHT (British title: SAWDUST AND TINSEL)
(GYCKLARNAS AFTON)
P, Sandrews. Sc, Ingmar Bergman. Ph, Sven Nykvist (in-
teriors) and Hilding Bladh (exteriors). A, Harriet Andersson,
Åke Grönberg, Hasse Ekman.
A LESSON IN LOVE (EN LEKTION I KÄRLEK)
P, Svensk Filmindustri. Sc, Ingmar. Bergman. Ph, Martin
Bodin. A, Gunnar Björnstrand, Eva Dahlbeck, Harriet An-
dersson.

1954 DREAMS (British title: JOURNEY INTO AUTUMN) (KVINNO-
DRÖM)
P, Sandrews. Sc, Ingmar Bergman. Ph, Hilding Bladh. A,
Eva Dahlbeck, G. Björnstrand, Harriet Andersson, Ulf Palme.

1955 SMILES OF A SUMMER NIGHT (SOMMARNATTENS
LEENDE)
P, Svensk Filmindustri. Sc, Ingmar Bergman. Ph, Gunnar
Fischer. A, Gunnar Björnstrand, Eva Dahlbeck, Jarl Kulle,
Margit Carlqvist, Harriet Andersson, Ulla Jacobsson.

1956 THE SEVENTH SEAL (Det sjunde inseglet)
P, Svensk Filmindustri. Sc, Ingmar Bergman. Ph, Gunnar
Fischer. A, Max von Sydow, Gunnar Björnstrand, Nils Poppe,
Bibi Andersson, Bengt Ekerot.

1957 WILD STRAWBERRIES (Smultronstället)
P, Svensk Filmindustri. Sc, Ingmar Bergman. Ph, Gunnar
Fischer. A, Victor Sjöström, Bibi Andersson, Ingrid Thulin,
Gunnar Björnstrand.
BRINK OF LIFE (Nära livet)
P, Nordisk Tonefilm. Sc, Ulla Isaksson and Ingmar Bergman.
Ph, Gunnar Fischer. A, Eva Dahlbeck, Ingrid Thulin, Bibi
Andersson, Barbro Hiort af Ornäs.

1958 THE MAGICIAN (British title: The Face) (Ansiktet)
P, Svensk Filmindustri. Sc, Ingmar Bergman. Ph, Gunnar
Fischer. A, Max von Sydow, Ingrid Thulin, Gunnar Björn-
strand, Bibi Andersson.

1959 THE VIRGIN SPRING (Jungfrukällan)
P, Svensk Filmindustri. Sc, Ulla Isaksson and Ingmar Berg-
man. Ph, Sven Nykvist. A, Max von Sydow, Birgitta Petters-
son, Gunnel Lindblom.
THE DEVIL'S EYE (Djävulens öga)
P, Svensk Filmindustri. Sc, Ingmar Bergman. Ph, Gunnar
Fischer. A, Bibi Andersson, Jarl Kulle, Stig Järrel.

1961 THROUGH A GLASS DARKLY (Såsom i en spegel)
P, Svensk Filmindustri. Sc, Ingmar Bergman. Ph, Sven
Nykvist. A, Harriet Andersson, Gunnar Björnstrand, Max
von Sydow, Lars Passgård.

1963 WINTER LIGHT (Nattvardsgästerna)
P, Svensk Filmindustri. Sc, Ingmar Bergman. Ph, Sven
Nykvist. A, Ingrid Thulin, Gunnar Björnstrand, Max von
Sydow, Gunnel Lindblom.
THE SILENCE (Tystnaden)
P, Svensk Filmindustri. Sc, Ingmar Bergman. Ph, Sven
Nykvist. A, Gunnel Lindblom, Ingrid Thulin, Birger Malm-
sten, Jorgen Lindstrom.

1964 ALL THESE WOMEN (För att inte tala om alla
dessa kvinnor)
P, Svensk Filmindustri. Sc, Ingmar Bergman, Erland Josephson. Ph, Sven Nykvist. A, Jarl Kulle, Bibi Andersson,
Harriet Andersson, Eva Dahlbeck.

1966 PERSONA
P, Svensk Filmindustri. Sc, Ingmar Bergman. Ph, Sven
Nykvist. A, Bibi Andersson, Liv Ullmann.

1968 HOUR OF THE WOLF (Vergtimmen)
P, Svensk Filmindustri. Sc, Ingmar Bergman. Ph, Sven
Nykvist. A, Liv Ullmann, Max von Sydow, Erland Josephson,
Bertil Anderberg, Ingrid Thulin.

1968 SHAME (Skammen)
P, Svensk Filmindustri. Sc, Ingmar Bergman. Ph, Sven
Nykvist. A, Liv Ullmann, Max von Sydow, Gunnar Björn-
strand.

Ingmar Bergman wrote the screenplay only for the following films:

1944 TORMENT (British title: Frenzy) (Hets)

1947 WOMAN WITHOUT A FACE (Kvinna utan ansikte)

1948 EVA

1955 THE LAST COUPLE OUT (Sista paret ut)

❀ MAJOR PRIZES
WON BY BERGMAN FILMS

SMILES OF A SUMMER NIGHT
　　Special Prize, Cannes Film Festival, 1956

THE SEVENTH SEAL
　　Special Prize, Cannes Film Festival, 1957
　　Grand Prix International de l'Académie du Cinéma (French
　　　　Motion Picture Academy), 1958
　　Golden Banner, Religious Film Festival, Valladolid, Spain,
　　　　1960

BRINK OF LIFE
　　Best Director Award, Cannes Film Festival, 1958
　　The three leading actresses in this film (Eva Dahlbeck, Ingrid
　　　　Thulin, Bibi Andersson) shared the Best Actress Award

WILD STRAWBERRIES
　　Grand Prize, Berlin Film Festival, 1958
　　Grand Prize, Mar del Plata Film Festival, Argentina, 1959
　　Critics' Prize, Venice Film Festival, 1959

National Board of Review (United States), Best Foreign Film, 1959

Nominated for Best Screenplay, American Academy of Motion Picture Arts and Sciences, 1959

THE MAGICIAN (THE FACE)

Special Prize, Venice Film Festival, 1958 (for "the best directing, poetic originality and style")

Pazinetti Prize (Italian film critics) for "best foreign film of 1959"

THROUGH A GLASS DARKLY

The Academy Award "Oscar" for the best foreign film of 1961 (Santa Monica, U.S.A.), April 10, 1962

The International Catholic Filmbureau (OCIC): A prize for most outstanding picture shown during the Berlin Festival, 1962

Finnish Film Critics' prize, 1963, for best foreign picture

Bambi Prize: Award for best foreign picture 1962–63 given by a German magazine

WINTER LIGHT

The Silver Laurel Medal, 1964

Grand Prix de l'Office Catholique International du Cinéma, 1963

THE SILENCE

Karlovy Vary, 1964 Diploma

The Golden Laurel Trophy

(The Selznick Award given to Ingmar Bergman, 1963, for his complete production)

PERSONA

Best Picture of 1967, National Society of Film Critics

Best Director Award, National Society of Film Critics

Best Actress Award, Bibi Andersson, National Society of Film Critics

Best Picture 1966–67, Swedish Film Industry

Best Actress, Bibi Andersson, Swedish Film Industry

SHAME

Best Picture of 1968, National Society of Film Critics

Best Director, National Society of Film Critics

Best Actress, Liv Ullmann, National Society of Film Critics

Best Foreign Language Feature of 1968, The Foreign Language Press Association